ISLAMIC ECONOMIC ALTERNATIVES

Islamic Economic Alternatives

Critical Perspectives and New Directions

Edited by
Jomo K. S.

Faculty of Economics and Administration
University of Malaya
Kuala Lumpur

اقرأ

Ikraq
Kuala Lumpur
1993

First published 1992
Malaysian edition 1993

Published by
Ikraq
11 Lorong 11/4E
46200 Petaling Jaya
Selangor

Originally published by
MACMILLAN ACADEMIC AND PROFESSIONAL LTD
Houndmills, Basingstoke, Hampshire RG21 2XS
and London

Printed in Malaysia by Vivar Printing Sdn Bhd

British Library Cataloguing-in-Publication Data
Islamic economic alternatives: Critical
perspectives and new directions.
I. Jomo, K. S.
330.1

ISBN 0-333-54920-1

The publication of this volume has been made possible by the Yayasan Pembangunan Ekonomi Islam Malaysia (Malaysian Islamic Economic Development Foundation).

For the true Jihad and Mujahideen
and the memory of
Abu Dzar and Ali Shariati

Contents

Acknowledgements

This book was originally conceived after years of frustration with much of what passes as Islamic economic discourse, whether it be mechanical *ulama* citations and elaborations from the Quran and Sunnah, or fairly standard neoclassical economic formulations interwoven with Arabic – even Quranic – terms to provide an Islamic veneer. The victory of the Iranian people's revolution against the Shah heightened the international Muslim community's expectations of intellectual breakthroughs and policy innovation. Fortunately, the subsequent disappointment has only strengthened, rather than undermined our resolve to develop and elaborate an ethical economics authentically rooted in Islam. Hence, once again, this volume truly represents a collective enterprise, of intellect as well as faith. In this effort, I have been encouraged and supported by many colleagues both in Malaysia and abroad. In particular, I would like to acknowledge Shamsul, Shabery, Ishak, Husin, Halim, Asghar and Suroosh. Professor S. N. H. Naqvi has also been a constant source of encouragement. In the final stages of preparation of this volume, Aslam, Farid, Rokiah, Kock Wah and Juliana Azlina rendered crucial assistance selflessly. None of these friends should be incriminated for any remaining faults and problems in this book, though all of them deserve to be commended for the contribution this volume seeks to make. Finally, Nadia and Emil distracted me often enough to delay the preparation of this volume, constantly reminding me that the most exalted labour is undoubtedly the labour of love.

I should like to thank the following for permission to reproduce material which originally appeared, in a somewhat different form, in publications produced by them: Cambridge University Press for the two articles by Timur Kuran (*International Journal of Middle East Studies*, 1986, 1989); The Association for Social Economics for Sohrab Behdad's contributions; Zed Press (London) for material by Ziaul Haque and Omar Asghar Khan from Asghar Khan (ed.), *Islam, Politics and the State; the Pakistan Experience* (1985); the Pakistan Institute of Development Economics (Islamabad) for material by S. N. Navqi *et al.*; the Institute of Developing Economics (Tokyo) for material by Jomo K. S. from *The Developing Economies*

(1977); the Institute of Islamic Studies (Bombay) for material by Asghar Ali Engineer from *Islam and its Relevance in our Age* (1984).

Jomo K. S.

Notes on the Contributors

Rafiq Ahmed has been Vice-Chancellor of the Islamia University, Bahawalpur, Pakistan, since 1981. He received his D. Phil from Oxford University.

H. U. Beg has been Secretary of the Ministry of Finance, Pakistan, since 1979.

Sohrab Behdad is Associate Professor of Economics, Denison University, Granville, Ohio.

Asghar Ali Engineer is the author of numerous articles and books on Islam, including *The Origin and Development of Islam*, *The Islamic State* and *Islam And Its Contemporary Relevance To Our Age*, and is Director of the Institute of Islamic Studies, Bombay.

Ziaul Haque has been with the Islamic Research Institute, Islamabad, and was editor of the journal, *Islamic Studies*. He is now with the Pakistan Institute of Development Economics (PIDE). He has a doctorate in Arabic and Islamic Studies from the University of Chicago and is author of several books on Islam, including *Landlord and Peasant in Early Islam*.

Omar Asghar Khan has an MPhil from Cambridge University and has taught Economics at the University of the Punjab.

Timur Kuran is Associate Professor of Economics at the University of Southern California, Los Angeles. He is the author of various articles on the evolution of values and institutions and on Islamic economics.

Syed Nawab Haider Naqvi is director of the Pakistan Institute of Development Economics (PIDE), has a Ph.D in economics from Princeton University and is the author of many works on development and Islamic economics, including *Ethics and Economics: An Islamic Synthesis*.

Mian M. Nazeer has been Dean of the Faculty of Arts, University of Peshawar, Pakistan, received his doctorate in economics from Amsterdam University and is the author of *The Islamic Economic System: A Few Highlights*.

Introduction

There has been growing interest in Islam and Islamic economic alternatives in recent times, both within and outside the Muslim world. Even the International Monetary Fund (IMF) is reported to have publicly endorsed Islamic banking principles in the mid-1980s. This book introduces some of the more notable recent contributions on Islamic economic alternatives available in the English language.

Since the mid-1970s, there has been a veritable boom in writings on Islamic economics, as on various other aspects of Islam. Interestingly, much of this is in the English language. Various efforts to compile updated bibliographies on the subject (e.g. Siddiqui, 1981; Akram Khan, 1983) can hardly keep up with the output.

Much of what claims or is taken to be Islamic economics falls into two main categories. First, there are the compilations, commentaries and elaborations on the Quran, the Sunnah (the Prophet's Traditions) as well as other texts by various Muslim scholars and authorities. More often than not, such efforts claim that these provide an adequate basis for a comprehensive Islamic economic framework superior to all other existing or even idealised economic systems.

Some proponents, especially from among the *ulama*, tend to emphasise that economic aspects cannot be divorced from other aspects of human life, and hence, that economic reform is contingent on and consequent of spiritual transformation and commitment. Often, this approach asserts that worldly matters are ultimately determined by human intent, sacred or otherwise. Order or disorder, stability or instability, justice or injustice – all seem to be determined by the righteousness, or otherwise, of human motivation.

In this sense then, the impact, scope and significance of particular economic institutions or relations prescribed or proscribed by such interpretations of Islam do not pose much of a problem. Unless specifically condemned, almost anything goes, as long as the intention (for God, for the faith) is alright. This *carte-blanche* implication of the apparently orthodox approach helps explain the considerable ambiguity and controversy in efforts to identify and elaborate Islamic economic alternatives.

The apparent inadequacies of the orthodox approach have given rise to attempts, mainly by Western-trained economists of the Muslim faith, to elaborate a more comprehensive Islamic economic system consistent with the Islamic prescriptions and proscriptions referred to earlier. In the main, the results of such efforts have involved the grafting or excision of these do's and don'ts respectively either on to an essentially pure market economy, i.e. liberal capitalism (e.g. Rauf, 1970), or else on one combined with a welfare state said to be consistent with Muslim principles (e.g. Chapra, 1979). Such perspectives often also imply a conservative neoclassical or marginalist economic perspective, or else a more liberal Keynesian one. Such approaches have caused some cynical observers to refer to the Islamic economic system as capitalism without *riba*, and perhaps, plus *zakat* and *niat* – a charge most would emphatically denounce, though usually by assertion, rather than persuasion.

There is also another – less common – caricature which equates the Islamic economic system with 'communism plus god', though this writer has yet to find any serious economic writing which even vaguely approximates such a position. Very common, however, is the view that Islam is unequivocally committed to justice, which can only be assured by essentially egalitarian economic institutions and relations, sometimes associated with some variety of socialism. For instance, socialist principles of distribution – in accordance with labour and need – are said to be prescribed by Islam. At the more theoretical level too, Islam is said to embody an essentially labour theory of value, rather than one based on subjective preference or marginal utility, as in neoclassical economics. The most common objections – i.e. that Islam favours commodity exchange and individual property rights – have been rebutted by reference to the 'market socialism' option, and by emphasising Islam's recognition of communal rights and state ownership.

* * *

This volume, however, is not inspired by either the orthodox approach or both (opposing) variants of the modernist approach. Rather, it is primarily interested in three types of endeavours. First, it is necessary to look more closely at the inadequacies of the two main approaches just described. Second, acceptable elements and guidelines for the conceptualisation of Islamic economic alternatives are identified. Third, these are elaborated by critically examining some of what has happened and should happen in the name of Islam.

Timur Kuran's opening contribution provides a useful critical review of notions of the Islamic economic system, as envisaged by most Muslim economists in recent years. He argues that they have failed to develop a coherent and consistent vision of an Islamic economic system, and to operationalise the Islamic economic injuctions said to be necessary to realise an Islamic economic system. In the second article, Kuran demonstrates the rhetorical, contradictory and inadequate notions of economic justice found in such work. He also examines some Muslim economists' claims about the impact of Islamic morality for economic behaviour, which is the supposed basis tor rejecting conventional economic assumptions about *homo economicus* in favour of *homo Islamicus*. Unfortunately, he notes, Muslim societies have not lived up to such idealised notions. More generally, he attributes the minor impact of Islamic economics to its unrealistic assumptions (about human nature, and social realities and their potential for transformation), its many ambiguities – which allow for interpretations least threatening to the status quo – as well as problems of poor organisational capacity and inadequate skills. In an important earlier review, Ziauddin Sardar (1985) blamed this failure of Muslim economists on their conservatism and essentially Occidental outlook, resulting in Islamic prescriptions from an essentially Western perspective. Most tragically, critics have noted, there is little apparent self-consciousness of the intellectual *cul-de-sac* that Islamic economics has gotten into.

Leaving aside the theoretical incoherence and other inadequacies of the arguments for an Islamic economic system, Sohrab Behdad distinguishes three main approaches in the Islamic economic literature – a *laissez faire* interpretation and two populist varieties, involving varying degrees of state control. Such variety, he argues, can all equally claim legitimacy in Islam because of the ambiguity of property rights in religious prescriptions. Nevertheless, he argues, the three approaches are essentially capitalist, or at least compatible with capitalism, though his third approach – associated with the late Muhammad Baqir Al-Sadr – allows for the most state intervention, the nature of which may not necessarily be capitalist.

Ziaul Haque takes this argument further by insisting that the original message of Islam, particularly of the Quran, was revolutionary. Subsequently, he argues, this essentially revolutionary and just message of Islam was subverted by those who established dynasties to rule in the name of Islam. Various economic, social and political institutions were established to consolidate their power by invoking Islam to secure legitimacy. Honest, progressive and egalitarian Islamic interpretations and initiatives could barely resist the corrupting powers responsible for this regression. However, such backward institutions and interpretations later came to stand in the way of modernisation under the aegis of capitalism. Hence, in this phase, according to Haque, a third more modernist and reformist approach has developed, reflecting the interests and priorities of a new, often Western-educated bourgeois Muslim elite frustrated with the backwardness of 'feudal Islam', but also threatened by the revolutionary implications of the original Islam. Haque identifies recent Islamisation programmes in several Muslim countries, especially their economic components, with the recent ascendance of such elites.

Asghar Ali Engineer's discussion provides a succinct summary of a radical perspective on Islam's relevance to contemporary economic challenges. He argues that Islam's commitment to justice (*adl*) and benevolence (*ehsan*) must be correctly interpreted to face modern economic challenges under capitalist hegemony. Production and distribution should be directed by ethical principles. Charity must not offend human dignity and should not be seen as a permanent solution, but rather, only as a transitional palliative. Engineer argues that Islam endorses a labour theory of value, which is the basis for its critique of unjust distribution. He argues that the only legitimate profit is payment for services, e.g. for marketing, transport, etc., whereas industrial profits are unacceptable since they are derived from the exploitation of labour. Engineer also emphasises the essentially just principle of *zakat*, which should not be limited by historical quantums appropriate to a different economic milieu. He also argues that the Islamic injunction against *riba* is not merely against interest, or a fixed rate of return, but rather against economic excess, surplus or exploitation, whether in the form of rent, profits or speculative gain. Finally, he emphasises the necessity of rethinking Islamic economic injunctions and institutions in the light of different economic milieus.

The following article critically re-examines Max Weber's thesis about Islam as a cultural obstacle to capitalist development (see Turner, 1974) by critically reviewing Maxime Rodinson's tome on the subject. While agreeing with Rodinson that Weber is wrong in arguing that Islam is doctrinally antithetical to capitalism, it also maintains that Islam provides the ethical and historical basis for a contemporary rejection of capitalism on moral grounds. Not unlike other religions then, Islam is not unequivocally and categorically either supportive of or in opposition to most economic systems, including capitalism. Rather, it is those who profess a particular faith who invoke its cultural and doctrinal heritage in support of their own moral, political and ideological positions. Of course, Islam's own history lends itself more readily to some interpretations rather than others, and it is often here that doctrinal contention is most fierce.

The Islamic resurgence of the last two decades has inspired a host of new Islamic economic institutions and policy reforms. (For a good critical review of the more notable economic initiatives associated with contemporary Islamisation, particularly in the areas of banking, finance and redistribution (especially *zakat*), see Kuran, 1991.) Omar Asghar Khan looks at some economic dimensions of Pakistan's Islamisation experience under the rule of General Zia-ul Haq (1977–88), especially during the early 1980s. He argues that economic Islamisation under Zia was primarily concerned with the disguise or avoidance of interest in the modern financial sector and the promotion of ostensibly Islamic institutional arrangements. Khan argues that while such contracts were practised at the time of the Prophet, there is nothing particularly Islamic about them. He also shows how such a policy emphasis has actually favoured landlord and capitalist interests. Khan emphasises that the prohibition of interest does not and cannot in itself eliminate contemporary socio-economic exploitation, while acknowledging that usury was, by far, the most unpopular type of exploitation in many pre-capitalist societies. Hence, Zia's Islamisation avoided addressing the roots of injustice and exploitation while appearing to conform to Islamic economic injunctions.

The final article contains summary proposals for economic reform – inspired by a progressive interpretation of Islamic ethics – by a team associated with the Pakistan Institute of Development Economics (PIDE). Their 'agenda' identifies key Islamic economic reform proposals, working from the assumption that Islam offers a comprehensive alternative way of life. Rejecting the avoidance of interest – in favour of profit – as inadequate, if not cosmetic, they argue for thoroughgoing reform of production, distribution and consumption relations to minimise wealth and income disparities as well as to eliminate rentier incomes associated with Pakistan's 'feudal-capitalist' system. Their essay outlines some key economic reforms, considered necessary or desirable in the Pakistani context and consistent with Islamic ethical principles, for the kind of socio-economic transformation necessary to establish an Islamic society based on justice and benevolence.

Taken together then, the articles in this volume critically review

Islamic economic alternatives at two levels. On the one hand, many of the articles, especially Kuran's opening essays, are critical of much of the existing literature purporting to present, discuss and elaborate Islamic economic alternatives. On the other hand, most of the contributions complement one another in pointing the way to what are considered to be more comprehensive, authentic and progressive economic alternatives based on and inspired by Islam's message, especially its ethical principles.

This is not to imply that there is a strictly and narrowly defined and articulated Islamic economic system. Instead, it is quite possible to conceive theoretically of a variety of economic relations, institutions and structures consistent with such principles. Rather, the approach developed in this volume allows for a variety of economic arrangements which should be developed contextually, i.e. bearing in mind the particular economic heritage, circumstances and environment encountered.

Neither do most of the writers included insist that Islam has developed a distinct school of economics, except in the unusual sense asserted by Baqir Al-Sadr. On the one hand, this implies that Islam is not obliged to re-invent the wheel, in this case, economic theory. On the other hand, however, this does not mean that the thinking behind the Islamic economic alternative articulated in this book is arbitrary or eclectic. Nor can it afford to ignore or gloss over the important epistemological issues involved. Nevertheless, there seems little doubt that a genuine Islamic economic perspective is far more consistent with a labour theory of value and distribution, rather than a more neoclassical theory of marginal utility, or subjective preference.

Clearly then, much more needs to be done. This book has tried to focus attention on and arouse interest in this interesting challenge to conventional economic thinking as well as conservative Muslim economic thought. This volume has also tried to consolidate the heterogenous and uneven progress in contemporary Islamic economic thought, and to identify the key challenges and tasks ahead. If this effort succeeds in broadening and opening up debate about Islamic economic alternatives, such fresh contributions – especially from outside the mainstream discussion – can only help to advance and sharpen the progress and development of Islamic economic alternatives, *insya Allah.*

NOTES

1. Abdul-Hamid Ahmad Abu-Sulayman, 'The Theory of the Economics of Islam', in Ismail R. A. al-Faruqi (ed.), *Contemporary Aspects of Economic Thinking in Islam* (Muslim Students Association of the United States and Canada, American Trust Publications, 1970).
2. Sohrab Behdad, 'Islamic Economics': A Utopian-Scholastic-Neoclassical-Keynesian Synthesis!' *Research in the History of Economic Thought and Methodology*, 7 (1989).
3. Umar Chapra, 'The Islamic Welfare State and Its Role in the Economy', in Khurshid Ahmad and Zafar Ishaq Ansari (ed.), *Islamic Perspectives* (Leicester: Islamic Foundation, 1979) pp. 208–17.
4. Asghar Ali Engineer, *The Origin and Development of Islam: An essay on its socio-economic growth* (Bombay: Longman, 1980).
5. Monzer Kahf, *The Islamic Economy: Analytical Study of the Functioning of the Islamic Economic System* (Muslim Students Association of United States and Canada, American Trust Publication, 1978).
6. Homa Katouzian, 'Shi'ism and Islamic Economics: Sadr and Bani Sadr' in Nikki R. Keddie (ed.) *Religion and Politics in Iran – Shi'ism from Quietism to Revolution* (New Haven, Conn.: Yale University Press, 1983).
7. Muhammad Akram Khan, *Islamic Economics: Annotated Sources in English and Urdu* (Leicester: Islamic Foundation, 1983).
8. Muhammad Asghar Khan (ed.), *Islam, Politics and the State: The Pakistan Experience* (London: Zed Books, 1985).
9. Timur Kuran, 'The Economic Impact of Islamic Fundamentalism', forthcoming in Martin Marty (ed.) *Remaking The World: The Impact of Fundamentalism* (Chicago: University of Chicago Press, 1991).
10. S. N. H. Naqvi, *Ethics and Economics: An Islamic Synthesis* (Leicester: Islamic Foundation, 1981).
11. Muhammad Abdur Rauf, 'Islam and Contemporary Economic Systems', in Ismail R. A. al-Faruqi (ed.), *Contemporary Aspects of Economic Thinking in Islam* (Muslim Students Association of the United States and Canada, American Trust Publications, 1970).
12. Muhammad Baqir Al-Sadr, *Iqtisaduna* (Our Economics) (Teheran: World Organization for Islamic Services, 1982).
13. Ziauddin Sardar, 'Islamic Economics: From Partial To Axiomatic Approach' in *Islamic Futures: The Shape of Ideas to Come* (London: Mansell, 1985).
14. Muhammad Nejatullah Siddiqui, *Muslim Economic Thinking* (Leicester: Islamic Foundation, 1981).
15. Sayyed Mahmud Taleqani, *Islam and Ownership*, trans. by Ahmad Jabbari and Farhang Rajaee (Lexington, Ky: Mazda Publishers, 1983).
16. Bryan S. Turner, *Weber and Islam: A Critical Study* (London: Routledge and Kegan Paul, 1974).
17. Hossein Modarressi Tabataba, *Kharaj in Islamic Law* (London: Tabataba, 1983).

1 The Economic System in Contemporary Islamic Thought

Timur Kuran

Since the late 1940s, and especially since the mid-1960s, a wealth of pamphlets, articles, and books have appeared that constitute the corpus of what is now known as 'Islamic economics'. This literature, whose exponents call themselves 'Islamic economists', purports to provide the blueprint of an economic system consonant with the original sources of Islam. The central feature of the proposed system is that individuals are guided in their economic decisions by a set of behavioural norms, ostensibly derived from the Quran and the Sunna. Two other features stand out: *zakat*, a tax considered the basis of Islamic fiscal policy, and the prohibition of interest, viewed as the centrepiece of Islamic monetary policy. Most Islamic economists consider this trio – the norms, *zakat*, and no interest – the pillars of the Islamic system.[1]

Although some details of the system remain to be worked out, there is widespread agreement within the Islamic school that since the pillars of the desired model are already in place, it is possible to predict how an Islamic economy would operate. The next three sections of this paper examine each of the pillars in turn and offer some thoughts as to whether they are capable of supporting the intended structure.

Certain readers may object to the following evaluation on the grounds that the Islamic economists' claims and proposals are based on irrefutable divine revelations. To counter this potential objection I should point out that Islamic economists go to great lengths, like secular social scientists, to buttress their case with logic, scientific theory, and empirical evidence. It is reasonable, then, to subject their works to the same review process that is undertaken routinely throughout the social sciences. This may entail criticising them for using faulty logic or spurious evidence. It would be inconsistent to accept their contention that they are offering reasoned arguments but then allow the flaws in their writings to disappear behind a veil of divine revelation.

A critical survey of Islamic economics, if it is to fit in an essay, requires taking a sample of writings as representative of the entire literature. The sample used here comprises the following English-language sources: the papers presented at international conferences on Islamic economics held between 1976 and 1981; the major economic treatises available as of this writing through Islamic bookstores and research institutes, including publications of the International Center for Research in Islamic Economics (Jeddah), the Institute of Policy Studies (Islamabad), the Islamic Foundation (Leicester), Sh. Muhammad Ashraf (Lahore), and Islamic Publications (Lahore); and finally, a number of widely-cited recent articles published in scholarly journals devoted to the dissemination of the Islamic viewpoint. The pioneering tracts of Sayyid Abul A 'la Maududi and Sayyid Qutb are excluded from the sample, even though they are still in print and widely read. I have favored recent publications, which, while drawing on such early works, tend to be relatively more sophisticated.

Some of the major assumptions and arguments in the burgeoning Islamic literature are common to a variety of other economic doctrines, notably the Judaic, Christian, Gandhian, Buddhist, and Marxian. But while many of the following criticisms also apply to other proposed systems, I shall not present a comparative critique. Nor shall I deal with imperfections in *existing* economic systems. The issue here is not whether existing systems can be improved but whether Islamic economics offers a viable alternative.

BEHAVIOURAL NORMS

Roles in Proposed System

In the system envisaged by the Islamic economists the individual is guided by a set of behavioural norms derived from the Quran and the Sunna, the latter comprising recollections of Prophet Muhammad's words and deeds. An Islamic education ensures that the behavioural standards specified by these norms are enforced, for the most part, by the individual's own conscience. The primary role of the norms is to make the individual member of Islamic society, *homo islamicus*, just, socially responsible, and altruistic. Unlike the incorrigibly selfish and acquisitive *homo economicus* of neoclassical economics, *homo islamicus* voluntarily foregoes temptations of immediate gain when by doing so he can protect and promote the interests of his fellows. According to Afzal-ur-Rahman, author of a trilogy on the Islamic system, the Islamic norms provide 'a practical solution of [*sic*] the modern economic problem'.[2]

The Islamic norms can be grouped in two categories: production norms, which also include norms involving trade activities, and consumption norms.[3] Regarding the former category, proponents of the Islamic system are careful to point out that Islamic man is free to produce and trade for personal profit. They move on, however, to state that in exercising this freedom he is required to avoid causing harm to others.[4] He is also obliged to refrain from earning more than his efforts justify. This means that he must pay 'fair' wages, charge 'reasonable' prices and be content with 'normal' profits.[5] It means, moreover, that he must not engage in speculation and monopolisation, or make deals, like insurance contracts, that allegedly involve gambling, uncertainty, and exploitation.[6]

In his consumption activities, the Muslim is bound by three sets of norms. First, he must not devote resources to activities, like adultery, or commodities, like wine, which are deemed illegitimate. Second, he is required to show moderation in consumption, and therefore, to refrain from 'displaying pomp and grandeur'.[7] One side effect of moderation in consumption, it is argued, is the elimination of the scarcity problem through a lowering of aggregate demand; another is the prevention of demand-pull inflation.[8] Finally, the Muslim must make voluntary donations to less fortunate members of the Islamic community. One Islamic economist notes in this connection that 'the ideal is not merely to give others from the surplus . . . of income over expenses but even to sacrifice and forego one's own share if the need of others is more urgent'.[9]

These and other similar norms, say the Islamic economists, would perform better than a planning board or the so-called invisible hand in fulfilling society's needs. Mian M. Nazeer of Peshawar University argues that if the consumption and production decisions of individuals were guided by the Islamic norms, 'the composition of demand and the range of goods and services provided by the market [would] be in consonance with one another'.[10] Implicit in all such statements is the assumption that the norms would perform equally well by Islamic standards in any society, regardless of its history, level of development, size, or degree of heterogeneity.

The principal ingredient in all of the proposed norms is altruism. Social problems will be solved as people put the interests of society before their own. A question of importance is how the Islamic economists define 'society''. Their working definition appears to vary from context to context. In writings on specific fiscal and monetary institutions they equate 'society' with any primarily Muslim nation, such as Algeria or Indonesia. In others, particularly abstract essays on the ultimate Islamic order, they seem to have in mind nothing less than the entire community of believers, the *umma*, which currently incorporates about a sixth of humanity.

Critique

There are at least two reasons for questioning the soundness of the arguments regarding the effectiveness of the Islamic norms. First of all, the implications of these norms are ambiguous in most of the contexts where they are expected to operate. A pious Muslim eager to follow them may be confused as to what wage is 'just' and what profit rate is 'normal'. He may be unclear about the meaning of 'moderation' in consumption. And he may be unsure about the practical implications of the injunction against causing harm to others through his productive activities. The ambiguity inherent in the Islamic norms suggests that his actions may subject him to charges of opportunism by other equally pious individuals who happen to interpret the relevant norms differently. Accusations of this sort would threaten the legitimacy of the Islamic order, reducing people's incentives to abide by the norms. The obscurity of the norms also suggests that they are susceptible to modification over time. Modifications could be instigated either by self-serving persons or by altruistic individuals trying to strengthen the norms through clarification and systematisation.

The ambiguity problem is, of course, very general, arising as it does in the day-to-day interpretation of any social principle. In all existing social systems, well-intentioned people who subscribe to the same principles of justice and efficiency often clash over the application of these principles.

The second basis for questioning the argument that the Islamic norms would achieve wonders in a modern society is the substantial amount of evidence pointing to an inverse relationship between the size of society and the effectiveness of norms of altruism. Various studies by sociologists and economists show that in a small commune or tribe, where people live in fairly continuous contact and share similar experiences and preferences, individual members tend to display considerable altruism toward the community at large.[11] This makes it economical for the community to base exchanges on interpersonal trust and for its members to rely on one another's support in the exigencies of daily life. On the other hand, in a large society, where people's perceptions of reality and their preferences vary widely, individuals generally feel far greater loyalty toward some segments of the community than others; their sympathies tend to be concentrated on people with whom they can identify on the basis of such characteristics as kinship, locality, tradition, and occupation. In such a society the typical person is largely indifferent to the well-being of most other members, even though he might pay lip-service to the ideal of universal brotherhood. The role of trust in exchange diminishes, making it necessary to protect buyers and sellers through legal institutions. Furthermore, people come to doubt whether in times of need they can count on the assistance of others, and they demand formal insurance. If these observations are correct, then one is justified in questioning whether *generalised* altruism, the intent of the proposed norms, is achievable in a modern society with millions of people.

One might think that since the evidence uncovered by modern social science comes primarily from the European and North American experiences, its relevance to the Muslim world is marginal. To counter such doubts I shall demonstrate, later in this section, that the Muslim experience is consistent with the Western experience. For now, however, I will move on with the argument.

These criticisms should not be taken to mean that the Islamic norms would be totally ineffective in a large society. Even in the largest societies in existence, norms of altruism play an important role in governing relationships within groups like the household, the residential community, and the work team – not to mention cartels and political lobbies. Regarding the exchange process within such groups, norms economise on transaction costs by lessening the need for formal contracts and enforcement mechanisms.[12]
It is quite possible, therefore, for at least a portion of the Islamic norms to serve some constructive purpose in a large society: they could reduce cooperation costs by reinforcing altruism and trust within subsets of the society. As for generalised altruism, one would

expect it to come about only in very special circumstances, such as a foreign invasion or a natural disaster – and then just for a limited time.

At least one Islamic writer, Waqar Ahmed Husaini, recognises that in an Islamic society of many millions people might acquire complex affiliations that superseded their devotion to the community at large. He is nonetheless optimistic that the Islamic spirit would prevent the individual's ties with subgroups from weakening the community's cohesion: 'Special interest groups such as labour and professional unions . . . might exist; but their goal and function might be information gathering and dissemination, rather than *a priori* unconditional loyalty to special or vested interests . . .'.[13] But unlike Husaini, most Islamic economists do not acknowledge that a society's size might hinder the establishment of generalised altruism.

A factor reinforcing the argument that norms of altruism are relatively ineffective in a large society is that, unlike the member of a small society, a person living in a large one cannot expect to influence the general welfare perceptibly through personal acts of altruism. This suggests that even if he ascribes to the superiority of the Islamic economic society, the member of a large society may be tempted to violate the norms on which this system rests. But if most people were to deviate from the norms in the belief that their personal influence is negligible, the system would collapse. This dilemma, known in neoclassical economics as the 'free-rider' problem, confronts societies in countless contexts. Societies are not, of course, incapable of resolving the dilemma. They successfully confront it in some contexts by making adherence to the norms intrinsically pleasurable to follow and in others through various forms of coercion.[14] But in many contexts, for example environmental preservation, a satisfactory solution remains elusive. To my knowledge, the Islamic economists have so far evaded the free-rider dilemma, too. Without offering a single example of a large society that has resolved this problem through religious faith, they have simply assumed that in a society of pious Muslims rational processes would not displace moral motives.

There remains the point that altruism, if taken too far, can produce undesirable results. If everyone in a burning skyscraper were to insist on being the last to leave, the consequence would be unmitigated disaster.

Role of the State

We have seen that the Islamic economists appear convinced that members of a modern Islamic society would correctly interpret the norms laid out for them, and what is more, conform to these norms by their own volition. People, they believe, would abide by the norms even when given the option of doing otherwise, because they would have internalised them. On this note, one Islamic economist writes that 'in Islam what the Communist[s] seek to achieve . . . through the state is to be established by the agency of man himself'.[15]

Does this mean, then, that the state's role in the Islamic system is only ceremonial? After all, one of the principal functions of any existing state is to resolve free-rider problems by *coercing* agents into behaving in accordance with the perceived public interest. There is an immense literature, going back at least to Hobbes, on the conflicts between state action and individual freedom. Contributors to this literature include some renowned Muslims, among them 'Ali 'Abd ar-Raziq, an Islamic reformist who published extensively in the early part of this century. 'Abd ar-Raziq wrote that 'there is no state which is not based on the sword, and sustained by virtue of violence and subjugation'.[16]

While contemporary Islamic economists hold widely divergent views on the role of the state, many maintain (in at least parts of their writings) that the economic role of the Islamic state is to be minimal.[17] According to them, the state's main role is to prevent violations of the norms. Thus, it is to impose price ceilings when sellers charge 'unreasonable' prices, and pass legislation to foster cooperation when the relevant norms turn out to be deficient. Beyond this, there is no consensus. For just about any type of programme, whether job creation, development of natural resources, or prevention of land fragmentation, one can find supporters as well as opponents among the Islamic economists. Interestingly, some advocates of restricting the state's role see no contradiction in proposing an extensive list of governmental duties.[18]

What is not clear is why the state should be required to enforce the norms, if people would, as the Islamic economists claim, dutifully conform on their own. Further, the contention that the system would be largely free of coercion is perplexing in view of the fact that many programmes advocated by Islamic writers involve massive resource transfers and sharp restrictions on individual freedom. The prevention of land fragmentation, for instance, can only be accomplished through legislation that constrains people's choices regarding land bequests. One is left with the impression that the Islamic economists either do not *really* believe that coercion will be absent, or are assuming that individuals will somehow internalise the state-imposed constraints and voluntarily transfer resources to the state.

A related issue is whether individuals running the state apparatus can realistically be expected to forego the temptations of wielding the powers at their disposal to their own advantage. Most writers are confident that the officials of an Islamic state would not abuse their powers. They offer four distinct reasons for this optimism. First, as members of an Islamic society, officials would have been inculcated with the Islamic norms. This means, if norms provide unambiguous behavioural guidance, that the actions of officials would conform to Islamic social objectives. Second, the leadership would be 'established on the basis of consent of the people'.[19] Third, in performing their functions elected officials would routinely consult the community or its representatives to ensure that important decisions are reached by consensus (*ijma*ᶜ). Finally, the community would be vested with 'the power to dismiss the officers of the state'.[20] This power, it is said, would effectively eliminate the temptation to abuse public resources.

Even a cursory consideration of these four arguments reveals that the Islamic economists' optimism is unwarranted. The first point can be dismissed on the grounds, already discussed, that the Islamic norms are ambiguous. Ambiguity implies that a state official commands no definitive criteria for determining whether his actions conform to Islamic principles.[21] The second point, that officials would be chosen by consensus, is unrealistic, at least insofar as it applies to large societies, where people's experiences and preferences tend to differ enormously. The third point, that the political leaders would consult the community, overlooks the fact that people's opinions can be manipulated for the advantage of a select few. Since in a large, complex society the average individual has neither the capacity nor the motivation to become informed about the multitudes of issues that influence his well-being,[22] he can be persuaded by organised groups, including those at the helm of state, to support policies that are not in his best interest. As for the last point, it disregards the risks incurred by a citizen articulating his desire to replace an official.

Some of these difficulties can be mitigated, to be sure, by decentralising the state's operations and controlling officials through organisational checks and balances. But such considerations are alien to the philosophical outlook of Islamic economists.

Evidence from Islam's Past and Present

The Islamic economists do not consider themselves defenceless in the face of the foregoing criticisms. The historical record of Islam proves, they contend, the possibility of creating a society whose members adhere to the Islamic norms and which embodies a benevolent state. 'For about a thousand years,' claims the Pakistani writer Ikram Azam, '. . . there was no accumulation of wealth in a few hands, no hoarding and no profiteering, as these had been tabooed by Islam . . . the state was responsible for providing a living wage or relief to every inhabitant . . . there were neither slums nor multi-millionaires . . .'[23] Other writers do not go so far as to claim that the system performed stunningly for an entire millennium. The majority believe that the system performed ideally during the Prophet's lifetime and subsequently during the tenure between 632 and 661 A D of the four 'rightly-guided' caliphs, but that the system began to fall ever shorter of the ideal thereafter.[24] Nonetheless, they maintain that the record of this brief 'golden age' constitutes sufficient proof that their preferred order can be established in the modern world.

Even this more modest account of early Islam is questionable. Historical research indicates that even in the first few decades of Islam physical force played a role in enforcing the Islamic norms, and that some norms, like those requiring moderation in consumption and sharing with the poor, were nonetheless inconsistently followed.[25] The evidence also demonstrates that the support enjoyed by officials of the Islamic state fell considerably short of the ideal. Muslims had varying perceptions of the state's role and of the limits of their rulers' authority. And many complained, often to no avail, of the sinfulness of various officials, including the caliph. Revealingly, three of the four 'rightly-guided' caliphs met violent ends at the hands of fellow Muslims. The evidence suggests, contrary to what is often claimed, that the early Islamic community was not a perfectly just and harmonious society – and certainly not up to the high standards put forth by contemporary Islamic economists. It was a society where people were able, at least occasionally, to get away with reprehensible acts, either by using physical force or by manipulating the public conception of Islamic norms.

All this is not to say that early Islamic society was not relatively more united than coeval non-Muslim societies, or that it was not run more efficiently from an economic standpoint. My point is simply that the picture of early Islam is not spotless as the Islamic economists would have us believe.

It is appropriate to point out that even the earliest Islamic society, chose, as it expanded, to supplement its norms by coercive measures. On the eve of the community's (*hijra*) migration from Mecca to Medina, when it numbered no more than eighty people,[26] relationships among members were governed almost entirely by norms. In Medina, with the community growing at a phenomenal rate – it had 1,500 members shortly after the *hijra*[27] – the sense of brotherly cooperation that had prevailed in Mecca weakened, and as my earlier argument regarding community size would suggest, formal institutions were created to bolster the norms. It is at this stage that Islam's voluntary redistribution mechanism was supplemented by the formal tax-cum-subsidy scheme known as *zakat*, and that coercion started to play a major role in controlling prices and preventing speculation.[28]

Despite the historical evidence, the Islamic writers tend not to recognise that the Islamic economic system was highly dynamic in its early years. They consider the system to have maintained essentially its original form throughout the tenure of the Prophet and the first four caliphs. This mythical conception allows them to maintain the mistaken belief that the Islamic norms could play a central role in a modern society. Surely, if these did not enjoy complete adherence even in the community which boasted the Prophet among its thousand-plus members, one should not expect them to be very effective in contemporary societies of many millions.

In fact, one might expect the norms to be increasingly less effective with the passage of time. All indications are that the trends which surfaced as the Prophet's community began to grow, and which have continued unabated until now, will not be reversed in the future. Consider the advanced industrial societies, where the movement from the personal life of isolated settlements to the largely impersonal life of the metropolis has gone farthest. In these societies coercion by the state and by other organisations plays a key role in the social order; formal institutions adopted in the course of modernisation have not been replaced by norms of brotherly cooperation.

Let us stick, however, with the Muslim world. A large literature demonstrates that even in the most pious segments of Muslim society the individual's commitments to the Islamic community are taking a back seat to his commitments to occupational, territorial, and ethnic networks.[29] Apparently, while many Muslims continue to subscribe to the principle of equal treatment of all believers, and while most are reluctant to acknowledge that they themselves ever violate this principle, their devotion to the Muslim community is in fact being overridden by their other interests. The class conflicts and ethnic divisions that we observe throughout the Middle East, North Africa, and elsewhere are, of course, nothing new for Islamic civilisation. In no corner of the Islamic world has Muslim solidarity, in its extreme form envisioned by the Islamic economists, ever become a reality for any protracted length of time. While it is true that Islam has helped achieve social cooperation in certain limited contexts, it is equally true that the divisive forces that have accompanied modernisation in non-Muslim societies have also been part of the Muslim experience.

The Islamic economists have a tendency to attribute divisions within Islam to Western influences. For instance, in their official communiqué, the participants in the First International Conference on Islamic Economics, held at Mecca in 1976, ascribe such divisions to slavish imitations of capitalist and Marxist ways.[30] This sort of argument, which mistakes universal social processes for Westernisation, explains neither why Muslims have felt compelled to imitate Westerners nor why they persistently have chosen not to adopt the ways they consider to have been followed during Islam's golden age.

ZAKAT

The Proposed Scheme

By tradition, *zakat* (literally, 'purifier') is one of the five requirements of Islam, the others being belief in one God, prayer, one month's fast, and pilgrimage to Mecca for those who can afford the trip. As the only requirement with an explicitly economic objective, *zakat* is accorded a prominent place in contemporary writings on the Islamic economic system. It is considered to be the central, if not the only, component of fiscal policy.

The most striking aspect of the *zakat* scheme advocated by Islamic economists is that it applies to few of the forms of wealth and sources of income observed in any existing economy, developed or underdeveloped. This is so even though the proposed scheme encompasses a variety of taxes, like *ʿushr*, which historically were collected under other names. Regarding wealth, one can distinguish two main categories of holdings that are said to be subject to *zakat*: precious metals and livestock. Provided they have been in a single individual's possession for an entire year, articles in these categories are subject to *zakat* at a rate that varies according to a complex set of criteria.[31] Gold and silver are subject to a 2.5 per cent tax. In the second category, *zakat* is levied in kind for some species, in money for others. A person who owns up to twenty-four camels, pays one goat for every five camels. Horses, on the other hand, 'are taxable according to their value at 2.5 per cent'.[32] Among the animals for which the owner is not obliged to pay *zakat* are mules and elephants, the former because they 'do not breed', the latter because they 'breed seldom or after a long time'.[33]

The sources of income to which *zakat* applies are mining and agriculture. In the former category, the rate is set at 20 per cent. In the latter, the rate varies according to the source of irrigation: 5 per cent of the product if the land is irrigated by the owner and 10 per cent otherwise.[34] Numerous writers consider various agricultural commodities to be exempt from *zakat*. Some hold that vegetables are exempt because of their perishability.[35] Others maintain, because of a statement by the caliph ʿUmar I, that while dates and grapes are subject to *zakat*, peaches and pomegranates are not.[36]

In each category of wealth *zakat* is paid by people whose holdings exceed a certain minimum called *nisab*. Those whose holdings fall below the *nisab* are exempt. For gold and silver the *nisabs* are, respectively, 7.5 tolas (3 ounces) and 52.5 tolas (21 ounces) – exactly the levels stipulated by Prophet Muhammad.[37] This means, as of 1984, that each member of an Islamic economy can hold roughly US $1,100 worth of gold and $200 worth of silver without paying zakat. It is not clear whether there are additional exemptions based on other considerations. Some writers maintain that children and the insane should be exempt from *zakat* obligations, but there is no agreement on the matter.[38]

The beneficiaries of *zakat* fall into several categories. The poor, the handicapped, the unemployed, and orphans are all entitled to assistance, as are dependents of prisoners, travellers in difficulty, and debtors whose debts stem from 'legitimate' activities. *Zakat* resources are also to be used to free prisoners and slaves, to spread Islam, and to pay the salaries of the *zakat* collectors.[39] While there is wide agreement among Islamic economists regarding the list of beneficiaries, there is none concerning the exact allocation among the various categories. Some advocate dividing each year's *zakat* fund equally among the categories, while others would rather grant the head of state the right to disburse resources as he sees fit.[40]

This redistribution scheme, whose essence I have tried to capture through a few illustrations, is viewed by the Islamic system's proponents as a potent weapon against numerous economic problems. *Zakat*, they say, would reduce income inequality and serve as a legitimate social insurance scheme.[41] Another effect of *zakat* would be the stimulation of demand, since its beneficiaries would have a relatively high marginal propensity to consume.[42]

These effects, one might argue, are also attainable through an alternative taxation scheme. But the Islamic economists see an immense difference because of *zakat*'s religious nature. Afzal-ur-Rahman writes: 'the very fact that Zakat is paid to seek the pleasure of God is enough to encourage people to use their capital as far as possible for productive purposes, so that they may earn more wealth and pay more Zakat, thereby earning still greater pleasure of God'.[43] In a similar vein, Sheikh Mahmud Ahmad, an educational advisor to the Pakistani government, contends that *zakat* would wash away the 'greed and acquisitiveness of the wealthy, [making] them alive to and responsible for solving the problem of poverty'.[44] On a separate note, Mohammad Abdul Mannan of the International Center for Research in Islamic Economics claims that the problem of evasion, which haunts all secular tax schemes, is unlikely to exist with *zakat*.[45]

Preliminary Critique

The Islamic argument regarding *zakat* is open to criticism on at least three counts. Most obviously, all existing economies feature tax-cum-subsidy schemes designed to redistribute wealth and income. And in most, further redistribution is brought about through a diverse array of other measures, including entry regulations, price controls, affirmative action policies, and emergency relief programmes – to say nothing of elaborate social security systems. It is true, of course, that in some countries redistribution is chiefly from the poor to the rich. But such perverse redistribution could also arise in a country featuring a *zakat* scheme. Since *zakat* rates vary from one commodity to another, with many rates set at zero by default, it is not at all clear that *zakat's* burden would fall primarily on the rich.

This brings us to another problem, that the scope of *zakat* is far too restrictive for its intended purpose. In its proposed form, *zakat* would serve a major redistributive function only in a primitive agricultural economy resembling that of seventh-century Arabia. In any contemporary economy, whether Saudi Arabia, Morocco, or Pakistan, a substantial portion of the national product is derived from the manufacturing, transportation, communication, and service sectors, which receive virtually no attention in the current *zakat* proposal – even though rates on certain livestock, fruits and grains are specified with care. If the proposed *zakat* scheme were put into effect today, the burden would fall primarily on low-income peasants, and virtually none on shipping tycoons, industrial bosses, and bureaucrats. While the imposition of *zakat* on such commodities as cows, goats, camels, dates, grapes, and wheat might well reduce inequality in an agricultural economy, one would expect this to have the opposite effect in a contemporary economy, even an underdeveloped one.

The third basis for criticism is that the proposed scheme is suited not to an economy where relative prices fluctuate freely, but to one where they are fixed at the levels of seventh-century Arabia. If rates on animals are expressed in terms of other animals, and the *nisabs* for precious metals in terms of weight, two equally wealthy people (as measured by market prices) may have highly unequal obligations. I already hinted at one such possibility by pointing out how imbalanced the *nisabs* for gold and silver are if measured at today's prices: the *nisab* of a person who holds his wealth in gold is about 5.5 times more valuable than that of a person whose wealth is in silver. The *nisabs* for livestock and grains entail similar inequities.[46]

There is, of course, a simple solution to the last problem: turn all the levies into *ad valorem* taxes payable in money. Under this system, each person with wealth above a specified minimum would be obligated to place a certain per cent of his wealth in a relief fund. Parity among the obligations of people with wealth embodied in different commodities would be maintained even if relative prices changed drastically. But as far as most Islamic economists are concerned, such an innovation would spell *zakat's* abandonment. They feel that *zakat* is synonymous with the specific forms and rates set fourteen centuries ago by the Prophet and his companions – change these, they say, and you have done away with *zakat*.

The Contemporary Experience

The pitfalls of instituting the traditional system of *zakat* in a contemporary economy are confirmed by examining two of the several major schemes currently in operation. An empirical study by two Malaysian economists shows that in Malaysia the recently imposed *zakat* scheme accentuates inequality.[47] Malaysia collects *zakat* from paddy-producing agricultural households, 88 per cent of which lie below the poverty line, while exempting most property owners and wage earners for whom no explicit allowance is made in the traditional sources of Islam. Within the agricultural sector, the *zakat* burden is progressive at the lower end of the income scale because of the usual exemptions; but it is regressive at the upper end, due in part to evasion. This latter finding obviously calls into question the claim that because of its religious nature, *zakat* would not be afflicted by the evasion problem.

In contrast to the Malaysian scheme, the Saudi Arabian one has a somewhat broader base than the scheme used by the first Islamic community. According to Abdin Ahmad Salama of Riyadh University, a series of rulings issued by the Great Mufti, beginning in the 1950s, extended the *zakat* obligation to some types of profit and dividend income as well as to non-traditional assets such as machines, houses, and hotels; however, this revolutionary broadening of the base was subsequently curtailed by exempting assets not meant for sale. Thus, a hotel, a factory, or an automobile is no longer '*zakat*able', unless the owner is trying to sell it. Regarding livestock and agricultural products, *zakat* is levied strictly in the traditional manner. Amazingly, in view of the widespread sensitivity to tampering with traditional rates, the legal *zakat* obligation on many types of wealth and income was reduced in 1959 from 2.5 to 1.25 per cent, following complaints from Nejd and Hejaz. People were left to distribute the remainder of their religious obligations at their own discretion. Four years later the *zakat* department reverted to collecting the full 2.5 per cent from all eligible Saudi Arabians.[48]

In 1973–4, the most recent fiscal year for which Salama provides complete data, total *zakat* revenue amounted to a miniscule 0.01 per cent of Saudi Arabia's gross national product, and it covered a small fraction of the government's expenditure on poverty relief.[49] One reason these figures are so low is that people were evading their *zakat* obligations, either by taking advantage of loopholes or by disguising their assets and earnings. Like their brethren in Malaysia, Saudi citizens are apparently willing to avoid paying *zakat* if they can get away with it. The *zakat* department is finding that it has a serious evasion problem, similar to the tax evasion problem faced by secular administrations all around the globe.[50] In any case, even if the present scheme were enforced more strictly, *zakat* revenue would hardly cover Saudi Arabia's poverty relief and social security programs.[51]

Historical Evolution of *Zakat*

The problems associated with the *zakat* schemes currently in operation, and with the Islamic economists' proposals, stem partly from a failure to understand the context in which *zakat* evolved and the rationale for the particular forms it assumed. *Zakat* was not developed all at once as the uninformed reader of contemporary tracts could easily come to believe. Rather, it was developed in piecemeal fashion to meet the community's rising revenue needs. As with any reasonable taxation scheme, commodities that could not be taxed at low cost with the available technology were exempted. For instance, certain jewels that are effectively indivisible and that could not be appraised accurately in the absence of an organised market were deliberately declared tax-free.[52] The evolution of *zakat* on horses provides another revealing example. Horses were exempt during Muhammad's lifetime when they were rarely raised for trade. The expected revenue was evidently not worth the effort. By the caliphate of ʿUmar I, however, there emerged a booming market for horses, so *zakat*'s coverage was extended to horses.[53] This last example signifies that, at least in the early years of Islam, *zakat* was not conceived as a perfect and unchangeable system of redistribution. It was regarded as a scheme that could change with time – which supports my earlier statement that during Islam's early years the structure of the economy was not considered immutable.

The fact that *zakat* was levied in kind for some commodities is attributable to the low degree of monetisation in the seventh-century Arabian economy. The particular *nisabs* undoubtedly reflected the prevailing perception of minimum human needs. As for the rates, it is likely that special-interest groups played a role in their evolution. We know that from the very beginning they generated controversy. The contending schools of Islamic law often took different sides, and they failed to resolve many of their differences.[54] Within each school, for reasons that cannot be analysed here, *zakat* eventually became an ossified, dysfunctional ritual, increasingly divorced from its original purpose. An important consequence of this development was that subsequent Muslim rulers found it personally hazardous to tamper with *zakat*.

Some of the confusion among contemporary Islamic economists over the form and rates of *zakat* – such as their disagreements about the obligations of the insane and the applicability of *zakat* to vegetables – mirror unresolved ancient controversies. Such confusion is, of course, inevitable as long as they base their proposals on traditional positions without first resolving traditional inconsistencies.

Reforming *Zakat*

Not all Islamic economists have been totally averse to modifying the rates and forms of *zakat*. Recognising the senselessness of superimposing the traditional system on a modern economy, and seeing that contemporary applications – like the Saudi Arabian scheme – have had to incorporate a few innovations, some have begun to favour a reformation. In 1962, a group meeting in Damascus found it appropriate to impose *zakat* on industrial machinery at 10 per cent. While challenging this particular rate on the grounds that it would retard industrial growth, Mannan supports the extension of *zakat* to forms of wealth and income unknown in the early days of Islam. He also favours allowing the modification of particular rates, resting his case partly on the fact that the caliph ʿUmar 'imposed *Zakat* on horses, whereas before him horses were exempt from *Zakat*'.[55] Another ardent advocate of reform bases his plea on the Quran's vagueness on the sources and rates of *zakat*. Taking this to mean that the details were left to the Muslim community's transitory judgment, he reaches the conclusion that some characteristics of the system used by the first Muslims can be discarded by a modern Islamic state.[56]

But the advocates of reform have displayed hardly any inclination to lead the way in designing a *zakat* scheme in tune with modern realities. Not only that, but most of them devote extensive passages, in the very chapters or articles in which they plead for reform, to the rates for camels, while neglecting to suggest a rate for automobiles. More amazing still is the fact that many writers are inconsistent in their positions on reform. For example, Salama, some of whose findings concerning the Saudi Arabian scheme are reported above, advocates expanding the zakat base 'to include all incomes earned', after having maintained that 'no authority on earth has any right to alter the *Zakah* rates'.[57]

Other Islamic economists have devised ingenious ways of combining reformism with staunch orthodoxy. One such economist is F. R. Faridi of King Abdulaziz University, who favours both a traditional *zakat* scheme and an activist fiscal policy whose instrument would be a separate 'Islamic tax system'.[58] In Faridi's scheme, the government sets targets for variables such as aggregate savings and employment, and then ventures to meet these by choosing appropriate *zakat* rates. If it feels that the consequent transfers have resulted in an 'unbalanced intersectoral allocation of the community's resources' or some other situation 'that runs counter to the overall objectives of the Islamic society', it simply makes the necessary corrections, in the spirit of a Keynesian fine-tuner, through the tax system. A simple example will highlight what Faridi's proposal might entail. Suppose *zakat* requires A to give B $300, and that the state considers this transfer to be inflationary due to B's higher marginal propensity to consume. To counteract this effect, the state imposes an Islamic tax of $200 on B and gives a subsidy of the same amount to A. The net transfer from A to B falls to $100, but the state can proudly claim that *zakat* is being fully implemented in its traditional form.

There are, finally, Islamic economists who vigorously oppose modern reforms even though they seem to approve of the changes undertaken in Islam's early years. Among them is Afzal-ur-Rahman who first writes that 'the source[s] and the rate[s] of *Zakat* . . . can never be changed by any person or Government', and then later notes that ʿUmar's decision 'to levy *Zakat* on horses was a need of the time. . . . Horses were never bred for trade on a large scale in the time of the Holy Prophet, and so the decision of the Holy Prophet could not have covered a thing which did not exist at that time'.[59]

Zakat and the Behavioural Norms

Perhaps the greatest puzzle in the Islamic economists' *zakat* proposals becomes apparent when these are juxtaposed with their claims regarding the Islamic norms. Why does an Islamic society need an obligatory levy if, as they contend elsewhere in their writings, individuals would voluntarily perform the altruistic acts prescribed by the behavioural norms? The puzzle disappears when one takes account of the problem of community size discussed earlier. In a large community one cannot rely on voluntary redistribution alone to overcome the problem of poverty. Charity must be supplemented by obligatory taxes.

For evidence in support of this explanation we do not have to go beyond the beginnings of Islam. The earliest Islamic community did not resort to any specific taxes, but relied solely on voluntary charity. As a formal obligation, *zakat* made its first appearance about two years after the *hijra*, or over a decade after the community's formation, at a time when it was expanding rapidly and becoming increasingly heterogeneous.[60]

Once again, we see that the history of Islam's early period contains valuable lessons concerning the need to devise new institutions to cope with new circumstances. But these lessons require sound historical interpretation, which is not an area where the Islamic economists are strongest. One writer observes that *zakat* was imposed after the Islamic community had grown substantially, but he fails to draw from this any lesson regarding the applicability to today's huge societies of the behavioural norms he and his colleagues advocate.[61]

PROHIBITION OF INTEREST

Rationale for the Prohibition

Well-known throughout recorded history, the institution of interest has been a potent source of dissension everywhere. Until very recently, for instance, the Western world was sharply divided over the moral and economic merits of interest. And today, although interest is widely recognised as a permanent fixture of the economic system, feverish controversies prevail over its determinants – which include the productivity of capital, liquidity preference, and positive time preference – as well as over its socially optimal rate. Within the Islamic school of economics the prevalent view is that interest is neither indispensable nor ineradicable. In the belief that the Quran unequivocally bans interest, most Islamic economists maintain that interest should be prohibited regardless of its level and of the nature and purpose of the loan involved. Confident that a prohibition of interest is enforceable, they believe that it would greatly improve the performance of an economic system.[62]

Actually, it is not at all clear that the Quranic ban covers the institution of interest as we know it today. What the Quran bans is the ancient Arabian practice of *riba*, which entailed the doubling and redoubling of debt when the borrower failed to make restitution on time. In pre-Islamic Arabia, *riba* was responsible for the effective enslavement of substantial numbers of people, whose debts mounted exponentially following a single default. The purpose of the Quranic ban must have been the elimination of this potent source of inequality and communal friction. If the ban was in fact intended to apply to *all* forms of interest, this was not clear even to the early Muslims, whose extensive doubts concerning the issue have been documented by Fazlur Rahman.[63]

This has not kept the Islamic economists from categorically opposing interest. They contend that historical controversies notwithstanding, a ban on interest makes a great deal of sense. One problem with interest, they say, is that it results in 'unearned gain', by which they mean that the lender makes money without exerting any effort. Financial intermediaries who lend at a higher rate of interest than they offer to depositors are characterised by one scholar, for example, as 'abominable creatures who fatten on the labour of others'.[64] Closely related is the argument that guaranteeing a fixed percentage return to the lender while the borrower's return from his business is uncertain violates Islamic standards of justice.[65] Another criticism of interest is that it 'transfers wealth from the poor to the rich, increasing the inequality in the distribution of wealth'. A consequence of this redistribution, given that recipients of interest income tend to have a lower propensity to consume than payers, is lower aggregate demand.[66] Some scholars further contend that interest has undesirable attitudinal effects. 'Interest', says one Islamic economist, 'inculcates love for money and the desire to accumulate wealth for its own sake. It makes men selfish, miserly, narrow-minded and stonehearted.'[67] In the same vein, another writes that interest 'drives away from the heart of a person the feeling of human brotherhood and converts him into a "Shylock" always insisting on his pound of flesh, no matter how distressed his fellow being may be'.[68] Among the other evils attributed to interest are that it deprives society of the labour and enterprise of the rentier class,[69] and that it 'provides banks with unproductive channels to employ their capital'.[70]

Islamic Alternatives to Interest

It is one thing to ban interest, quite another to develop sound alternative institutions for allocating resources between the present and the future and for inducing people to save and invest. The Islamic economists have found the task problematic, partly because the Quran provides little guidance.

The director of the Pakistan Institute of Development Economics,

Syed Nawab Haider Naqvi, is convinced that in an interestless economy people would save and invest optimally only if forced to do so by the state. So he wishes to empower a planning agency with the right to decide how society should allocate its resources.[71] But this is a minority position, as evidenced by the adverse reactions it evoked at the Mecca seminar on the Monetary and Fiscal Economics of Islam.[72] The dominant view is that the practice of profit sharing would ensure the adequacy of savings and investment.

Under profit sharing, depositors, lenders, and investors receive not a fixed percentage return (which would constitute interest), but instead a predetermined share of any income generated by the projects financed through their contributions. They also share in any losses, again according to a predetermined formula. Among the several variants of profit sharing which have received attention in the contemporary literature, the most important is *mudaraba*, also known as *qirad*.[73]

In the ideal interest-free system put forth by the Islamic economists, people earn a return on their capital only by subjecting themselves to the risks involved in profit and loss sharing. Thus, an individual who wishes to make money on his retirement savings has to incur the risk inherent in a *mudaraba* account. If he wants to avoid this risk, his alternative is to have the bank simply hold his funds, without investing them, in which case he not only gets no return but might also pay service charges. Similarly, a bank cannot lend to a firm for a fixed payment. It can lend only on condition that it shares in the firm's profits and is exposed to its losses.

Participants in a *mudaraba* venture are in principle free to choose whatever profit-and-loss-sharing ratio they consider appropriate. Yet there is a concern that if full freedom of choice is allowed, the weaker participants might be exploited, and that, moreover, the supply of money might slip out of control. Echoing the preferences of most Islamic economists, Pakistan's Council of Islamic Ideology recommends government regulation.[74] Another problem, according to at least some Islamic writers, is that enterprises could underreport the profits stemming from the funds they borrowed. The principal remedy offered for this problem is to let banks audit the accounts of firms to which they lend.[75] A few Islamic economists recognise that banks could find auditing the accounts of small firms unduly expensive. To prevent such firms from being squeezed out of the credit market, they recommend having the government either subsidise audits of these firms, or simply guarantee the loans they receive.[76]

Short-term loans made to firms for their liquidity requirements present yet another sort of difficulty: they are generally not attributable to specific projects. To cope with this problem, one writer recommends making these loans interest-free, rationing them if demand exceeds supply.[77] Others have suggested schemes that involve service fees or average rates of return.

It is appropriate to ask, as we did earlier in a more general context, how the Islamic economists reconcile their advocacy of regulatory measures with their claim that opportunistic behaviour would be absent from a society imbued with Islamic norms. The answer is that regulatory measures will largely be redundant once a full-fledged Islamic order has been established. They are expected to play an important role only during the period of transition, which, the Islamic economists stress, has just barely begun even in societies that have explicitly committed themselves to an Islamic way of life.

Regarding loans, we have so far considered only those intended to finance productive ventures. What about personal loans taken in order to meet consumption expenses? Recognising that profit and loss sharing is inapplicable to such loans, the Islamic economists suggest making all consumption loans interest-free.[78] In the system they envisage, individuals lend on an interest-free basis to their brethren in need. In addition, banks set aside a portion of their deposits, whose origin is left unspecified, for such loans.

The Islamic economists recognise that in the absence of interest, which performs an equilibration function in existing economies, the demand for consumption loans could exceed the supply, necessitating some form of rationing. Most do not, however, specify the sort of rationing scheme they have in mind. An exception is M. Fahim Khan of the Islamic University in Islamabad, who suggests that as far as banks are concerned rationing should be based on two criteria: clients' credit records and the nature of their needs. Illustrating the scheme, he writes that an 'old client' who needs a 'loan for his son's education' has priority over a 'new client' who wants a 'loan to buy an air conditioner'.[79] Khan does not say whether an old client who wants to buy an air conditioner has priority over a new client desiring to finance his son's education. Nor does he say whether a bank has any obligation to provide consumption loans to non-clients in need.

In any case, it is believed that rationing would be an uncommon occurrence in an Islamic society, because the two institutions discussed in earlier sections would keep the demand for consumption loans under control. In the first place, the demand would be curtailed by Islamic norms that exhort people to shun 'borrowings for lavish expenditure, artificial standard of living [and] conspicuous consumption'.[80] Secondly, people with the most urgent needs would receive assistance from *zakat* funds, obviating their needs for bank loans.

Another problem that receives attention is the possibility that recipients of interest-free consumption loans would peddle their funds for interest on the black market. The temptation to do this would certainly be present, as very profitable firms that can obtain legal business loans only on a profit-and-loss-sharing basis would prefer to borrow at an interest rate equal to the normal rate of return. The solution to this problem, as with many others, is sought in the Islamic norms. People, the argument goes, will no longer desire to do business on the basis of interest once their 'false values' have been eradicated by Islamic training.[81] A few writers hold that Islam's behavioural norms are so crucial to the enforcement of a ban on interest that an immediate prohibition 'would be just like constructing a huge university building without making any provision for teachers'.[82] But most favour the prohibition of all forms of interest without delay, in the belief that the use of interest can be reduced dramatically even if few members of society have been inculcated with Islam's value system.

Regarding the treatment of interest-free loans under inflation, there is no consensus. Some writers consider full indexation to be the Islamically just approach.[83] But others say that indexation would violate the *Shariʿa* principle requiring the same quantity to be returned as borrowed. Just as, they say, someone who borrows five bushels of wheat must return exactly five bushels even if the price of wheat has in the meantime changed, so too must the person who borrows $100 return $100 even under galloping inflation. Significantly, in its lengthy report on interest, the Council of Islamic Ideology takes no clear stand on the issue.[84]

Critique

There are a number of flaws in the proposed alternatives to interest. It is true, however, that profit and loss sharing constitutes a useful scheme. In many markets, and for various types of lenders, borrowers, savers, and investors, profit and loss sharing is the preferred mechanism for allocating returns even when interest is a legally available option. This is supported by the fact that in many places, including the Arabian peninsula, profit and loss sharing has been practiced since long before Islam.[85] In contemporary societies, Muslim and non-Muslim, the practice takes a variety of forms, including money-market funds, industrial partnerships, and joint ownership of firms by workers.

It hardly follows, though, that it is reasonable to make profit and loss sharing the basis of *all* productive ventures. Replacing interest with profit and loss sharing redistributes not just returns but also risks. And while some segments of society, such as diversified firms, are willing to bear high risks, others are not. Consider the problem facing a handicapped octogenarian who relies on her savings for a living. By forcing her to open a *mudaraba* account instead of an interest-bearing account, the Islamic economists would make her bear risks that are borne better by others. She would, of course, possess the option of having the bank simply hold her funds, but this would deprive her of income.[86] This octogenarian's dilemma – income of security – illustrates a general problem that would afflict borrowers and lenders alike. People engaged in financial deals would be deprived of the right to allocate risks among themselves according to their relative willingness to bear it.

A second reason why interest may be preferable to profit and loss sharing is that by fixing borrowers' obligations, interest removes their incentives to behave opportunistically. Because of informational asymmetries between borrower and lender, these incentives are present in both depositor-bank and bank-firm partnerships. In each of these cases, the borrowing enterprise has full knowledge of its revenue and cost structures, whereas the lender can only form estimates. Given this unavoidable asymmetry, the borrower can understate its earnings and overstate its costs. Alternatively, it can deliberately let its costs soar by granting, say, inordinately high benefits to its employees. In the event of such opportunism, lenders might want to pre-negotiate a lower bound on their returns, opening the door to interest.

While sensing the possibilities of opportunism that exist under profit and loss sharing, the Islamic writers do not regard interest as a legitimate solution. They suggest that the problem can be overcome partly by inculcating members of society with Islamic norms and partly by supervising borrowers' activities. The suggestion that opportunistic behaviour can be controlled through Islamisation is belied, however, by the experiences of the recently established Islamic banks, which I shall touch on later. As for the second component of the suggestion, it overlooks the fact that effective supervision can be prohibitively costly. Suppose, for the sake of illustration, that a bank lends to a firm operating at the forefront of electronics. The cost of supervision is apt to be very high, because this has to be done by specialists in the industry's latest technical developments. It is not correct that the bank's 'keen business outlook and experience' can only make the firm's investments healthier. Nor is it obvious that bank supervision would necessarily benefit 'the march of economic progress'.[87] Banks, like all other enterprises, specialise in only certain areas of knowledge, and it may not always be economical for them to engage in detailed supervision of their customers' operations. In cases where supervision would be too costly, the bank, and by implication, its depositors, might well wish to settle for a fixed return, even if this makes them they forego the upside earnings potential.

All these problems of feasibility and efficiency aside, the logic behind the prohibition of interest raises doubts about the merits of predetermined wages, to which few Islamic economists object. Consider a firm operating in an uncertain environment. If this firm pays its employees according to a predetermined scale, all risks are borne by the shareholders: while workers would earn the same return on their efforts regardless of the firm's revenue, shareholders could either make or lose money. Clearly, then, it would be inconsistent to ban interest without also banning fixed wages. The very logic used to justify *mudaraba* requires employees to share in the firm's risk.

One of the few Islamic economists who detects the inconsistency in allowing fixed wages but not interest is Syed Aftab Ali of the Bureau of Statistics in Ottawa. In the belief that 'the existing [capitalist] institutional framework . . . restricts the choice of risk taking only to owners of capital',[88] Ali suggests that all workers receive wages tied to the profitability of their firms. The problem with Ali's proposal is that some workers prefer fixed wages even if they must accept an earnings cut to get them. From an efficiency standpoint, fixed wages are appropriate when employees are more risk-averse than the firm and have limited access to information about the firm's financial flows. In any case a ban on fixed wages is unenforceable.

Regarding interest-free consumption loans, the Islamic argument is open to criticisms analogous to those related to profit and loss sharing. It is quite reasonable to expect people to make such loans to relatives and close friends. In all societies, Muslim and non-Muslim, most people are usually willing to help those with whom they routinely associate, not only through interest-free consumption loans, but also in other ways, including outright donations. In a small community like an isolated village, this might mean that in his moment of need an individual receives assistance, which may take the form of interest-free loans, from a substantial fraction of the community. Interest-free loans to strangers constitute quite a different matter. There is no evidence that such loans have been sufficiently common in any large society to justify extensive reliance on them in the proposed Islamic society where each individual would be unknown to the vast majority of members.

A question that has received insufficient attention concerns the possibility of excess demand for interest-free consumption loans. The Islamic economists' position on the matter has already been outlined: they argue that excess demand can be dealt with through rationing, but that in any case the problem would rarely arise, as Islamisation would put a damper on demand. Aside from the unresolved issue of how rationing is to take place, there is the issue of whether rationed demanders can obtain loans from countries where interest is legal. The Islamic writers do not consider this possibility, although some of them recognise that there will exist outside opportunities to engage in interest-based transactions. Faridi would prevent Muslims from taking advantage of these opportunities by prohibiting capital mobility between interest-free and 'interest-laden' societies.[89] His suggestion amounts, of course, to a tacit acknowledgement of the futility of expecting behavioural norms to prevent violations of the injunction against interest.

Evidence from the Past

The Islamic economists' ultimate defence against these and other criticisms hinges on their interpretation of Islam's golden age. They believe that both interest-free consumption loans and profit-and-loss-sharing ventures were common among the early Muslims. Further, they believe that the system was not plagued by the problems I have described.

Although they offer hardly any evidence in support of their claims, their basic interpretation is not implausible. Throughout history consumption loans have been interest-free in predominantly agricultural communities that are small, isolated, and operating at the brink of subsistence. In such communities, where technological and transactional considerations inhibit the establishment of a formal insurance system, an individual member's survival depends on others' assistance whenever his own production falls short of his subsistence needs. Assistance may take the form of outright charity or an interest-free loan; the loan must be interest-free because otherwise fraternal assistance would turn into a business deal, reducing people's sense of security. Thus, the rationale for the prohibition of interest is the protection of the community's viability.[90] Not surprisingly, the ancient Jews abolished interest when they became an isolated tribe, and the medieval Christians put greatest emphasis on the Biblical prohibition of usury in times of contracting population and shrinking agricultural output.[91]

As for profit and loss sharing, conditions in the earliest Islamic community were undoubtedly conducive to its widespread use. In that community everyone knew each other personally and by modern standards could assess the profitability of each other's economic activities rather well.[92] Therefore, both the motivation to behave opportunistically and the possibilities for doing so must have been substantially more limited than they are in any modern economy.

The real issue, however, is not whether interest-free loans and profit and loss sharing were common in the early years of Islam, but whether interest-based financial deals were uncommon. A wealth of evidence gathered by Maxime Rodinson shows that especially after Islam's first few decades the Quranic prohibition of interest was routinely violated throughout the Muslim world, even by pious individuals.[93] Violations occurred in the context of various ruses, (*hiyal*), which were developed by Muslim jurists to circumvent the prohibition of interest while safeguarding the letter of the Quran. The following example illustrates a widely-practiced ruse. Person A sells an object to person B for $110, to be paid after a year, but promptly buys it back for $100, payable immediately. While technically no interest payment is involved, this double transaction is equivalent to a single transaction in which A lends $100 to B for one year at 10 per cent interest. Evidently, people were exhibiting such a pressing need for borrowing and selling at interest that the jurists found it prudent to legitimise their roundabout methods.

The fact that the prohibition of interest ceased to be observed on a general scale soon after Islam's birth is not surprising in view of the economic rationale I offered for it earlier. If it is indeed true that the prohibition serves an insurance function in small communities operating close to subsistence, one would expect its effectiveness to have progressively declined as the Islamic community grew and prospered. Just as the prohibition lost its appeal among Jews and Christians in times of territorial expansion and economic growth.[94] so too would Muslims have deemphasised and reinterpreted it as their own community grew in size and wealth.

The Contemporary Experience with Islamic Banks

The Islamic economists' empirical defence of their claims concerning the desirability and feasibility of a ban on interest is not confined to a recitation of what they believe to be the early Islamic record. They draw additional support from the records of the Islamic banks recently established in Saudi Arabia, the Gulf Emirates, Egypt, Sudan, Jordan, and Pakistan, among other places. They point out that all of these banks have proved profitable even though they have been offering depositors a higher yield than their interest-paying rivals. Impartial investigators, including Ingo Karsten whose research was conducted under the auspices of the International Monetary Fund, have verified that the Islamic banks have been successful from the standpoint of both owners and clients.[95]

But let us be cautious in interpreting the evidence. Before jumping to conclusions about the superiority of Islamic banking over traditional banking, one must consider that in the countries involved both the dividends of the Islamic banks and the interest rates offered by traditional banks are controlled by monetary authorities, who may well be under special orders to enhance the attractiveness of the Islamic banks. While I know of no study concerning subsidies to Islamic banks, some evidence of the matter can be gleaned from comments made at the Islamabad conference on the Monetary and Fiscal Economics of Islam by Fouad Agabani of the Faisal Islamic Bank of Sudan.[96] According to Agabani, not only are the Faisal Bank and its employees exempt from taxation, but the Bank enjoys most-favoured-enterprise status in all of its dealings with the government.

Yet even if the Islamic banks did not enjoy such privileges, it would not be surprising that *mudaraba* accounts yield greater returns than interest-bearing accounts. Since *mudaraba* accounts are riskier, few people would be attracted to them unless they provided higher yields. But it does not follow that *everyone* would become better off if all banks were forced to offer only *mudaraba* accounts. Depositors with a strong preference for security, who currently choose to hold their savings in regular accounts in spite of the higher expected earnings of the *mudaraba* accounts, would become worse off if forced to hold a risky portfolio.

A related issue is whether the establishment of Islamic banks may, as some Islamic economists claim, have provided a stimulus to aggregate savings. While there exist no reliable data on the matter, the claim is certainly plausible. This is so because in most countries with Islamic banks the stock market performs inadequately, and because from the standpoint of the individual saver-investor, *mudaraba* accounts serve the same function as stocks. The bulk of the individuals who have switched to Islamic banks are probably relatively less risk-averse savers who, if the economy were more developed, would be holding stocks. If this conjecture is correct, one can infer that the establishment of Islamic banks has stimulated savings by introducing a new financial service. This does not mean, however, that savings could be increased further by abolishing the traditional banking system, for as noted earlier, the highly risk-averse customers of traditional banks may not feel comfortable with *mudaraba*.

What about the other features that the Islamic economists say would characterise Islamic banking? None of the Islamic banks studied by Khan had ever provided an interest-free consumption loan.[97] Another of his findings is that the banks are exhibiting a marked preference for investing in 'projects which give quick returns'. One bank, the Kuwait Finance House, has invested almost exclusively in short-term commercial deals and in the notoriously speculative real estate market. This finding suggests that Islamic banks operate as profit maximisers, not as social-welfare maximisers intent on upholding Islamic principles of justice. But Khan refrains from drawing this conclusion and attributes his finding to 'the prevalent trend in local markets'.[98]

It appears, moreover, that participants in profit-sharing ventures engage in many types of behaviour that, we are told, should be absent in an Islamic setting. Agabani complains that some of his bank's clients tend 'to ignore the terms of [their] contracts . . .'; that they are 'prone to hoarding'; and that they are 'reluctant to liquidate [their] operations in the agreed time, . . . preferring to wait for "golden chances" to sell at "appropriate" periods'.[99] The experiences of the Faisal Bank suggest that Islamic banks are not immune to the problem of opportunism, which haunts non-Islamic banks in a multitude of contexts. Although it is too early to judge the problem's seriousness, it is safe to say that, just like their non-Islamic counterparts, the Islamic banks will have to rely on the force of law to get their clients to abide by provisions of their contracts.

We come at last to the most crucial question of all: whether Islamic banks are finding it practical to eliminate interest. Judging by the Council of Islamic Ideology's recent report, they are not. Like the medieval jurists before them, contemporary Islamic economists are apparently being pressured by practitioners to legitimise a variety of practices that amount to interest in disguise. One of the practices accepted by the Council (on condition that it not be used indiscriminately) is *bay mu'ajjal*, which is intended for short-term loans to industrialists, farmers, and traders. The Council illustrates *bay mu'ajjal* through the following example involving a firm that needs to buy fertiliser on credit. 'If the current cost of a bag of fertiliser to the bank is Rs. 50, the bank may sell it . . . at Rs. 55 subject to actual payment of this price after an agreed period.'[100] If one assumes that the period in question is one year, this deal is technically indistinguishable from a one-year loan of Rs. 50 given at 10 per cent interest.

Another ruse approved by the Council is 'financing on the basis of normal rate of return'. Under this method a public agency estimates the normal rate of return in each industry, and banks then provide loans on condition that their returns from these loans not fall below the relevant normal rates. If this were all, the method would have to be viewed as involving unadulterated interest. It does contain, however, an additional proviso. If a borrower's actual profit turns out to be above the normal rate, it *voluntarily* transfers the difference to the bank. On the other hand, if the actual rate falls short of the normal rate, the firm may have its obligation reduced by convincing public officials that it has not cheated. The Council feels that this method does not violate Islamic principles. Yet it is wary that because of 'existing moral standards' the practice might 'degenerate into pure interest with the passage of time'. It recommends that the method be restricted to transactions involving small entrepreneurs.[101]

Among other legitimate ways of getting around the prohibition of interest, the most ingenious one is called 'time-multiple counter-loans'. The Council uses the following example to illustrate this method. Person A wishes to borrow Rs. 100 from bank B for three months. To obtain the loan, A agrees to maintain a deposit of Rs. 10 with B for thirty months. A repays Rs. 100 to B at the end of three months, and B repays Rs. 10 to A after having profited from the use of this sum for a full thirty months.[102] This deal is technically free of interest, as it involves no fixed charge. But it is closer in spirit to interest than to profit sharing, since both A and B keep 100 per cent of the profits generated by their borrowings.

Given all this, it would be hard to argue that the Islamic banks are operating according to the ideals put forth by Islamic economists. Faced with realities of the market place, the banks seem to be finding it prudent to abandon profit and loss sharing for interest – concealed, of course, in Islamic garb.

CONCLUDING REMARKS

The foregoing discussion, which has scrutinised the three most fundamental features of the proposed Islamic system, raises serious questions about the claim that it provides a functional alternative to existing systems. The suggested behavioural norms are riddled with ambiguity and also unlikely to enjoy widespread adherence in a large society. In practice, many of them would have to be treated as state-enforced laws. There is no way of ensuring, moreover, that state officials would behave in an Islamically 'correct' manner. These criticisms are borne out by the fact that throughout most of the past fourteen centuries, members and officials of Muslim communities have had a tenuous link with Islam's behavioural norms, even when they have more or less agreed as to what these norms mean.

Another major feature of the envisaged system, *zakat*, is essentially a redistribution scheme resembling those already in operation all over the world, except that it is far less comprehensive and rather regressive. The problems with the proposed *zakat* scheme stem largely from the Islamic economists' attachment to the particular rates and exemption limits set by the early Muslims. Since these rates and limits were generally expressed in kind, they would constitute an illogical taxation scheme in the contemporary world where relative prices differ enormously from those in seventh-century Arabia. Although a few writers have toyed with the idea of reforming the traditional scheme, they have yet to specify the nature of the reforms they favor.

As for the prohibition of interest, it is effectively unenforceable in a large, heterogeneous society. While the *mudaraba* accounts, which are presented as an alternative to interest-bearing bank accounts, constitute a beneficial financial instrument in the absence of a well-functioning stock market, they do not obviate relatively risk-averse individuals' needs to lend at interest. There is no reason to believe, moreover, that all banks would be content with lending to firms on a profit-and-loss-sharing basis, or that firms would necessarily desire to borrow on this basis. The problems are similar in the case of interest-free consumption loans: in a large society people would not voluntarily make such loans, except to personal acquaintances. Unless one can show that people's need to borrow and lend at interest would disappear with the establishment of an Islamic system, it is reasonable to expect interest to persist, if in thinly-disguised form. This argument is supported by the fact that even within the existing Islamic banking system, no less than in medieval financial circles, various indirect forms of interest have been legitimised.

The unrealistic assumptions, contradictory proposals, and fallacious inferences that permeate the Islamic economists' writings can be traced to two basic methodological flaws. First of all, there is a serious tension between their professed desire to derive the entire blueprint of the Islamic economy from the Quran and the Sunnah, and their realisation that these sources do not offer a comprehensive economic framework. Indeed, the Quran is a book of moral principles that contains few specific injunctions, while the Sunnah expresses the perceived institutional and normative ideals of the first few generations of Muslims that produced it.[103] Neither one deals with the pressing economic issues of the present age, which could not have been imagined in the seventh century. It follows that if a *functional* alternative to existing economic systems is to be developed, its intellectual foundations must either be created anew or be drawn from sources outside the Quran and the Sunna. Most Islamic writers are aware of this, but they are by and large unwilling to break away from the few specifics found in the traditional sources. And when they do break away from ancient specifications, they do so without acknowledgement. We saw, for instance, how they have ratified several forms of interest while steadfastly maintaining their unconditional opposition.

The other major methodological flaw in Islamic economics is that it shuns confrontation with historical evidence. Among the documented facts that it has largely disregarded are that generalised altruism gave way to incessant factional struggles as soon as the Islamic community began to grow; that the community split into many discordant nations only a few decades after Prophet Muhammad's death; and that the spirit of the ban on interest was routinely violated throughout Islamic history. This flaw also shows up in the Islamic economists' interpretation of Islam's golden age. Ignoring evidence that even in Prophet Muhammad's time institutions were modified or abandoned as circumstances warranted, they maintain in many contexts that the institutional structure of the first Islamic economy emerged all at once and in unalterably perfect form. This interpretation, which forms the basis of the argument that the early Islamic institutions are suited to the modern world, is erroneous, as I have tried to show.

There is, of course, much one can learn from the experiences of early Islamic society. One should not, however, expect to find the ideal institutions for a modern society embodied therein. The value of such study is, rather, the lesson that successful economic growth and development require a measure of institutional flexibility.

NOTES

Author's note: The earliest version of this paper was presented at the Fourth Conference on Major International Economic Issues, held in honour of Professor John Elliott at the University of Southern California on 5–6 January 1984. I am grateful to Nikki Keddie and Jeffrey Nugent for having given me the benefit of their thoughts on that version, and to an anonymous reader and the editor of the *International Journal of Middle East Studies* for their suggestions that led to further improvements. An abbreviated version was presented at the Middle East Studies Association Conference held in San Francisco on 28 November–1 December 1984.

1. For explicit statements to this effect, see F. R. Faridi, '*Zakat* and Fiscal Policy', in Khurshid Ahmad (ed.), *Studies in Islamic Economics* (Leicester: The Islamic Foundation, 1980), pp. 119–20; and Ziauddin Ahmed, Munawar Iqbal and M. Fahim Khan (eds), *Fiscal Policy and Resource Allocation in Islam* (Islamabad: Institute of Policy Studies, 1983), pp. 2–5.
2. Afzal-ur-Rahman, *Economic Doctrines of Islam*, vol. I (Lahore: Islamic Publications, 1980), p. 56. For a similar contention, see Muhammad Abdul-Rauf, 'The Islamic Doctrine of Economics and Contemporary Economic Thought', in M. Novak (ed.), *Capitalism and Socialism: A Theological Inquiry* (Washington, D.C.: American Enterprise Institute, 1979), p. 129.
3. The first half of the present section constitutes a brief summary of a paper, 'Behavioral Norms in the Islamic Doctrine of Economics: A Critique', *Journal of Economic Behavior and Organization*, 4, 4 (December 1983), 353–79, in which I outlined in detail and critiqued these norms. The rest of this study concentrates on issues not covered in that earlier paper.
4. See, for example, Abdul-Rauf, 'The Islamic Doctrine', pp. 134–40; Monzer Kahf, *The Islamic Economy: Analytical Study of the Functioning of the Islamic Economic System* (Plainfield, Indiana: Muslim

Students' Association, 1978), ch. 4; and Mian M. Nazeer, *The Islamic Economic System: A Few Highlights* (Islamabad: Pakistan Institute of Development Economics, 1981), p. 18.

5. Such criteria are found in virtually all of the Islamic writings. For some examples, see Muhammad Nejatullah Siddiqi, *The Economic Enterprise in Islam* (Lahore: Islamic Publications, 1972), pp. 100–14; Ikram Azam, *Pakistan and Islamic Economics* (Lahore: Amir Publications, 1978), pp. 38–49; Muhammad Akram Khan, 'Inflation and the Islamic Economy: A Closed Economy Model', in M. Ariff (ed.), *Monetary and Fiscal Economics of Islam* (Jeddah: International Center for Research in Islamic Economics, 1982), pp. 245–8; and Syed N. H. Naqvi, *Ethics and Economics: An Islamic Synthesis* (Leicester: The Islamic Foundation, 1981).
6. While some writers are opposed to all forms of modern insurance, others find nothing wrong with insurance *per se*; they object only to profits derived from it. For an outline of the controversy, see Muhammad Nejatullah Siddiqi, *Muslim Economic Thinking: A Survey of Contemporary Literature* (Leicester: The Islamic Foundation, 1981), pp. 26–8; and Azam, *Pakistan*, ch. 6. Also prohibited, in the view of some scholars, are transactions in which the quantity is not numerically specified but the price is. Accordingly, an agreement to buy or sell a day's catch of fish at a price fixed in advance is in violation of Islam's normative system. See Anwar Iqbal Qureshi, *Islam and the Theory of Interest* (Lahore: Sh. Muhammad Ashraf, 1967), pp. 88–92.
7. M. Umar Chapra, 'The Economic System of Islam', four parts, *The Islamic Quarterly*, 14 (1970) 152. See also Siddiqi, *The Economic Enterprise*, pp. 15–22; and Kahf, *The Islamic Economy*, ch. 2.
8. See Abdul-Rauf, 'The Islamic Doctrine', p. 146; and Khan, 'Inflation', pp. 242–5.
9. Chapra, 'The Economic System', p. 153.
10. Nazeer, *The Islamic Economic System*, p. 16.
11. See Reuven Brenner, *History – The Human Gamble* (Chicago: University of Chicago Press, 1983), ch. 2; and David Collard, *Altruism and Economy: A Study in Non-Selfish Economics* (New York: Oxford University Press, 1978).
12. For a detailed argument along these lines, see Oliver E. Williamson, *Markets and Hierarchies* (New York: Free Press, 1975).
13. S. Waqar Ahmed Husaini, *Islamic Environmental Systems Engineering* (London: Macmillan, 1980), pp. 113–14.
14. See Mancur Olson, *The Logic of Collective Action* (Cambridge: Harvard University Press, 1965); and Russell Hardin, *Collective Action* (Baltimore: Johns Hopkins University Press, 1982).
15. Inamul Haq, *Principles and Philosophy of Democratic Socialism in Islam* (Karachi: By the author, 1966), p. 2. See also Muhammad Muslehuddin, *Economics and Islam* (Lahore: Islamic Publications, 1974), pp. 88–90; Syed N. H. Naqvi, *Individual Freedom, Social Welfare and Islamic Economic Order* (Islamabad: Pakistan Institute of Development Economics, 1981), pp. 9 and 25; and Afzal-ur-Rahman, *Economic Doctrines*, vol. I, p. 42.

16. As quoted by Hamid Enayat, *Modern Islamic Political Thought* (Austin: University of Texas Press, 1982), p. 64.
17. See, for instance, Abdul-Rauf, 'The Islamic Doctrine', pp. 136–7; and Siddiqi, *Muslim Economic Thinking*, p. 13.
18. In *Economic Doctrines*, for instance, Afzal-ur-Rahman assigns many major duties to the state although elsewhere in the same trilogy he opposes an interventionist state.
19. Husaini, *Islamic Environmental Systems*, p. 93. On this point and the other three, see also Muhammad Nejatullah Siddiqi, *Some Aspects of the Islamic Economy* (Lahore: Islamic Publications, 1978), esp. pp. 61–73; Chapra, 'The Economic System', pp. 238–9; Muslehuddin, *Economics and Islam*, ch. 3; and Husaini, *Islamic Environmental Systems*, ch. 5.
20. Siddiqi, *Some Aspects of the Islamic Economy*, p. 72.
21. The free-rider problem, on the other hand, is less pronounced for a state official than for the average citizen, because the former can perceptibly influence the welfare of society through his actions.
22. See Anthony Downs, *An Economic Theory of Democracy* (New York: Harper, 1957), chs 11–14.
23. Azam, *Pakistan*, p. 97. The author attributes this passage to a 1952 book by S. A. Siddiqi.
24. See, for instance, Husaini, *Islamic Environmental Systems*, chs 2 and 5. Strictly speaking, this entire period is an object of affection and reverence for the Sunnis but not the Shi'is. The latter, who regard the first three caliphs as impostors, believe that apart from Prophet Muhammad's lifetime, the Islamic social order has existed only during the short caliphate of 'Ali.
25. Maxime Rodinson, *Islam and Capitalism* (New York: Pantheon, 1973), ch. 3, provides a wealth of evidence on economic practices in early Islam. On communal disunity and the role of the state in enforcing the norms, see Marshall G. S. Hodgson, *The Venture of Islam*, vol. I (Chicago: University of Chicago Press, 1974), ch. 3; M. A. Shaban, *Islamic History A.D. 600–750 (A.H. 132)* (London: Cambridge University Press, 1971); and Montgomery W. Watt, *Islam and the Integration of Society* (Evanston: Northwestern University Press, 1961).
26. Hodgson, *The Venture of Islam*, vol. I, pp. 167–72.
27. Salih Tuğ, *İslam Vergi Hukukunun Ortaya Çikişi* (Ankara: Ankara Üniversitesi, İlahiyat Fakültesi Yaylnlarl, 1963), p. 29.
28. For evidence of these and other coercive practices, see Montgomery W. Watt, *Muhammad at Medina* (Oxford: Oxford University Press, 1956), chs 5–9; Maxime Rodinson, *Muhammad* (New York: Pantheon, 1980); and Hodgson, *The Venture of Islam*, vol. I, pp. 146–230.
29. See, for instance, Daniel Lerner, *The Passing of Traditional Society: Modernizing the Middle East* (New York: Free Press, 1958); and S. N. Eisenstadt, 'Convergence and Divergence of Modern and Modernizing Societies: Indications from the Analysis of the Structuring of Social Hierarchies in Middle Eastern Societies', *International Journal of Middle East Studies*, 8, 1 (January 1977), 1–27.
30. See Khurshid Ahmad (ed.), *Studies*, p. 353.

31. Detailed commentaries on *zakat* are given by Afzal-ur-Rahman, *Economic Doctrines of Islam*, vol. III (Lahore: Islamic Publications, 1976), chs 14–18; Shaikh Mahmud Ahmad, *Economics of Islam*, 2nd ed. (Lahore: Sh. Muhammad Ashraf, 1952), ch. 4; and Mohammad Abdul Mannan, *Islamic Economics: Theory and Practice* (Lahore: Sh. Muhammad Ashraf, 1970), pp. 284–302. For a brief survey, see Siddiqi, *Muslim Economic Thinking*, pp. 22–5. Recent expositions include Z. Ahmed et al. (eds), *Fiscal Policy*, chs 1–4; and Faridi, '*Zakat*'.
32. S. M. Ahmad, *Economics of Islam*, p. 91. See also Afzal-ur-Rahman, *Economic Doctrines*, vol. III, pp. 218–24.
33. Ibid., p. 206.
34. S. M. Ahmad, *Economics of Islam*, p. 90; and Afzal-ur-Rahman, *Economic Doctrines*, vol. III, pp. 206–7.
35. Ibid., p. 205; and Azam, *Pakistan*, p. 100.
36. Afzal-ur-Rahman, *Economic Doctrines*, vol. III, p. 217.
37. S. M. Ahmad, *Economics of Islam*, p. 89; and Afzal-ur-Rahman, *Economic Doctrines*, vol. III, pp. 225–6.
38. See Abdin Ahmed Salama, 'Fiscal Analysis of Zakah with Special Reference to Saudi Arabia's Experience in Zakah', in Ariff (ed.), *Monetary and Fiscal Economics*, p. 344.
39. See Afzal-ur-Rahman, *Economic Doctrines*, vol. III, ch. 16.
40. Ibid., p. 243.
41. See Mannan, *Islamic Economics*, pp. 298–301; Afzal-ur-Rahman, *Economic Doctrines*, vol. III, pp. 198–203 and 250–2; and Muslehuddin, *Economics and Islam*, p. 80.
42. Afzal-ur-Rahman, *Economic Doctrines*, vol. III, pp. 248–50; and M. M. Metwally, 'Fiscal Policy in an Islamic Economy', in Z. Ahmed et al. (eds), *Fiscal Policy*, p. 64.
43. Afzal-ur-Rahman, *Economic Doctrines*, vol. III, p. 246.
44. S. M. Ahmad, *Economics of Islam*, p. 78.
45. Mannan, *Islamic Economics*, p. 296.
46. Abdool Aziz Shaik, one of the few Islamic economists who is at once an ardent advocate of *zakat* and a critic of using the traditional exemption limits today, notes that the *nisab* for cows is five times higher than that for goats. Shaik's calculations, which are based on current South African prices, also show that the *nisab* for goats is, in turn, twelve times higher than that for silver. See his 'Concept of *Zakah*: A Survey of Quranic Texts and Their Explanations in Shariah and Contemporary Economics', in M. Raqibuz Zaman (ed.), *Some Aspects of the Economics of Zakah* (Gary, Indiana: Association of Muslim Social Scientists, 1981), p. 28
47. Ismail Muhd Salleh and Rogayah Ngah, 'Distribution of the *Zakat* Burden on Padi Producers in Malaysia', in Zaman (ed.), *Some Aspects*, pp. 80–153.
48. Salama, 'Fiscal Analysis', sect. 3.
49. Ibid., Tables 1 and 6.
50. Ibid., p. 354.
51. Ibid., pp. 361–2.
52. See Shaik, 'Concept of *Zakah*', p. 26; and Tuğ, *İslam Vergi Hukuku*, p. 56.

53. See Nicholas P. Aghnides, *Mohammedan Theories of Finance* (Lahore: Premier Book House, 1961), pp. 236–9.
54. On these differences, see ibid., esp. pp. 181–273.
55. Mannan, *Islamic Economics*, p. 293.
56. Husaini, *Islamic Environmental Systems*, pp. 134–9.
57. Salama, 'Fiscal Analysis', pp. 364 and 342.
58. See F. R. Faridi, 'A Theory of Fiscal Policy in an Islamic State', in Z. Ahmed et al. (eds), *Fiscal Policy*, pp. 27–45.
59. Afzal-ur-Rahman, *Economic Doctrines*, vol. III, pp. 197 and 223.
60. See Tuğ, *İslam Vergi Hukuku*, pp. 16–82.
61. See Muslehuddin, *Economics and Islam*, pp. 76–7.
62. For a general survey of the Islamic position on interest, see Muhammad Nejatullah Siddiqi, 'Islamic Approaches to Money, Banking and Monetary Policy: A Review', in Ariff (ed.), *Monetary and Fiscal Economics*, pp. 25–39. Detailed expositions are contained in the proceedings of the recent seminars on the Monetary and Fiscal Economics of Islam, Ziauddin Ahmed, Munawar Iqbal and M. Fahim Khan (eds), *Money and Banking in Islam* (Jeddah: International Centre for Research in Islamic Economics, 1983); and Ariff (ed.), *Monetary and Fiscal Economics*. Other contributions include Qureshi, *Islam and Interest*; Afzal-ur-Rahman, *Economic Doctrines*, vol. III, chs 1–13; Mannan, *Islamic Economics*, pp. 157–76 and ch. 9; S. M. Yusuf, *Economic Justice in Islam* (Lahore: Sh. Muhammad Ashraf, 1971), ch. 6; and Muhammad Samiullah, 'Prohibition of *Riba* (Interest) & Insurance in the Light of Islam', *Islamic Studies*, 21, 2 (Summer 1982), 53–76. For critical reviews of this literature, see Ingo Karsten, 'Islam and Financial Intermediation', *International Monetary Fund Staff Papers*, 29, 1 (March 1982), 108–42; and Siddieq M. Noorzoy, 'Islamic Laws on *Riba* (Interest) and Their Economic Implications', *International Journal of Middle East Studies*, 14, 1 (February 1982), 3–17.
63. Fazlur Rahman, '*Riba* and Interest', *Islamic Studies*, 3, 1 (March 1964), 1–43.
64. Yusuf, *Economic Justice*, p. 86. See also Afzal-ur-Rahman, *Economic Doctrines*, vol. III, pp. 59–60.
65. See Siddiqi, *Some Aspects*, pp. 91–2; and S. M. Ahmad, *Economics of Islam*, p. 41.
66. Siddiqi, *Muslim Economic Thinking*, p. 63. See also Afzal-ur-Rahman, *Economic Doctrines*, vol. III, pp. 57–61.
67. Ibid., p. 55.
68. Samiullah, 'Prohibition of Riba', p. 54. See also S. M. Ahmad, *Economics of Islam*, p. 41.
69. See Siddiqi, *Muslim Economic Thinking*, p. 63; and Qureshi, *Islam and Interest*, p. 47.
70. S. M. Ahmad, *Economics of Islam*, p. 28. See also Azam, *Pakistan*, p. 76; and Afzal-ur-Rahman, *Economic Doctrines*, vol. III, pp. 57–8.
71. Syed N. H. Naqvi, 'Interest Rate and Intertemporal Allocative Efficiency in an Islamic Economy', in Ariff (ed.), *Monetary and Fiscal Economics*, pp. 75–95.
72. See, in particular, Muhammad Anas Zarqa's comments in Ariff (ed.), *Monetary and Fiscal Economics*, pp. 98–106.

73. For detailed accounts of profit and loss sharing in the Islamic system, see Muhammad Nejatullah Siddiqi, *Banking Without Interest* (Lahore: Islamic Publications, 1980); Mannan, *Islamic Economics*, pp. 221–31; and Mahmud Abu Saud, 'Money, Interest and *Qirad*', in K. Ahmad (ed.), *Studies*, pp. 59–84.
74. See Council of Islamic Ideology, 'Elimination of Interest from the Economy', in Z. Ahmed et al. (eds), *Money and Banking*, esp. p. 122. Another defence of state regulation is put forth by Muhammad Nejatullah Siddiqi, 'Economics of Profit-Sharing', in Z. Ahmed et al. (eds), *Fiscal Policy*, pp. 163–85.
75. See Council of Islamic Ideology, 'Elimination', pp. 125–6.
76. See, for instance, M. Umer Chapra, 'Monetary Policy in an Islamic Economy', in Z. Ahmed et al. (eds), *Money and Banking*, p. 42.
77. Siddiqi, *Banking Without Interest*, ch. 4.
78. See Council of Islamic Ideology, 'Elimination', p. 112; and Mannan, *Islamic Economics*, pp. 224–5.
79. M. Fahim Khan, 'Islamic Banking as Practised Now in the World', in Z. Ahmed et al. (eds), *Money and Banking*, p. 267.
80. Council of Islamic Ideology, 'Elimination', p. 145.
81. Ibid., p. 106.
82. Mannan, *Islamic Economics*, p. 166.
83. See, for instance, Munawar Iqbal's comments in Z. Ahmed et al. (eds), *Money and Banking*, pp. 52–7.
84. See Council of Islamic Ideology, 'Elimination', pp. 115–16.
85. See Abraham L. Udovitch, *Partnership and Profit in Medieval Islam* (Princeton, N.J.: Princeton University Press, 1970), p. 8 For some evidence from Bahrain, see Samar K. Datta and Jeffrey B. Nugent, 'Bahrain's Pearling Industry: How It Was, Why It Was That Way, and Its Implications', in Nugent and Theodore H. Thomas (eds), *Bahrain and the Gulf: Past Perspectives and Alternative Futures* (New York: Macmillan, 1985), pp. 25–41.
86. A side issue here is that this would keep her funds idle, a practice the Islamic economists condemn in other contexts as 'hoarding'. They seem to overlook the fact that some of the Prophet's closest companions, among them 'A'isha and 'Umar, invested money left in their safekeeping in profit-and-loss-sharing ventures. On this last point, see Udovitch, *Partnership*, p. 173.
87. Mannan, *Islamic Economics*, p. 229. The same argument is made by Siddiqi, *Banking Without Interest*, ch. 2.
88. Syed Aftab Ali, 'Risk-Bearing and Profit-Sharing in an Islamic Framework: Some Allocational Considerations', in Z. Ahmed et al. (eds), *Fiscal Policy*, p. 265.
89. Faridi, '*Zakat* and Fiscal Policy', p. 120.
90. An illuminating discussion concerning the prohibition of interest in primitive societies is presented by Richard A. Posner, 'A Theory of Primitive Society with Special Reference to Law', *Journal of Law and Economics*, 23 (April 1980), 1–53.
91. For a detailed exposition of the ban's appearance and decline in Judaism and Christianity, see Brenner, *History*, ch. 3. See also Benja-

min Nelson, *The Idea of Usury: From Tribal Brotherhood to Universal Otherhood*, enlarged 2nd ed., (Chicago: University of Chicago Press, 1969; first ed. 1949).

92. This is not to say that these activities involved no risks. Long-distance trading could be very hazardous. What made profit and loss sharing possible even in this instance was the relative difficulty of concealing the resulting income. See M. J. Kister, 'Mecca and Tamim (Aspects of their Relations)', *Journal of the Economic and Social History of the Orient*, 8 (November 1965), 113–63.
93. See Rodinson, *Islam and Capitalism*, esp. ch. 3.
94. See Brenner, *History*, ch. 3.
95. See Karsten, 'Islam and Financial Intermediation'.
96. These comments are in Z. Ahmed, et al. (eds), *Money and Banking*, pp. 277–84.
97. Khan, 'Islamic Banking', p. 267.
98. Ibid., p. 264.
99. See Z. Ahmed et al. (eds), *Money and Banking*, p. 283.
100. Council of Islamic Ideology, 'Elimination', p. 118.
101. Ibid., pp. 119–20.
102. Ibid., pp. 120–1.
103. Modern scholars have shown that most of the words and deeds attributed to the Prophet in authorised compilations of the Sunna, which date back to the tenth century, are inauthentic. Apparently, the Prophet was assumed to have said or done countless things on the basis of a long list of oral transmissions of this form: A attests that he heard it from B who was told by C that D was present when E, the Prophet's companion, mentioned that. . . . Many of these transmissions were undoubtedly fabricated by individuals seeking religious sanction for policies they favoured for nonreligious reasons. See Ignaz Goldziher, *Muslim Studies*, vol. 2 (ed. S. M. Stern, transl. C. R. Barber and S. M. Stern) (London: George Allen and Unwin 1971; first German ed. 1889); and Joseph Schacht, *The Origins of Muhammadan Jurisprudence*, 3rd. ed. (London: Oxford University Press, 1959).

2 Economic Justice in Contemporary Islamic Thought

Timur Kuran

In the massive contemporary literature that has come to be known as 'Islamic economics',[1] the claim is repeatedly made that an Islamic economic system would achieve a greater degree of economic justice than existing capitalist and socialist systems. An Islamic system, it is said, would be free on the one hand of the exploitation and severe inequalities that characterise capitalism, and on the other of the class struggles and intolerable restrictions that are the hallmarks of socialism.[2]

The objective of this paper is to describe and evaluate the notion of economic justice that appears in this literature. I begin by defining the main principles of justice to which the Islamic economists subscribe. Then I present a synopsis of the injunctions they put forward as means of ensuring that society adheres to these principles. By and large, I go on to argue, these injunctions rest on a faulty model of human civilisation, and they leave far more room for interpretation than the Islamic economists acknowledge. In many contexts, moreover, the injunctions bring the principles of justice into conflict, both with one another and with other Islamic principles. On the basis of these observations, I suggest, finally, that an Islamic society would inevitably contain seeds of disharmony. The Islamic economists downplay the possibility of discord, but at the same time they pay considerable attention to mechanisms for minimising its scope and magnitude. Prominent among these are educational measures designed to engender a consensus that conforms to Islamic principles.

Islamic economics did not emerge as a discipline in its own right until the mid-1960s. Earlier years saw the appearance of some books, articles, and pamphlets, most notably the still widely-cited works of Sayyid Abul-A'la Maududi and Sayyid Qutb.[3] But these works showed neither an interest in nor an appreciation for the economic concepts and tools developed in recent centuries, primarily in Europe and North America. The Islamic economists who have appeared on the scene lately tend to be of a different mould: having been exposed to modern currents of thought, they are more willing to borrow ideas and methods from non-Islamic writings. Perhaps as a consequence, their standards of analysis are in some respects higher. Still, there are broad substantive continuities between the earlier and later writings. Like their predecessors, the contemporary Islamic economists ascribe immense importance to the prohibition of interest and to Islamic forms of redistribution. More importantly from the standpoint of the present article, they subscribe to the same two principles of justice. It is entirely appropriate, therefore, to treat the earlier and later writings as a single body of literature – provided one recognises that over time this literature has gained in sophistication.

In any case, I have chosen to restrict the analysis to the monographs, essays, conference proceedings, and journal articles published in English between 1970 and mid-1987. The bulk of these writings were issued by a handful of publishers: the Centre for Research in Islamic Economics (Jeddah); the Islamic Foundation (Leicester, United Kingdom); the Institute of Policy Studies (Islamabad); Sh. Muhammad Ashraf (Lahore); and Islamic Publications (Lahore). I shall pass over the writings that are providing ideological support to attempts to restructure the Iranian economy along Islamic lines, some of which have been published in English by Mizan Press (Berkeley, California). Including these writings in the present analysis would have required consideration of the doctrinal differences between the predominantly Sunni and the mostly Iranian, Shiʿi camps – differences that have split Islamic economists into two groups. I venture to say, though I shall not defend this statement here, that as far as economic justice is concerned, the inconsistencies, ambiguities, and disagreements that pervade the Sunni-dominated literature are very much a part of the Iranian Shiʿi-dominated literature as well.

Inconsistencies, ambiguities, and disagreements exist in all the great literatures that point the way toward a just world – including the diverse writings whose roots lie in Judaism, Christianity, Marxian socialism, and Third World nationalism. But the objective here is not to undertake a comparative analysis. It is to evaluate the notion of economic justice in one particular literature, that of contemporary Islamic economics. Only at the very end shall I come back to the parallels with other literatures, and then simply to put the whole argument into perspective.

PRINCIPLES

For a society to achieve economic justice, say the Islamic economists, it must conform to two general principles: equality and fairness.

The principle of equality forbids gross inequalities in the distribution of goods: 'moderate' inequality is acceptable, but 'extreme' inequality is ruled out. A society would not be considered properly Islamic if it allowed some of its members to live in luxury while others eked out an impoverished existence.[5]

The principle of fairness holds that people's economic gains are to be 'earned' and their losses 'deserved'. It requires the economic system to treat similar economic contributions similarly, and different contributions differently. 'There is to be no discrimination', says a leading Islamic economist, 'due to race or colour or position. The only criterion of a man's worth is character, ability, and service to humanity.'[6] In the same vein, another states that 'no economic entity [should be] deprived of its due share in the national product'.[7]

Of these principles, the first is concerned with the outcome of the economic process, the second with the process itself. The principle of equality bars the distribution of wealth generated by this process from being grossly unequal. The principle of fairness, by contrast, requires the economic transactions that determine the distribution to be equitable.

INJUNCTIONS

The literature offers numerous injunctions as means for bringing economic relations into conformity with the principles of equality and fairness. These take the form of prohibitions, restrictions, obligations, and responsibilities.

It would be impossible in just one section of an article to provide an exhaustive survey of these injunctions, in all their details and ramifications.[8] The synopsis that follows simply identifies the injustices the injunctions are intended to prevent, demonstrates how the injunctions vary in terms of specificity, and provides a basis for evaluating the logic on which they rest.

A much heralded obligation is the redistribution scheme known as *zakat*. It entails taxing certain holders of wealth and certain income earners at rates varying between 2.5 and 20 per cent, with the proceeds being used to aid disadvantaged members of society, including the poor, the handicapped, the unemployed, dependents of prisoners, orphans, and travellers in difficulty. The extent to which *zakat* is applied is a matter of some controversy. Some writers consider it to be limited to those categories of wealth and income for which rates were specified in the early years of Islam. Others consider it to include categories that were not known until recently, such as factories and motor vehicles. The reformist writers do not agree among themselves, however, as to the limits of the coverage and the applicable rates. But regardless of how they perceive *zakat*, all Islamic economists believe that it is a very powerful instrument for bringing an economy in line with the principle of equality.[9]

Another injunction regarded as having an important equalising effect is the Islamic law of inheritance, which distributes a deceased person's wealth among all his immediate relatives. One contributor to the literature describes the essence of the law as follows: '[A] person may not dispose of more than one third of his property by testamentary directions . . . The rest of the inheritance must be divided among the prescribed heirs in specified shares'.[10] The shares are determined according to the exact number and relationships of the survivors, so the distribution of estates assumes an endless variety of configurations. In accordance with the principle of fairness, full siblings of the same sex have identical entitlements, which rules out primogeniture. The law serves the principle of equality by preventing the growth of family estates.

In addition to such formal obligations, there are some informal injunctions intended to equalise the distribution of goods. Most important, the individual is to make charitable donations to those in need. In this connection, a Pakistani Islamic economist writes that 'capacity for contribution to social welfare . . . is to be measured by the amount one is able to spare after enjoying the standard of living which is commonly enjoyed by men of one's rank and station in life'.[11] As a consumer, meanwhile, the individual is encouraged to enjoy the earth's bounties, but without drifting into extravagance, even if he can afford to do so after having met his formal obligations. The following warning by a widely-quoted Islamic economist is typical: 'After a certain limit, consumption of cloth may turn into extravagance. As extravagance is prohibited, the individual must stop at this point'.[12] Extravagance violates the principle of equality because, by definition, it entails consumption well beyond the average level for society.

An injunction that appears in numerous guises is the obligation to behave altruistically, that is, to demonstrate an unselfish concern for the welfare of others. An individual is required by this injunction both to refrain from actions unduly harmful to others and to take positive steps in the public interest.[13] In the terminology of modern economics, he is to bring into his calculus the negative and positive externalities of his actions. This injunction, which is intended to serve both principles of justice simultaneously, comes into play primarily in discussions concerned with personal consumption, resource allocation, and industrial relations.[14] To give one example, an industrialist deciding whether to build a particular factory must take into account not only his expected personal profits but also the air pollution the factory would generate and the new employment opportunities it would provide. Many writers stress that the externalities to be considered are not limited by geographical, national, racial, familial, or occupational boundaries.[15]

The pursuit of monetary gain is legitimate, provided it does not involve unfairness. In this connection, an industrialist is to pay 'fair' wages to his employees and charge 'just' prices to his customers.[16] Moreover, he is to make every effort to share with his customers what he knows about the characteristics of the goods he is selling, including their possible defects.[17] To this end, he is to avoid equivocal speech and to refrain from concluding a deal until the buyer knows all there is to know. The main objective of this insistence on openness is to give the consumer a fair deal, that is, to protect him from exploitation. Some writers claim that the injunction also promotes the principle of equality.

Of all the injunctions cited, the most celebrated is the prohibition of interest. The rationale for the prohibition differs depending on whether the loan involved is a consumption loan or a business loan, although in both cases the principle of fairness is central. If interest is charged on a consumption loan, the lender makes money without exerting any effort and without giving the borrower something in return. If it is charged on a business loan, the lender's return is fixed, while that of the borrower is variable. (A bank deposit is treated as a special kind of business loan, where the depositor is the lender and the bank the borrower.)

How are the implied injustices to be avoided? In the case of a consumption loan, the lender is to earn no return at all: when the loan comes due, he is to get back only what he has lent. In the case of a business loan, the lender and the borrower are to share, according to a predetermined formula, the profits or losses from the investment financed by the loan. Mindful of the possibility that under interest a borrower could end up with a significantly higher return than the lender – as when an industrialist earns a 30 per cent return on an investment financed through a loan obtained at 5 per cent interest – the Islamic economists contend that a ban on interest would also have an equalising effect on the distribution of wealth.[18]

The prohibition of insurance as a profit-oriented business rests on similar reasoning. Most Islamic economists have no objection to insurance *per se*, just as they are not opposed in principle to lending and borrowing. They recognise that by spreading unanticipated losses among its members, a well-designed insurance scheme can serve the principle of equality. At the same time, they feel that profit from insurance constitutes unearned gain, 'the callous exploitation of the misery of . . . helpless common folk'.[19] To prevent exploitation, they say, the state must be empowered to take over most areas of the insurance business and to regulate the rest.[20]

Transactions involving speculation caused by avoidable ignorance are considered objectionable, again on the grounds that they may result in unearned gain for one party and undeserved loss for the other. Thus, the sale of a pregnant camel is prohibited, because her value depends on the sex of the offspring, which, until known, may generate speculation. Likewise, an orange tree in blossom may not be sold, because neither the quantity nor the quality of its yield can at this stage be predicted exactly. It is also considered illegal to trade a piece of cloth that has not been examined carefully by both parties, lest they misperceive the cloth's properties.[21]

Throughout the literature one finds injunctions against the activities of middlemen, a catchall category that includes such diverse groups as commodity speculators, real estate agents, and stockbrokers. Invariably, the opposition is based on the belief that such activities result in unearned gain. Commodity speculation, undertaken in the expectation of profiting from fluctuations of supply and demand, is the most frequent target of attack.[22] There is a consensus that speculation over basic commodities is highly unjust. Certain writers argue that speculation does not violate the principle of fairness when it involves non-basic commodities, although they fail to specify a set of criteria for distinguishing between the two categories.[23]

Modes of agricultural cultivation are also a concern of the Islamic economists. Sharecropping, a practice whereby a labourer cultivates a landowner's plot in return for a fixed share of the output, is the favoured mode of most writers, who consider it to be analogous to profit and loss sharing in industry and trade. They maintain that sharecropping entails praiseworthy cooperation by owners of complementary factors, land and labour, and that the landowner's returns are no less justified than those of a depositor in a profit-and-loss-sharing bank account.[24] Other writers oppose sharecropping on the grounds that a landowner who does not participate personally in cultivation is not entitled to a return.[25] Still others take an intermediate position. Among them is the author of a trilogy on Islamic economics, who writes:

> If there is a spirit of goodness and benevolence behind [a sharecropping] contract and either [party] expects only to receive his due . . . then it is the best form of cooperation, partnership and friendship. But if this spirit is lacking and the weakness of the cultivator becomes the instrument of [the] landlord's oppression and exploitation . . . then this form of cultivation is not permitted. . . .[26]

He adds that sharecropping should not be allowed where it would turn the landowner into an idler or a parasite.[27]

Predictably, perhaps, the practice of renting land, which involves a fixed payment from the labourer to the landowner, comes under harsh indictment. Like interest, it places the contract risk entirely on one party: the labourer's return depends on the size of his harvest, whereas the landowner's return is fixed. In addition, the practice enables the landowner to lead a comfortable life of leisure while the labourer struggles for his subsistence. Still, some authors are prepared to exclude a class of cases from the prohibition. A landowner can justly rent his land, they say, if he is pursuing socially beneficial activities, and in particular, if he is defending Islam.[28]

Various Islamic economists consider certain other market structures and forms of economic organisation to be unjust. There is widespread agreement that unregulated private monopoly gives rise to grievous injustices by allowing exceptionally high returns. 'Islam views with extreme disfavour', says a Nigerian proponent of Islamisation, 'the monopoly of resources by a few self-seeking millionaires.'[29] Some writers consider the publicly-held corporation of modern economies to be inconsistent with Islam's principle of fairness. The facility of liquidating the corporation's shares encourages, they say, its shareholders to desert it at the slightest sign of trouble, compounding in the process the remaining shareholders' expected losses. The majority, however, regard the modern corporation to be praiseworthy, on the grounds that it involves risk-sharing.[30]

ILLUSIONS

By and large, the Islamic economists consider the Islamic injunctions to provide a set of unambiguous guidelines for attaining economic justice. The following remark is typical:

> If the Islamic teachings on the earning of wealth are followed, the norm of justice to employees and consumers is applied, provisions for redistribution of income and wealth are implemented, and the Islamic law of inheritance is enforced, there cannot be any gross inequalities of income and wealth in Muslim society.[31]

There is a strong consensus, moreover, that the set of injunctions is not dynamic, but static: it is eternally applicable, without revision, to all societies.

One thus gets the impression that in an Islamic economy the attainment of *substantive* justice would be a *procedural* matter.[32] Regardless of economic and social conditions, the two substantive principles of justice would be met by having members of society follow the specified injunctions. This position harbours two distinct claims: first, that just behaviour entails conformity to the stated Islamic injunctions; and second, that these injunctions are just, in the sense that they are better suited than other sets of injunctions to serve the principles of equality and fairness. I wish here to evaluate the second claim – to question, that is, whether the injunctions put forth by the Islamic economists can reasonably be expected to secure their two principles of justice.

As we have seen, the purpose of *zakat* is to promote equality by redistributing wealth from the haves to the have-nots. It is by no means self-evident, however, that *zakat* would achieve this purpose. Since it entails taxing only some categories of income and wealth, and then at various rates, its distributional impact would depend on the composition of society's output. Its narrow version places the burden of taxation entirely on categories of income and wealth known in the early years of Islam, notably agriculture, mining, and precious metals. With industrialisation and explosion of the service sector, these sources of income and wealth have dwindled in importance, even in the least developed countries. Also, most of the poor households in today's world are concentrated in agriculture, and most of the rich outside agriculture.[33] It is not clear, therefore, that *zakat* would promote equality; it might well promote *in*equality. This conjecture is supported by a study of one of the narrow *zakat* schemes in existence.[34] What about the broader schemes that have been proposed? It is certainly possible that they would play an equalising role, although this remains to be demonstrated. The impact of any particular scheme will depend on the characteristics of the economy to which it is applied. A scheme that serves as a strong equaliser in a contemporary economy dominated by industry and agriculture could lose its potency as services for which rates have not been specified gain in importance.

Regarding the injunction to take into account negative and positive externalities of one's actions, it is appropriate to ask how individuals are to compute and predict these. In most contexts, this is an enormously difficult task, if only because human abilities to acquire, store, retrieve, and process information are severely limited. Thus, individuals willing to abide by this injunction would not necessarily succeed in doing so. The Islamic economists are confident, nonetheless, that in an Islamic system the individual would have no difficulty in distinguishing among collectively harmful and beneficial actions.[35] One basis for their confidence is their conviction that the Quran and the Sunna, the traditional sources of Islam, provide considerable guidance. Another, which will be criticised further on, is their belief that a consensus will form in many important contexts, and that this consensus will coincide with the public interest.

Overly optimistic assessments of human nature and capabilities also pervade discussions concerning other injunctions. On the subject of helping those in need, the Islamic economists have a tendency to write as if it were perfectly obvious what 'need' is. Likewise, when exhorting employers to pay fair wages, and sellers to charge just prices, they write as though everyone will attach identical meanings to 'fair' and 'just'. They simply evade the treacherous task of making these concepts operational. This should not obscure the fact that if ten members of an Islamic society, all well versed in Islamic economics, were asked to quantify the need of a certain person out of work, or the fair price of ripe tomatoes, or the just wage of a novice bricklayer, they might well produce ten different answers. It is true, of course, that on some issues agreement would be easy. No one trying to follow the injunction to help the needy would want to let an unemployed person starve. But on the nature and magnitude of assistance, there is no reason to expect agreement to be automatic.

We saw earlier that the Islamic economists would give the state an active role in preventing injustices associated with insurance. Further on, we will see that they accord to the state many other roles in preventing injustice. They take it for granted in this connection that the officials in charge of identifying and correcting injustices will be both able and willing to carry out their duties in full. Such optimism is unwarranted, partly because no state official has unbounded cognitive abilities, and partly because the powers at the disposal of an official constitute assets that can be used for self-enrichment.[36] Throughout the history of Islam there have been state officials, many of them very pious, who have abused their powers by putting public resources to personal use, conferring privileges on relatives and friends, subsidising prosperous groups at the expense of the poor, and in other ways.[37] This is not to say that the Islamic economists disagree with this interpretation of the past.[38] I touch on the historical record to draw attention to the fact that the Islamic economists have not offered a convincing explanation as to how the kinds of abuses observed in the past can be avoided in the future.

The prohibition of interest, deceptively straightforward in an abstract setting, poses a fundamental practical problem that many writers do not even acknowledge. Under inflation, is the borrower of a consumption loan obligated to compensate the lender for changes in purchasing power? Some of the writers who address the issue refrain from taking a position. And those who do take a position are divided, with some saying that fairness requires the indexation of loans, others that it bars indexation.[39] For those who favour indexation, an unresolved issue is whether the relevant price level is to be based on the lender's consumption basket or on that of the borrower.

Profit and loss sharing, the favoured alternative to interest in the case of a business loan, presents another problem that has received little attention. Suppose an old person takes his savings to the only Islamic bank in his neighbourhood, which offers him a profit-and-loss-sharing deal whereby it would receive 99 per cent of any profits and, correspondingly, incur 99 per cent of any losses. Is this deal fair from an Islamic standpoint? If the answer is 'no' or 'not necessarily', what are the lines of demarcation? One writer who takes up the issue states that the shares are to be determined by custom – as if a practice becomes fair by virtue of being customary.[40] Another writer, using a mathematical model, says that the shares are to be determined through the interaction of the supply and demand for contracts – as if, once again, an equilibrium allocation could never be lopsided.[41] As far as I am aware, only one writer recognises that the literature effectively evades the issue.[42]

The point of all these criticisms is not to suggest that one *ought* to impose even tighter restrictions on economic transactions, or that one *ought* to regulate every aspect of the economy. It is, rather, to expose as an illusion the Islamic economists' apparent belief that the Islamic injunctions would guarantee economic justice.

DISAGREEMENTS AND INCONSISTENCIES

This belief is all the more surprising when one considers that the Islamic economists do not themselves agree as to what the Islamic injunctions are. We have already seen how they differ in their positions on indexation, the scope of *zakat*, sharecropping, and publicly-held corporations. Another fundamental controversy concerns the limits of public ownership. Quoting verses of scripture and passages from the Islamic classics, some writers maintain that the principle of equality requires public ownership of trade facilities, industrial raw materials, and even land.[43] Citing different verses and passages, others hold that public ownership is not necessary in these areas, except when this would improve social welfare.[44] Thus, Islamic justifications exist both for sharply curtailing private property rights and for according them wide protection.

There is a similar controversy over the method of financing public projects. 'A progressive taxation system', says one prominent Islamic economist, 'seems to be perfectly in harmony with the goals of Islam.'[45] Another sharply disagrees: 'Progressive taxation assumes illegitimacy of the income of the rich. The rising slabs represent taxation with vendetta. Only a proportional tax at a fixed rate (on the pattern of *Zakat*) is to be levied on the accumulated wealth of the capable taxpayers without any distinction.'[46] Yet another Islamic economist sees merit in both positions: 'Proportional taxation becomes Islamic if income and wealth are already distributed according to Islamic economic egalitarian criteria . . . However, in the existence of maldistribution of income and wealth . . . a progressive system of taxation should be invoked.'[47]

Underlying this particular controversy is the fact that the principal of equality is subject to many different interpretations. Indeed, writers who agree that 'moderate' inequality is acceptable often disagree over the limits of moderation.[48] It is worth noting that such disagreement is anything but new to Islam: even the early caliphs saw the limits differently.[49]

On the disbursement of *zakat* funds, writers disagree as to whether funds collected in one year can be spent in another. Some take the position that rollovers are inconsistent with the spirit of *zakat*.[50] Others disagree, on the grounds that cyclical fluctuations in economic activity require disbursements to be greater in some years than in others.[51]

These and other disagreements belie the Islamic economists' belief that in an Islamic economy the attainment of substantive justice would be a procedural matter. On many central issues the Islamic economists subscribe to contradictory injunctions, which means that, even though they share the same substantive objectives, they disagree as to the procedures needed to reach these. A person trying to weigh the merits of an Islamic economy might wonder: whose Islamic economy is *the* Islamic economy?

If we ignore actual and potential disagreements among the Islamic economists, we notice that the injunctions defended by any given writer are not always consistent with each other. Take the prohibition of interest on business loans and bank deposits, which, as I remarked earlier, is defended on the grounds that fairness requires the borrower and the lender to share risk. This interpretation of the principle of fairness would also seem to require employees to earn variable, as opposed to fixed, wages. Yet, many of the most vehement opponents of interest favour fixed wages, and some say explicitly that variable wages are unjust.[52] If wages were variable, the argument goes, a fall in a firm's revenues might so lower its employees' wages that they would have trouble obtaining even the bare necessities of life. This situation would violate the principle of equality.

Leaving aside the question of why in such instances *zakat* funds or other reservoirs of altruism could not be brought into play, let us pursue the implications of coupling fixed wages with the absence of interest. It means, for instance, that a grocery worker is shielded from market risk as an employee, but not as a saver, should he put part of his earnings in an income-producing bank account. Correspondingly, the owner of the grocery store bears the entire risk of his operation, while his neighbour the banker shares his own risk with the grocer's employee. I am not arguing that in practice grocers, bankers, and employees would find this arrangement undesirable or unreasonable. They may or may not, depending on a host of factors. My point is simply that the Islamic economists do not apply the principle of fairness consistently.

A subtler inconsistency involves the injunction against speculation caused by avoidable ignorance. Through examples, the Islamic economists try to show that the injunction would effectively block all transactions where the buyer and the seller might have avoidable differences over relevant characteristics of the traded commodities. But these examples do not make a case. Consider, first, the prohibition against selling a pregnant camel and the associated suggestion that one may sell her after she has given birth and the sex of her offspring has been revealed. Does *all* avoidable ignorance end with the termination of pregnancy? Not at all. The mother could have a brain tumor, detectable through modern veterinary technology, which would make her expected life span very short. In practice, therefore, she could change hands with both the buyer and the seller expecting her to live ten more years, instead of the six months she actually has left. The buyer would then suffer what the Islamic economists call an undeserved loss, and the seller would enjoy an unearned gain.

For another example, take the ban on selling an orange tree in blossom, which carries with it the permission to sell the tree after it has borne fruit. Islamic treatises would have us believe that there is no avoidable ignorance once the oranges have ripened. In fact, the juiciness, sweetness, and vitamin C content of ripe oranges – to mention three of the characteristics that make them desirable – become known with greater precision when they are cut open, eaten, and analysed. Traders of ripe oranges can thus reduce their ignorance through scientific sampling and testing.

The inconsistency, then, is to insist on the elimination of some types of ignorance, without demanding even the reduction of others that traders are capable, in the present state of technology, of reducing substantially. This inconsistency is the inevitable result of attempting to eliminate *all* avoidable ignorance. Since one can always avoid more ignorance through more tests, the approach will lead to arbitrary decisions, unless one bans trade altogether. In modern economies the ignorance of traders is reduced through mechanisms such as commodity standards, product brands, and warranties.[53] Some ignorance is deliberately tolerated, apparently because traders consider the cost of elimination to be prohibitive. But the trade-offs involved rarely appear in the Islamic economists' repertoire.

The specific prescriptions that permeate the contemporary literature, like those involving pregnant camels and orange trees in blossom, are by no means new. They figure prominently in classical Islamic jurisprudence as solutions to recurrent commercial problems that threatened social stability. If in the absence of a particular piece of information a transaction tended to breed resentment, Islam's jurists tied the legality of the transaction to the availability of this information. They hoped thereby to minimise the incidence of disputes.[54]

The jurists did not always agree among themselves as to which informational imperfections were problematic enough to call for regulation. Nor, when in agreement on this count, did they always agree on the nature of regulation. In a recently published study Nabil A. Saleh records, in encyclopaedic fashion, the differences that existed among the various schools of law.[55] He documents, for instance, that while the Shafi'i, Hanbali, and 'Ibadi jurists categorically prohibited the sale of unripe fruits, the Malikis and some of the Hanafis allowed 'the sale of fruits . . . which ripen in succession during one harvest, if such sale accompanies the sale of what has already ripened'.[56] Apparently, there were also differences over the definition of ripeness. For the Malikis, Shafi'is, Hanbalis, and 'Ibadis, fruits ripened – and, hence, became ready for sale – when they turned sweet. For the Hanafis, in contrast, they ripened upon passing the flowering stage and attaining their final appearance.[57] Surprisingly, Saleh does not consider the inconsistencies he detects to hinder the task of defining the Islamic economic order. On the contrary, he suggests that his study will *facilitate* Islamisation, even though he ignores the question of how one is to choose among the conflicting positions.[58]

PRIORITIES

Certain inconsistencies in the contemporary literature are attributable at least partially to the fact that justice is not the sole objective of the Islamic economic system. Among the other objectives are efficiency, growth, employment, and industrialisation. A few authors appeal to such goals in justifying their reluctance to ban all transactions involving avoidable ignorance.[59]

The apparent inconsistencies involving modes of cultivation are also traceable to other goals, although I am unaware of explicit arguments to this effect. As we saw earlier, the Islamic economists would prohibit the renting of agricultural land, except in cases where the owner is engaged in socially beneficial activities, notably the defence of Islam. A landowner defending Islam is presumably away from home for extended periods of time, and unlike his counterparts who stay home, he might not be able to monitor at low cost the productivity of his property. Allowing him to extract a fixed rent, as opposed to a variable share, eliminates the need for monitoring. As such, the fixed-rent contract can be interpreted as a compromise that promotes cost efficiency in monitoring over justice.

Other inconsistencies can be attributed to clashes between the principles of justice themselves. Take the contradiction between the prohibition of interest and the requirement that wages be fixed. Each of these cases features a clash between fairness and equality. In the former case, the clash is resolved in favour of fairness; in the latter, in favour of equality. The resolutions differ because of an implicit assumption that workers are much poorer than investors. From this assumption – which does not always correspond to reality – it follows that workers would suffer more severely from a decline in wages than investors would from a drop in their returns. Hence, the principle of equality prevails in the case of wages, but not in the case of investment returns.

Certain disagreements among the Islamic economists can likewise be ascribed to clashes between the two principles of justice. The dispute concerning progressive versus proportional taxation and the potential disputes over such notions as need, fair wage, and just price can all be linked to variations in the weights accorded to fairness and equality.

A few Islamic economists recognise in some contexts that the principles of fairness and equality may conflict with each other or with a goal such as efficiency. One writer thus remarks that 'Islam emphasizes the priority of justice over efficiency . . . This is not to say that efficiency is not a relevant consideration, but only that it is not decisive'.[60] Illustrating the implications of this ordering, he notes that it calls for a ceiling on firms' profits, although he does not discuss how the ceiling is to be determined.[61] On the subject of resource allocation, another writer provides a long list of relevant criteria, from consumer preferences to project profitability to Islamic ideology. It may prove impossible, he says, to satisfy all of them at once, in which case they must be weighted according to importance. He does not specify how the weighting is to be done.[62] Yet another writer detects a conflict over inflation. After noting that erosion of the purchasing power of money does injustice to the providers of interest-free consumption loans, he states:

> This implies that any activity . . . which significantly erodes the real value of money should be considered to be a national issue of paramount importance and treated with a sense of concern. Nevertheless, there are other goals which are of equal, or greater, importance. If there is an unavoidable conflict between the realisation of these goals, and a compromise becomes inevitable, then the goal of stable real value of money may be somewhat relaxed provided that the damage done by such relaxing is more than offset by the realisation of other indispensable national goals and provided that such relaxing is undertaken only as long as absolutely necessary and does not become a permanent feature of the policies of the Islamic state.[63]

But which other goals are 'indispensable', and how is one to determine when they 'more than offset' the damage done by inflation? On these crucial points, we are offered little guidance.

Most writers do not even bring up the issue of priorities. They appeal to one principle on the question of wages, another on interest; then, on modes of cultivation, they switch principles in mid-discussion, without, however, offering a rule to govern such switches. This style of argumentation is characterised by philosophers as 'intuitionist', since it involves using intuition to strike a balance among different principles.[64] In intuitionist arguments, compromises are struck among principles as a matter of course, but because the established priorities remain implicit, they offer limited assistance in novel contexts.

Interestingly, a leading Islamic economist admits in one of his latest books that in resolving conflicts among Islamic goals 'the appeal to intuition cannot be avoided altogether'.[65] But he immediately reverses himself, dismissing the arbitrariness that intuitionism imparts to one's judgments. Islam's holy laws [*Shariʿa*], he claims, specify how the various considerations are to be weighted. He goes on to argue that 'the so-called controversy between equity and efficiency is not real in Islam'.[66]

It is important to realise that no intellectual enterprise as ambitious as Islamic economics can be entirely free of inconsistencies or avoid intuitionist argumentation. Our cognitive limitations as human beings preclude us from producing a fully coherent blueprint of the socioeconomic system we favour. They force us to segment our blueprint, to bring to the issues and problems that concern us disparate constellations of impulses, aspirations, assumptions, and logical processes. They prevent us, moreover, from articulating the complete rationale behind every feature of the blueprint.[67]

This is not to say that the flaws of Islamic economics outlined here are excusable. While it may be true that total coherence is a mirage, it is also true that blatant inconsistencies can be avoided through careful and systematic reflection. Yet as we have seen, even the few Islamic economists who notice certain inconsistencies attempt to deal with these in the most superficial manner. They eschew the painstaking task of making doctrine comprehensible – a task to which generations of judges and social thinkers, in both Muslim and non-Muslim societies, have devoted their careers.[68] The task involves more than bringing coherence to abandoned injunctions of past centuries – as when an attempt is made to explain why fourteen centuries ago the caliph ʿUmar I declared that dates are subject to *zakat*, but not pomegranates.[69] It involves bringing coherence to current practices as well. Consider the ongoing policy of Saudi Arabia and the Gulf emirates, according to which non-Muslims from the Far East are given preference in certain employment categories over Muslims.[70] In various countries many well-qualified Muslims are out of work, yet workers from the Far East are less likely to cause political trouble. Given these facts, is Saudi Arabia's employment policy justified by Islamic standards? As far as I can ascertain, the literature provides little help in resolving issues of this sort.

The Islamic economists might reject the bulk of this appraisal, for in a good many of their writings they maintain that Islamic thought is equipped with a sound methodology for resolving inconsistencies and handling novel issues. A major component of this methodology, they say, is analogical reasoning (*qiyas*), whose purpose is to apply established priorities to new contexts.[71] It is true that in medieval Islamic treatises one finds extensive philosophical commentaries on analogical reasoning, as well as scores of applications.[72] However, these do not amount to an operational system for the *coordinated* determination of priorities. And this is hardly surprising. For reasons just explained, establishing similarities between a novel case and familiar cases involves a measure of arbitrariness even in the best of circumstances. Also, a decision-maker's perceptions and values are inevitably colored by his personal experiences and by local conditions.[73] Islamic jurists, in fact, often produced a series of judgments on a single case.

Even if I am wrong, and classical jurisprudence does provide an operational system for the determination of priorities, one would not know this from contemporary Islamic economics. Nowhere in this literature does one find articulated a set of general rules to govern analogical reasoning. Instead, one finds in abundance unsynthesised, disparate examples of analogical reasoning by medieval Islamic writers. When contemporary Islamic economists resort to analogical reasoning themselves, they do so in what seems to be the most arbitrary manner.

CONSENSUS

As I mentioned at the outset, the Islamic economists claim that an Islamic economy would be free of the economic injustices allegedly rampant in capitalist and socialist economies. In various contexts, however, it is not clear what Islamic justice requires. Nor is it clear what compromises are to be struck on account of other considerations.

These ambiguities have a far-reaching practical implication: even in a society composed entirely of pious Muslims eager to build the economic system championed by the Islamic economists, no-one would possess definitive criteria for judging whether particular economic actions, practices, and institutions were just. Two members, equally well-meaning and learned, could easily differ as to whether a certain market institution conformed to Islam's twin principles of justice. Because of their differences, moreover, they could suspect each other of subscribing to un-Islamic principles. Their suspicions would disturb the envisioned social harmony.

Yet most Islamic economists minimise, and some dismiss altogether, the possibility of discord. In the belief that the institutions of an Islamic society would be geared toward the reconciliation of individual differences, they maintain that people would eventually attain a consensus (*ijma*ʿ).[74] Some writers seem quite confident that this consensus would not conflict with Islamic principles. One says in this connection that 'when new situations have been met by analogy or otherwise', the consensus of the community would prevent it from 'drifting into heresy'.[75] He builds his case partly on a saying commonly attributed to Prophet Muhammad: 'My people shall never agree on error'.

There are two distinct circularities in this position. First, the ability to determine whether or not a consensus is acceptable presupposes a consensus on what is properly Islamic. As we have seen, however, the Islamic economists do not even agree among themselves as to the implications of the Islamic principles. Second, the authenticity of the Prophet's saying is itself based on the consensus of the Islamic community. There is no guarantee that this consensus will endure, for scholarship has shed serious doubt on whether the saying belongs to the Prophet.[76]

In any case, the Islamic economists are not really prepared to leave the economy's design to the community's consensus. They would not lend their approval to a consensus they perceived to conflict with Islamic principles – to one, for example, that consented to the legalisation of interest. Revealing a refusal to take the Prophet's saying literally, they also offer concrete measures to ensure the acceptability of the community's consensus. Coercion, some say flatly, is not one of these: people are not to be forced, on pain of punishment, to support opinions or interpretations with which they disagree. The emphasis is to be on teaching the Islamic interpretation of history, inculcating Islamic principles of justice, and fostering a sense of brotherly cooperation. Through these educational measures, the argument goes, beliefs, opinions, and preferences will become harmonised, and people will thus become better equipped for the establishment of a consensus meeting Islamic stipulations.[77]

This argument, too, is problematic, for it rests on a pair of premises shown above to be doubtful. The first is that there is a unique Islamic economic system, characterised by a well-defined ensemble of institutions, practices, and behaviours. The second is that there exists a class of knowledgeable leaders – presumably the Islamic economists themselves – who can teach people what the system entails. Both premises conflict with the fact that the Islamic economists are seriously divided over many basic features of the economy. How can one expect teachers who have not achieved a consensus among themselves to forge a consensus in the wider community?

A measure of consensus is essential, of course, to the smooth functioning of any society. If people are to live and work together in harmony, they must agree on what is good or right, at least on basic social issues.[78] The Islamic economists are justified, therefore, in according consensus a primary role in establishing their preferred social order. Where they err is in thinking that more Islamic research and teaching will lead to *a particular* consensus – to communal acceptance of a *God-given* set of injunctions, which unambiguously defines *the* just economy. They overlook that individuals' perceptions of justice are shaped in significant measure by their personal experiences, over which no Islamic establishment can possibly exercise full control. Which consensus, if any, comes into being will thus depend on people's experiences. Moreover, since each generation goes through a different set of experiences, one particular consensus might give way over time to another, or disappear altogether.[79]

There is nothing novel about the Islamic economists' conviction that inconsistencies and disagreements will disappear through the formation of consensus. Since the eighth century Islamic scholars have accorded consensus an indispensable role in the creation and maintenance of social stability.[80] Yet a veritable consensus never did emerge – not even on the definition of consensus itself. Whereas al-Shafiʿi, the founder of Sunni Islamic jurisprudence, defined consensus in terms of the entire community of believers, other jurists were apt to perceive it in terms of the leading scholars.[81] Nor did educational efforts to bring about consensus put an end to the sharp divisions within the community over major social and economic issues.

The medieval jurists of Islam might be excused for underestimating the strength of the forces that make Muslims differ in their interpretations. After all, the religion was still in its infancy at the time they wrote, and the methods that they were proposing for achieving consensus had just begun to be tested. Today's Islamic economists have much less justification for trusting that consensus will emerge and endure. Over the past fourteen centuries Islamic education has not prevented groups from pursuing diametrically opposite causes, all in the name of Islam. Under the banner of Islamic fairness, some have campaigned vigorously for raising certain prices that others, also touting the fairness principle, were clamouring to lower. To provide another illustration, the accumulation of wealth has been defended on the grounds of fairness and efficiency, just as it has been attacked on the grounds of equality. It is obvious, too, that interpretations of Islam have a propensity to change over time. Until relatively recently, for instance, slavery was a tolerated institution, which was regulated by the Islamic establishment.[82] Today, many Muslims consider slavery unjust. Revealingly, the Islamic economists ignore the subject, except in listing the freeing of slaves among the uses of *zakat* funds.[83]

CONCLUDING REMARKS

Despite their ambitious claims, the Islamic economists have not established that the injustices they find in existing social orders would be absent from an Islamic order. They have shown neither that the distribution of wealth would be relatively more equal in an Islamic order nor that an Islamic order would be fairer, even by their own standards of fairness. The injunctions they propose are riddled with inconsistencies, and their conviction that Islam's consensus mechanism would eliminate these collides with the fact that they themselves are divided over many crucial matters.

As I mentioned at the outset, some of the flaws found in Islamic economic thought afflict other ideologies as well. Just consider the diverse schools of social thought that have developed around that electrifying cry of the French Revolution, 'Liberty, Equality, Fraternity!' Each can be faulted for failing to specify how these three goals are to be attained and for harbouring inconsistencies. In fact, whenever and wherever an attempt has been made to bring about these goals, major conflicts have erupted over what they require. Witness how the limits of liberty have never ceased to be a source of controversy. It has become apparent, too, that the goals sometimes pull in opposite directions. Thus, economic liberties have been found to generate inequality, and many egalitarian measures have rested on various forms of coercion. It is significant that in a number of Western countries schools of legal scholarship have emerged that are very critical of the practices of their community. These schools find many practices to be incompatible with the principles from which they were ostensibly derived, and the goals themselves to be deeply antagonistic.[84]

All this points to the presence of a *universal* process preventing social doctrines from becoming totally clear and consistent. I argued earlier that this process is linked to the incontrovertible fact that human cognitive powers are limited. The Islamic economists see the matter differently. While agreeing that other doctrines are deeply flawed, they believe that Islamic thought, being divinely inspired, is exempt from the perils of human weakness. They thus ignore the fact that, like the doctrines they indict so harshly, Islamic economics rests on human reasoning and interpretation.

This is not to say that all systems of thought are alike in every way. They differ in the severity of the ambiguities, inconsistencies, and illusions they harbour. They also differ substantively. A very major difference between Islamic economics and other doctrines that enjoy currency lies in the emphasis placed on liberty. In many doctrines, liberty is a supreme goal, on a par with fairness and equality. In Islamic thought, by contrast, liberty is barely an issue. It enters writings only through unsupported assertions to the effect that in an Islamic order transgressions of individual liberty would be minimal. The positions taken by Islamic economists make clear, however, that in the event of conflict between an Islamic injunction and individual liberty, it is liberty that must yield.

NOTES

Author's note: A summary of this paper was presented at a conference on 'The Economic Dimensions of Middle Eastern History', held in honour of Professor Charles Issawi at Princeton University on 24 May 1986. Another abbreviated version was presented at a session on 'Economic and Ethical Issues in Islamic Thought', organised jointly by the American Economic Association and the Association for Comparative Economic Studies, and held in New Orleans on 28 December 1986. I am indebted to Frederic Pryor and Bruce Thompson for their thoughtful comments, which led to refinements. At a later stage, I benefited from the constructive criticisms of the editor and three anonymous readers of the *International Journal of Middle East Studies*.

1. For a survey of the literature by a leading Islamic economist, see Muhammad Nejatullah Siddiqi, *Muslim Economic Thinking: A Survey of Contemporary Literature* (Leicester: The Islamic Foundation, 1981). Critiques of the literature include Timur Kuran, 'Behavioral Norms in the Islamic Doctrine of Economics: A Critique', *Journal of Economic Behavior and Organization*, 4 (4) (December 1983), 353–79; idem., 'The Economic System in Contemporary Islamic Thought: Interpretation and Assessment', *International Journal of Middle East Studies*, 18 (2) (May 1986), 135–64; and Frederic L. Pryor, 'The Islamic Economic System',

Journal of Comparative Economics, 9 (2) June 1985), 197–223.

2. For extensive comparisons, see Yusuf al-Qardawi, *Economic Security in Islam*, transl. Muhammad Iqbal Siddiqi (Lahore: Kazi Publications, 1981, first Arabic ed. 1966), ch. 2; Mohammad Abdul Mannan, *Islamic Economics: Theory and Practice* (Lahore: Sh. Muhammad Ashraf, 1970), ch. 3; idem., *The Frontiers of Islamic Economics* (Delhi: Idarah-i Adabiyat-i Delli, 1984), ch. 5; Syed Nawab Haider Naqvi, *Ethics and Economics: An Islamic Synthesis* (Leicester: The Islamic Foundation, 1981), ch. 4; and Adeleke Dirisu Ajijola, *The Islamic Concept of Social Justice* (Lahore: Islamic Publications, 1977), esp. part 1.
3. A representative work of Maududi is *The Economic Problem of Man and its Islamic Solution* (Lahore: Islamic Publications, 1975). Qutb's most relevant work is *Social Justice in Islam*, transl. J. D. Hardie (New York: American Council of Learned Societies, 1970, first Arabic ed., 1948).
4. The most influential of these writings are by Mahmud Taleqani, Mohammed-Baqer Sadr, and Abol-Hasan Bani-Sadr. The crucial chapters of Taleqani's leading works have been translated into English by R. Campbell, under the title *Society and Economics in Islam* (Berkeley, Calif.: Mizan Press, 1982). For commentaries on the Shiʿi literature, and for some further sources, see Shaul Bakhash, *The Reign of the Ayatollahs* (New York: Basic Books, 1984), ch. 7; and Homa Katouzian, 'Shiʿism and Islamic Economics: Sadr and Bani Sadr', in N. R. Keddie (ed.), *Religion and Politics in Iran* (New Haven: Yale University Press, 1983), pp. 145–65.
5. For some explicit statements, see Ajijola, *Islamic Concept*, pp. 194–8; Afzal-ur-Rahman, *Economic Doctrines*, vol. I (Lahore: Islamic Publications, 1980), pp. 62–6; M. Umer Chapra, 'The Economic System of Islam', four parts, *The Islamic Quarterly*, 14 (1970), 14–16; Ahmad Hasan, 'Social Justice in Islam', *Islamic Studies*, 10 (1971), 211; Ausaf Ahmad, 'A Macro Model of Distribution in an Islamic Economy', *Journal of Research in Islamic Economics*, 2 (1) (1984), 1; and Mohsin S. Khan, 'Islamic Interest-Free Banking', *International Monetary Fund Staff Papers*, 33 (1) (1986), 2.
6. Chapra, 'The Economic System', p. 11.
7. Ausaf Ahmad, 'A Macro Model of Distribution', p. 1. For a third such statement see Muhammad Nejatullah Siddiqi, *The Economic Enterprise in Islam* (Lahore: Islamic Publications, 1972), p. 38.
8. Several detailed surveys are available. Some are listed in note 1 above.
9. The narrow interpretation of *zakat* is outlined by Afzal-ur-Rahman, *Economic Doctrines of Islam*, vol. III (Lahore: Islamic Publications, 1976), chs. 14–16. Various broad interpretations are put forth by Mannan, *Islamic Economics*, 284–302; Monzer Kahf, 'Fiscal and Monetary Policies in an Islamic Economy' in M. Ariff (ed.), *Monetary and Fiscal Economics of Islam* (Jeddah: International Center for Research in Islamic Economics, 1982), pp. 125–37; and Masudul Alam Choudhury, *Contributions to Islamic Economic Theory: A Study in Social Economics* (New York: St Martin's Press, 1986), ch. 5. On the disagreements among the reformists, see the commentaries on Kahf's article, in Ariff (ed.), *Monetary and Fiscal Economics*, pp. 138–44. Certain authors who

subscribe to the narrow interpretation do not object to new taxes under other names. See, for example, F. R. Faridi, '*Zakat* and Fiscal Policy', in Khurshid Ahmad (ed.), *Studies in Islamic Economics* (Leicester: The Islamic Foundation, 1980), pp. 119–30. For a critical review of the writings on *zakat*, see Kuran, 'The Economic System', pp. 143–9.

10. Mannan, *Islamic Economics*, p. 182. The most detailed contemporary exposition of inheritance matters is contained in this source, pp. 176–86.
11. S. M. Yusuf, *Economic Justice in Islam* (Lahore: Sh. Muhammad Ashraf, 1971), p. 61.
12. Siddiqi, *Economic Enterprise*, p. 16. See also Mohammad Abdul Mannan, *The Making of an Islamic Economic Society: Islamic Dimensions in Economic Analysis* (Cairo: International Association of Islamic Banks, 1984), pp. 300–3.
13. See Chapra, 'The Economic System', pp. 9–10; Masudul Alam Choudhury, *An Islamic Social Welfare Function* (Indianapolis: American Trust Publications, 1980), pp. 5–14; Naqvi, *Ethics and Economics*, p. 64; and Siddiqi, *Economic Enterprise*, pp. 61–73.
14. For extensive examples, see Muhammad Abdul-Rauf, 'The Islamic Doctrine of Economics and Contemporary Islamic Thought', in M. Novak (ed.), *Capitalism and Socialism: A Theological Inquiry* (Washington, D.C.: American Enterprise Institute, 1979), pp. 134–40; and Siddiqi, *Economic Enterprise*, esp. chs 2 and 3. For a critique of this injunction, see Kuran, 'Behavioral Norms'.
15. See, for example, Chapra, 'The Economic System', p. 9.
16. On just prices and wages, see Mannan, *Islamic Economics*, ch. 8; and Yusuf, *Economic Justice*, pp. 77–80.
17. See Siddiqi, *Economic Enterprise*, pp. 52–4; and Mannan, *The Making of an Islamic Economic Society*, pp. 256–8.
18. For a survey of the Islamic position on interest, see Muhammad Nejatullah Siddiqi, 'Islamic Approaches to Money, Banking and Monetary Policy: A Review', in M. Ariff (ed.), *Monetary and Fiscal Economics of Islam* (Jeddah: International Center for Research in Islamic Economics, 1982), pp. 25–38. Also see Ziauddin Ahmed, Munawar Iqbal and M. Fahim Khan (eds), *Fiscal Policy and Resource Allocation in Islam* (Islamabad: Institute of Policy Studies, 1983), chs 5–8; M. Umer Chapra, *Towards a Just Monetary System: A Discussion of Money, Banking and Monetary Policy in the Light of Islamic Teachings* (Leicester: The Islamic Foundation, 1985); and Mohsin S. Khan and Abbas Mirakhor (eds), *Theoretical Studies in Islamic Banking and Finance* (Houston, TX: The Institute for Research and Islamic Studies, 1987). Critical reviews of the writings on interest include Ingo Karsten, 'Islam and Financial Intermediation', *International Monetary Fund Staff Papers*, 29 (1) (March 1982), 108–42; and Kuran, 'The Economic System', pp. 149–58.
19. Yusuf, *Economic Justice*, p. 90.
20. The most detailed statement on insurance is by Muhammad Nejatullah Siddiqi, *Insurance in an Islamic Economy* (Leicester: The Islamic Foundation, 1985). Other statements include Yusuf, *Economic Justice*, ch. 6; Mannan, *Islamic Economics*, ch. 14; and Muhammad Samiullah, 'Prohibition of Riba (Interest) and Insurance in the Light of Islam', *Islamic*

Studies, 21 (2) (Summer 1982), 53–76. For a concise account of the involved controversies, see Siddiqi, *Muslim Economic Thinking*, pp. 26–8. On the issue of regulation, see Muhammad Akram Khan, 'The Role of the Auditor in an Islamic Economy', *Journal of Research in Islamic Economics*, 3 (1) (Summer 1985), 31–42.

21. See Afzal-ur-Rahman, *Economic Doctrines of Islam*, vol. II, 2nd ed. (Lahore: Islamic Publications, 1980), ch. 6; Siddiqi, *Economic Enterprise*, pp. 54–7; and idem., *Insurance*, pp. 40–1.
22. See Afzal-ur-Rahman, *Economic Doctrines*, vol. II, pp. 44–5; Siddiqi, *Economic Enterprise*, pp. 57–60; and Ajijola, *Islamic Concept*, pp. 237–40.
23. See Chapra, 'The Economic System', p. 149.
24. See Siddiqi, *Muslim Economic Thinking*, pp. 15–16.
25. They include Yusuf, *Economic Justice*, pp. 23–7.
26. Afzal-ur-Rahman, *Economic Doctrines*, vol. II, p. 173.
27. Ibid., ch. 10, esp. pp. 175–7.
28. Ibid., pp. 193–207.
29. Ajijola, *Islamic Concept*, p. 181. Also see Yusuf, *Economic Justice*, p. 11; Siddiqi, *Economic Enterprise*, esp. pp. 115–35; and Mannan, *The Making of an Islamic Economic Society*, ch. 11.
30. Among the opponents of the modern corporation is Yusuf, *Economic Justice*, pp. 34–8. The proponents include Afzal-ur-Rahman, *Economic Doctrines*, vol. I, pp. 242–3.
31. Chapra, 'The Economic System', p. 16.
32. On the question of substance versus procedure, a very illuminating discussion relating to Islamic thought can be found in Majid Khadduri, *The Islamic Conception of Justice* (Baltimore: Johns Hopkins University Press, 1984), ch. 6. For general treatments, see John Rawls, *A Theory of Justice* (Cambridge, Mass.: Harvard University Press, 1971), esp. pp. 83–90; Brian Barry, *Political Argument* (London: Routledge and Kegan Paul, 1965), ch. 6; and Geoffrey Brennan and James M. Buchanan, *The Reason of Rules* (Cambridge: Cambridge University Press, 1985), ch. 7.
33. *World Development Report, 1980* (Washington, D.C.: The World Bank, 1980), esp. ch. 4.
34. The scheme is that of Malaysia. See Ismail Muhd Salleh and Rogayah Ngah, 'Distribution of the Zakat Burden on Padi Producers in Malaysia', in M. Raqibuz Zaman (ed.), *Some Aspects of the Economics of Zakah* (Gary, Indiana: Association of Muslim Social Scientists, 1981), pp. 80–153.
35. Witness Naqvi, *Ethics and Economics*, p. 64: 'The Islamic ethical principles not only determine individual choice and collective choice, but also provide a principle of integrating the two'. A supremely optimistic argument is put forward by Afzal-ur-Rahman, *Economic Doctrines*, vol. I, pp. 169–73.
36. There is an extensive literature on the benefits conferred by state power. See James M. Buchanan, Robert D. Tollison, and Gordon Tullock (eds), *Toward a Theory of the Rent-Seeking Society* (College Station: Texas A&M University Press, 1980). Most of the major contributions published since this collection was issued have appeared in the journal *Public Choice*.

37. Numerous examples are dispersed throughout Marshall G. S. Hodgson's trilogy, *The Venture of Islam: Conscience and History in a World Civilization* (Chicago: University of Chicago Press, 1974).
38. Strictly speaking, the Sunni Islamic economists believe that official corruption became rampant in A.D. 661 after the death of the fourth caliph ʿAli. The Shiʿis believe that corruption became widespread at an earlier date.
39. For the rationale behind the opposition to indexation, see S. M. Hasanuz Zaman, 'Indexation – An Islamic Evaluation', *Journal of Research in Islamic Economics*, 2 (2) (Winter 1985), 31–53; and Chapra, *Towards a Just Monetary System*, pp. 39–42. The pro-indexation argument has been put forth by Mannan, *The Making of an Islamic Economic Society*, ch. 14A. The issue was addressed inconclusively at the second seminar on the 'Monetary and Fiscal Economics of Islam', held in Islamabad in 1981. The proceedings of this seminar have been edited by Z. Ahmed, M. Iqbal, and M. Fahim Khan, under the title *Money and Banking in Islam* (Jeddah: International Center for Research in Islamic Economics, 1982).
40. See Umer Chapra, 'The Prohibition of *Riba* in Islam: An Evaluation of Some Objections', *American Journal of Islamic Studies*, 1 (2) (August 1984) 34.
41. See Choudhury, *Contributions*, ch. 6; also Zubair Hasan, 'Determination of Profit and Loss Sharing Ratios in Interest-Free Business Finance', *Journal of Research in Islamic Economics*, 3 (1) (Summer 1985) 13–29.
42. See Mohsin Khan, 'Islamic Interest-Free Banking', pp. 19–20. Khan also takes issue with the suggestion that profit and loss sharing would promote equality, indicating that this is not self-evident.
43. See, for example, Ahmad Hasan, 'Social Justice'; Ajijola, *Islamic Concept*, esp. pp. 208–24; and Naqvi, *Ethics and Economics*, esp. pp. 147–50.
44. Many of those who stress individual ownership are followers of Maududi. They include Chapra, 'The Economic System'; Yusuf, *Economic Justice*; and Monzer Kahf, *The Islamic Economy: Analytical Study of the Functioning of the Islamic Economic System* (Plainfield, Indiana: Muslim Students' Association of the United States and Canada, 1978).
45. Chapra, 'The Economic System', p. 245.
46. Yusuf, *Economic Justice*, p. 67 (emphasis in original).
47. S. Waqar Ahmed Husaini, *Islamic Environmental Systems Engineering* (London: Macmillan, 1980), p. 135.
48. The disagreements are discussed by Ausaf Ahmad, 'A Macro Model of Distribution', pp. 3–6.
49. Ibid., p. 5.
50. See, for instance, Kahf, *The Islamic Economy*, p. 65.
51. See Umer Chapra, 'Review of Kahf's *The Islamic Economy*', *Journal of Research in Islamic Economics*, 1, 2 (Winter 1984), 84.
52. See, for example, Afzal-ur-Rahman, *Economic Doctrines*, vol. I. pp. 145–52. Variable wages are favoured by certain writers, including Syed Aftab Ali, 'Risk-Bearing and Profit-Sharing in an Islamic Framework:

Some Allocational Considerations', in Z. Ahmed et al. (eds), *Fiscal Policy*, pp. 253–70.

53. See Yoram Barzel, 'Measurement Costs and the Organization of Markets', *Journal of Law and Economics*, 25 (1) (April 1982) 27–48.
54. See Abraham L. Udovitch, 'Islamic Law and the Social Context of Exchange in the Medieval Middle East', *History and Anthropology*, 1 (1985), 445–65.
55. Nabil A. Saleh, *Unlawful Gain and Legitimate Profit in Islamic Law* (Cambridge: Cambridge University Press, 1986).
56. Ibid., p. 59.
57. Ibid., p. 60.
58. Ibid., pp. 1–7.
59. See, for instance, Siddiqi, *Economic Enterprise*, pp. 56–7.
60. Syed Nawab Haider Naqvi, *Individual Freedom, Social Welfare and Islamic Economic Order* (Islamabad: Pakistan Institute of Development Economics, 1981), p. 23. The same point is made by Chapra, 'The Economic System', pp. 8 and 94.
61. Naqvi, *Individual Freedom*, p. 30.
62. Muhammad Abdul Mannan, 'Allocative Efficiency, Decision and Welfare Criteria in an Interest-Free Islamic Economy: A Comparative Policy Approach', in Ariff (ed.), *Monetary and Fiscal Economics*, pp. 43–62. See also his *Frontiers*, pp. 10–11.
63. Chapra, *Towards a Just Monetary System*, pp. 38–9.
64. On intuitionism, see Rawls, *A Theory of Justice*, pp. 34–45.
65. Mannan, *Frontiers*, p. 11.
66. The quote is from ibid., p. xii, although the same point is also made on p. 1 and, following the remarks on intuitionism, on p. 11.
67. See Herbert A. Simon, *Reason in Human Affairs* (Stanford, Calif.: Stanford University Press, 1983); and Michael Polanyi, *The Tacit Dimension* (Gloucester, Mass.: Peter Smith, 1983, first ed. 1966).
68. The argument that the role of judges and social thinkers is to bring order over doctrine is developed by Ronald Dworkin, *Law's Empire* (Cambridge, MA: Harvard University Press, 1986).
69. See Afzal-ur-Rahman, *Economic Doctrines*, vol. III, p. 217.
70. See Rodney Wilson, *Islamic Business: Theory and Practice*, revised ed. (London: The Economist Publications, 1985), p. 17
71. See Husaini, *Islamic Environmental Systems*, esp. pp. 79–81; and Mannan, *Islamic Economics*, pp. 23–6.
72. See Fazlur Rahman, *Islam*, 2d ed. (Chicago: University of Chicago Press, 1979), pp. 71–9.
73. On the biases that inevitably enter analogical reasoning, see John H. Holland, Keith J. Holyoak, Richard E. Nisbett, and Paul Thagard, *Induction: Processes of Inference, Learning, and Discovery* (Cambridge, Mass.: MIT Press. 1986), ch. 10.
74. See Husaini, *Islamic Environmental Systems*, p. 81 and ch. 5; and Mannan, *Islamic Economics*, pp. 21–3.
75. Mannan, *Islamic Economics*, p. 22.
76. The principal reason for doubting the saying's authenticity is that it

emerged several generations after the Prophet's death, at a time when many Muslims were becoming acutely aware of the fact that their institutions were not based on scripture alone. See C. Snouck Hurgronje, 'The "Foundations" of Islamic Law', in *Oeuvres Choisies – Selected Works* (eds G.-H. Bousquet and J. Schacht) (Leiden: E. J. Brill, 1975), p. 275.

77. See Chapra, 'The Economic System', esp. pp. 143–5; Afzal-ur-Rahman, *Economic Doctrines*, vol. I, sects 2–5 passim; and Choudhury, *Islamic Social Welfare*, ch. 1.
78. See Brennan and Buchanan, *The Reason of Rules*; and Edna Ullmann-Margalit, *The Emergence of Norms* (Oxford: Oxford University Press, 1977).
79. There is an extensive literature on the evolution of people's perceptions, to which researchers in several disciplines have contributed. For two broad statements, both by anthropologists, see Leslie White, *The Concept of Cultural Systems: A Key to Understanding Tribes and Nations* (New York: Columbia University Press, 1975); and Mary Douglas, *How Institutions Think* (Syracuse, N.Y.: Syracuse University Press, 1986). The involved dynamics have been explored by Timur Kuran, 'Preference Falsification, Policy Continuity and Collective Conservatism', *Economic Journal*, 97 (387) (September 1987), 642–65.
80. See George F. Hourani, 'The Basis of Authority of Consensus in Sunnite Islam', *Studia Islamica*, 21 (1964), 13–60; and Wael B. Hallaq, 'On the Authoritativeness of Sunni Consensus', *International Journal of Middle East Studies*, 18 (4) (November 1986), 427–54.
81. John L. Esposito, 'Law in Islam', in *The Islamic Impact*, in Y. Yazbeck Haddad, B. Haines, and E. Findly (eds), (Syracuse, N.Y.: Syracuse University Press, 1984), pp. 71–5.
82. See Bernard Lewis, *Race and Color in Islam* (New York: Harper and Row, 1971).
83. See Afzal-ur-Rahman, *Economic Doctrines*, vol. 3, pp. 237–8; and Choudhury, *Contributions*, p. 56.
84. See Duncan Kennedy and Karl E. Klare, 'A Bibliography of Critical Legal Studies', *Yale Law Journal*, 94 (2) (December 1984), 461–90.

3 Property Rights and Islamic Economic Approaches

Sohrab Behdad

In the past four decades, a growing segment of the political movements in the Muslim countries of the Third World has turned to Islamic ideology as its guiding principle (Sivan 1985, Enayat 1982, Rodinson 1978[1]). The Islamic popular movements strive to establish an 'Islamic economic system'. The characteristics of this ideal economic system are elaborated by 'Islamic economists' in the vast and diverse literature known as 'Islamic economics'.[2] An Islamic economic system is regarded by its proponents as a just and humane social order, in accordance with the teachings of Islam. This social order is 'neither capitalist nor communist, but it stands on its own and combines all the good features of a healthy and balanced society' (Mannan, 1986, pp. 346–7). The definition of the Islamic economy as a system of social relations of production remains, however, far from clear. The most significant theoretical controversy among Islamic economists is about the limits of private property rights in a 'true' Islamic economy.

This controversy reflects the populist orientation of the Islamic movements and the corresponding methodological eclecticism of Islamic economics. Islamic movements attempt to mobilise the poor, the well-to-do petty bourgeoisie and even certain strata of the bourgeoisie under the banner of Islamic justice. Islamic movements aim to establish a 'third path' by objecting to the inequities in the existing capitalist regimes while keeping a clear distance from the socialist movements. The definition of property relations in the idealised Islamic economic system, in contrast to these relations in capitalism and socialism, has become the key element in differentiating this 'third path' from the existing economic systems. Islamic economists are put to this task not only by their Marxist and mainstream economic critics but also, and more importantly, by the political imperatives of the movements which demand a platform addressing the existing economic inequities, on the one hand, and the fear of socialist expropriation of property, on the other.

Methodological eclecticism at the theoretical level is a prerequisite for populism at the political level. The methodology of Islamic economics is a juxtaposition of Neoclassical-Keynesian analysis with a world view shaped by utopian thoughts and bounded by Islamic scholasticism.[3] Thus, Islamic economics fails to provide a unique methodological framework ('paradigm') for the study of the social relations of production. It also fails to establish the characteristic elements of distinction between an Islamic economy and capitalism and between the transitional and developed forms of one with those of the other (see Behdad, 1992). (The line of demarcation with socialism, as I will demonstrate in this paper, is clear.) In the absence of a unique theoretical framework, the various ideological orientations in Islamic political movements seek to sanction, promote, or forbid certain economic practices and norms of conduct by interpreting the teachings of Islam in the context of the social conditions of modern Muslim countries. So, the determination of the extent of private property rights, or the limits on freedom of action of the owners of property in the idealised Islamic market (which is the nexus of social relations of production), becomes the problématique of Islamic economics.

Islam teaches compassion for the poor and destitute[4] and condemns the wealthy and arrogant.[5] Islam also praises worldly and material preoccupations, leaving no doubt that the quest for material possession is not only accepted, but also respected. Thus, Islam is open to a wide range of interpretations on property rights. It can serve as the ideology of radical populist movements longing for equality and redistribution of wealth.[6] It can also be the means of justifying concentration of wealth and existence of acute inequalities.[7]

The 'true' Islam established in any society as the result of the current Islamic resurgence will undoubtedly be a reflection of the balance between contending social forces. The resolution of the property rights issue, therefore, must be viewed in the context of the class struggle within any given Islamic society. My contention in this paper is to show that Islamic ideology itself would, however, impose definite limits upon the resolution of the property rights issue. These limits stem from Islamic jurisprudence, an integral element of Islamic ideology.

Because Islam has explicitly and extensively addressed worldly affairs, particularly economic and commercial relations, Islamic thought has been endowed by fourteen centuries of jurisprudential studies and judicial practices. Thus, the debate on property rights in Islamic economic thought is not only scholastic in the sense that these rights must be in accordance with God's revealed wisdom, which may be interpreted differently in different times and places. This debate is also jurisprudential since conformity with the Islamic legal tradition must be established. I maintain, in agreement with Maxime Rodinson (1978), that the interpretation of property rights according to Islamic Law (*shari'a*) and jurisprudence will counter any radical tendencies in Islamic reformist[8] movements. I will show that the framework of property relations proposed by Islamic reformers is at most that of a capitalist economy with an interventionist-welfare state, and the jurisprudential sanction for even such a non-radical change would require a radical reform in Islamic jurisprudence.

I will limit my analysis only to the works of contemporary Islamic economists; therefore, the views of Islamic jurists (*mujtahids* and *faqihs*[9]) and political leaders of past or present are not reviewed here. In this paper I assume some familiarity with the fundamentals of Islamic jurisprudence.

GOD'S ULTIMATE OWNERSHIP

There is no disagreement among Islamic economists in the belief that the ownership of property belongs to God (Siddiqi, 1981, p. 7). The Quran is explicitly clear about God's ownership. 'Unto Allah (belongeth) whatsoever is in heavens and whatsoever is in earth' (Quran, II:284.) The same or similar verses are repeated elsewhere in the Quran. (For example, see the Quran II:255, III:129 and XXII:64). Yet, the right of the individual to hold property is accepted and respected. The dichotomy of God-Man ownership is reconciled by the notion of trusteeship of Man and Man's accountability to God (see *inter alia*, Siddiqi, 1981, p. 7 and Naqvi, 1981, p. 77). 'Hast thou not seen how Allah hath made all that is in the earth subservient unto you?' (Quran, XXII:65). And, 'Believe in Allah and his messenger, and spend of that whereof He had made you trustee'[10] (Quran, LVII:7).

God's ultimate ownership is the source of the ambiguity in property rights in Islam.[11] God's ultimate ownership implies that His ownership supersedes the right of the individual to property. Thus, a state representing the will of God, i.e., an Islamic state, may impose limits on individual property rights. The restrictiveness of these limits will depend upon the extent of interference of individual property rights with the realisation of God's will in the society of Muslims. The Islamic state will be the judge of interference and the abrogator of the individual property rights. As long as the state is not Islamic, the issue of determination of limits of property rights according to Islam is merely academic. In the established Islamic states (e.g., Saudi Arabia, or prior to the secularisation of state in the present century, in most Muslim societies) where the existing property relations have gained historical legitimacy, the issue is confined to adjudication in the cases of conflict in the property rights of individuals. However, the problem becomes a highly critical political issue when, as in Iran, the establishment of a new Islamic state is the outcome of a populist revolution under the egalitarian banner of Islamic ideology. The problem also becomes apparent when Islamic reformist movements advocate populist social changes in a society under an Islamic rule (e.g., Pakistan and Egypt).

Three general approaches may be identified on the issue of private property rights among Islamic economists. I refer to these as '*laissez faire*', 'populist' and 'populist-state control' approaches.

Laissez faire Approach

The *laissez faire* approach[12] is best summarised by Faruqi:

> Islam teaches the greatest possible individualism. . . . This individualism knows no bonds except those imposed by the moral law. But when no moral violation is in evidence, Islam teaches that man may and should amass the greatest fortune he can, and these are his and his natural or adopted heirs to have, to keep and to enjoy. . . . *Man's acquisitions of wealth may have no limits in Islam. A person may amass boundless treasures. Indeed he can, theoretically at least, 'own' the whole world* (Faruqi, 1980, p. xii, emphasis added).

The moral limits according to Faruqi are that

> In his acquisition of wealth, man is not to lie, or cheat his neighbour . . . [must] uphold his promise and to fulfil his

> contract . . . not to steal . . . [or] exploit the destitution of his fellow men by subjecting them to work for him without full title to the fruits of their own work, as is usually the case with interest levied on borrowed capital (Faruqi, 1980, p. xii).

Charity will take care of 'poverty and destitution' and *zakat* (a wealth tax[13]) serves to 'sweeten or make innocent . . . man's enjoyment of wealth'[14] (Faruqi, 1980, p. xiii). According to Faruqi, these are the limits that separate Islam from 'extreme individualism and capitalism' (1980, p. xii). He does not, however, clarify what he means by capitalism or why these mechanisms of income redistribution should be considered fundamentally different from those which are relied on in capitalist economies.

Abdul-Rauf, noting the 'obvious' difference between Islam and 'the communistic system', sees little difference between Islam and capitalism. He maintains that it is 'difficult to necessarily differentiate the system of Islam from that of capitalism unless you include in the definition of capitalism certain inherent evils' (Abdur Ra'uf (Abdul-Rauf), 1980, p. 53).

The interpretation of Faruqi and Abdul-Rauf, among others, may be justified by many verses of the Quran, numerous *hadiths* ('reliable' references to Muhammad's actions or views) and rulings of *faqihs*. The Quran, by praising charity, sanctions inequality of wealth in a way not dissimilar to the medieval approach of Christianity. The Quran states, for example, 'And covet not the thing in which Allah hath made some of you excel others. . . . (Envy not one another) but ask Allah of His bounty'[15] (IV:32).

Many rulings of the past and contemporary *faqihs* also reflect this position. An interesting example is a recent ruling referred to by Abdul-Rauf (1979, pp. 14–15). After Muhammad's death, Abu Dharr, a Companion of Muhammad, challenged the luxurious life of the Ummayed governor of Syria by referring to a number of hadiths, including: 'Should this mountain of 'Uhud be turned into gold for me, I would not wish that the nightfall comes before I have disposed of it all in charity except two carats'. Uthman, the third Caliph of Muslims, fearing an uprising in Syria, sent Abu Dharr to exile, where he died. Al-Azhar, the authoritative theological school in Cairo, ruled in 1948 (nearly fourteen centuries after the incident) in favour of the Caliph. The ruling by al-Azhar was a response to the challenge of the growing populist tendency against the existing orientation in Islam. As Nowaihi points out, the proponents of *laissez faire* approach to private property rights claim that 'there is nothing in the classical works of Islamic jurisdiction to countenance [the] limitation [on property rights] (1980, p. 74).

Populist Approach

The populist approach claims that Islam has 'reserved' the right to ownership for individuals. This implies that although the right to private property is respected by Islam, the opportunity to exercise this right must exist for every individual. That is, no one should be without property. Most notable among the adherents to this approach is Abu Sulayman (1980) who argues that equality is the economic manifestation of *tawhid* (Divine Unity), the cardinal principal of Islam.[16] *Tawhid*, according to Abu Sulayman, 'is a coin with two faces: One implies that Allah is the Creator, and the other that men are equal partners' (1980, p. 14). He extends this interpretation of *tawhid* to property rights and concludes that all natural resources including land, capital and 'general circumstances' belong to the whole society, and no one can claim a bigger share than others[17] (1980, pp. 14, 16–17). This 'right of priority' must be 'protected against the tyranny and despotism of capitalists, chairmen and committees' (Abu Sulayman, 1980, p. 17).

Abu Sulayman maintains that if one cannot make use of certain resources over which one has priority, one should let someone else take advantage of it without claiming a share in the income from that resource (1980, p. 17). The extra income resulting from resources beyond one's equal share must be distributed among the 'weaker members of society'. This approach to the property rights issue may imply imposition of certain ceilings on large-scale ownership and has been generally supported by even right-wing populist movements such as Ikhwan al-Muslimun (Muslim Brotherhood) in Syria and Egypt and Jama'at-i Islami (Islamic Society) in Pakistan (Siddiqi, 1981, p. 9). The position is clearly appealing to small proprietors who would like to see a limitation imposed on the accumulation of riches by the wealthy without the fear of losing their own wealth under socialism.

To Abu Sulayman, the redistribution of property (priority of use), although justified in principle, is not appropriate. He maintains that since such redistribution will be required frequently and is 'disruptive to economic activity and social relations', taxation, charity and 'modern techniques' of income redistribution are recommended (Abu

Sulayman, 1980, p. 40). This recommendation of Abu Sulayman brings him much closer to the *laissez faire* approach than his analysis may imply. The difference lies merely in the rate of taxation and the extent of coercion by the state in payment of 'charity'. Clearly underplayed in Abu Sulayman's model of Islamic society is state ownership.

Populist-State Control Approach

The 'populist-state control' approach extends Abu Sulayman's interpretation of property rights by putting the state in a central position. Sadr, a *shi'i mujtahid* from Iraq, is the main proponent of this approach (1971 and 1978). Sadr argues that God has availed the natural wealth to the society to be used for the welfare of mankind. Through ownership, individuals must carry a social role as prescribed by the Divine Revelations. Therefore, the right to private property is subject to fiduciary principle and as such it is neither natural nor irrevocable (Sadr, 1978, pp. 32-3). An Islamic ruler may limit the use of property or confiscate it if the fiduciary principle is violated (Sadr, 1978, p. 34).

Sadr's emphasis on the social character of ownership sets stricter limits on private property rights than the proponents of the *laissez faire* approach are willing to accept. Sadr, on the other hand, prescribes a more positive role for the state's right to hold property than is envisioned by the populist approach. Sadr suggests that Islam, in contrast to socialism and capitalism, prescribes 'mixed' (private and state) ownership. In Sadr's view, the contrast between property relations in Islam and those in the other two economic systems is at the level of working principles of these systems, and not in actual practices[18] (1971, pp. 355-8).

According to Sadr, ownership in Islam is in three forms: state, public and private.[19] (1978, pp. 63-141). State and public forms of ownership are exercised by the Islamic ruler over what Islamic law calls *anfal*. *Anfal*, in Islamic jurisprudence, includes natural resources and spoils of war. The most important examples of *anfal* are land, mineral deposits and water. Properties confiscated by the state, for whatever reason, will also come under thls category.

The important implication of Sadr's view on 'mixed' ownership is legitimisation of a large state sector in the economy. This is more clearly seen when one considers Sadr's view on the responsibility of the state for maintaining a 'social balance' by providing 'an appropriate standard of living for individuals' (Sadr, 1978, pp. 329–50). Almost all Islamic economists would uphold, as a matter of principle, the view that the state should step in when the voluntary charity of individuals is not sufficient for maintaining subsistence for the poor and destitute (for example, Choudhury, 1986, Chapter 1 and Naqvi, 1981, Chapter 8). Chapra (1980) has been explicit in specifying many functions of a modern capitalist state (e.g., creating full employment, maintaining a high rate of growth, economic stability and the real value of money) for an Islamic state. However, what sets Sadr apart from other Islamic economists is the role that he prescribes for an Islamic state in maintenance of a 'social balance'. To Sadr, there should be a 'balance in the standard of living of all members of the society' with only *minimal* differences reflecting the physical and intellectual capacities of individuals (1978, p. 331). The significance of Sadr's view on the role of state in an Islamic society may be summarised as follows:

a) The Islamic state may legislate new restrictions on economic activities in addition to what is prescribed by the *shari'a* in order to maintain social balance in the face of historical changes in the conditions of production (1978, pp. 34 *et seq.*, 344–50).
b) Since (according to Sadr), in an Islamic economy, the growth of individual capital is limited, where production conditions require establishment of large enterprises, such enterprises must be established and controlled by the state (1978, p. 341).

Sadr's view is controversial not only from a political perspective, but also from a jurisprudential standpoint. The extent of state intervention in the market necessary for maintenance of a 'social balance' implies strict limitations of the activity of large capital and formation of a large state sector in the economy. The economy will remain, however, capitalist in character while the state may play an aggressive role in facilitating and regulating the accumulation process. This extensive state intervention cannot be carried out based on the existing jurisprudential tradition. Legislation of new restrictions by the Islamic state opens the door to jurisprudential controversies, to which we will return in a following section.

HOARDING AND *RIBA*: THE LIMITS TO PRIVATE PROPERTY

Ultimate ownership by God sets the general constraints on private property rights. These constraints are further specified by the *shari'a* in prohibition of hoarding and *riba* (excessive gain).

Hoarding

One may not leave consumption wealth or productive capacity unused. 'That which they hoard will be their collar on the Day of Resurrection' Quran (III:180). *Zakat* and charity are to discourage and reduce accumulation which may result in hoarding. Prohibition of hoarding, beyond discouraging abstinence in consumption of wealth and 'excessive' personal accumulation, has been limited in two principal cases in tradition. One is the case of hoarding by merchants as a way of cornering the market. The state may force the hoarder to sell the hoards at a 'fair value' (Ibn Taymiya, 1982, pp. 32–3 and Mannan, 1986, pp. 153–5). The other, and more controversial, case is hoarding land by leaving it unused, with which we will deal in the next section. Some Islamic economists have, however, attempted to extend the prohibition of hoarding by considering any unused capacity of production as hoarding. Extending the definition of hoarding from the sphere of circulation to the sphere of production is justified by Sadr's attempt (1971, 1978) to reinterpret Islamic jurisprudence in the light of changing historical circumstance in the Muslim societies from Muhammad's time. If any output level short of maximum capacity is regarded as hoarding, then the optimum output of a firm in an Islamic economy is its second break-even point (where the demand curve intersects the average cost curve from above).[20] Then, firms making an economic profit by producing less than the 'Islamic optimum output' could be regarded as hoarders. If hoarding is unlawful, then it must be the duty of the state to eliminate it when it does occur. Thus, prohibition of hoarding may justify appropriation of 'unused' private wealth by the state. This position is consistent with Abu Sulayman's notion of 'priority rights'. There is, however, little in tradition (Muhammad's conduct of affairs) to point to such conclusions, and there are few who extend the definition of hoarding to such limits.

Riba

Riba, literally means 'over and beyond'. The Quran explicitly condemns *riba*. 'Those who swallow *riba* cannot rise up save as he ariseth whom the devil hath prostrated by [his] touch'[21] (Quran, II:275). No transaction may bring a party anything beyond the 'fair exchange' value (Abu Sulayman, 1980, pp. 22–3). The most clear case of *riba* is usury, but it may be extended, and it has been, to include other forms of transaction, as we will see below.[22]

The concept of fair exchange value may appear similar to Aquinas' 'just price'. (See O'Brien, 1920, p. 102 *et seq.*) Fair exchange value in Islam is, however, neither socially determined nor administratively regulated. In response to a request to control prices, Muhammad said: 'God is the Taker, the Disposer, the Succourer and the Controller of prices. I very much hope that when I meet God no-one will claim against me for an injury I have caused him for blood or property' (Ibn Taymiya, 1983, p. 35). Fair exchange value, therefore, cannot mean other than the market return to labour and capital.[23]

That labour creates value is clear enough in Islamic thought. The Quran goes as far as stating, 'And that man hath only that for which he maketh effort' (LIII:39). This and similar statements in the Quran have provided the grounds for some scholars to raise questions about legitimacy of return on property (Abu Sulayman, 1980, pp. 17–19). Most Islamic economists, however, in agreement with the Islamic jurisprudential tradition, interpret 'effort' in the general sense of the word, including the effort of entrepreneurs in their profit-making activities. The Quran's explicit sanctions of gains from trade ('Allah permitted trading and forbidden *riba*', (II:275)) and Muhammad's frequent praise of merchants (he was one himself)[24] point to the indisputable legitimacy of profit in Islam. What distinguishes profit from *riba* is that profit is a return on capital where such return is not fixed in rate and is subject to risk.[25] Sadr, however, differs with this view. He maintains that capital in the form of means of production can receive no more than the rent for such means and has no claim over the final output. To Sadr, however, such a claim cannot be made by labour either. Since production is no more than reshaping the raw material, the final product belongs to the owner of raw material (Sadr, 1978, pp. 200–10). Sadr makes a great deal from this somewhat inverted physiocratic notion of production in order to establish the superiority of an Islamic economy to capitalism and socialism. There is, however, little significance in his distinction, at least in modern economies, where capital provides not only the means of production but also the material of production.

The specific limits of property rights as they may be applied to the ownership of land and capital must, therefore, be determined in light of the prohibition of hoarding and *riba* and within the context of God's ultimate ownership.

LIMITATION ON THE RIGHTS TO LAND AND CAPITAL

Since the Quran, in most cases, only refers to the general guidelines on the limits and responsibilities of ownership, the main source for jurisprudential rulings on property rights is Muhammad's tradition. This, however, reflects the tribal-mercantile society of Mecca and Medina with a small agricultural preoccupation and even smaller manufacturing activities.[26] Therefore, the interpretive value of tradition in contemporary societies is severely limited. This limitation has given rise to a number of debates on the specific limits of property rights in Islam.

On Land

The most controversial debate has been on the ownership of land, for the rather obvious reason that Islamic societies have been, and still are, essentially agrarian with significant tensions around land ownership. Land is the most obvious gift of God. 'Lo! the earth is Allah's. He giveth it for an inheritance to whom He will' (Quran, VII:128). On this basis, plain land (land in its natural form) may not be owned by individuals. There is little disagreement on this issue among Islamic economists. Plain land, according to Sadr, is under public or state ownership (respectively, for usable and unusable land) (1978, pp. 62–117). One may claim priority in use of plain land by improving it with one's labour and capital. This priority, however, may be conditional (*a la* prohibition of hoarding) to the continued use of land. Sadr is among the scholars who emphasise the conditionality of continued land use. He quotes a *hadith* of Muhammad stating, 'Land belongs to God, whoever leaves it uncultivated for three consecutive years will have it taken away and given to someone else'. (Sadr, 1978, p. 43. The issue is further elaborated in pp. 101–6, 114 and 152–5 of the same volume.)

The land ownership issue becomes less clear when land rent and sharecropping are considered. Is rent on land permitted by Islam? There is agreement among Islamic scholars that Islam does not permit rent for plain land (Siddiqi, 1981, p. 15). Abu Sulayman relies on the following *hadith* of Muhammad to prove that land rent is unlawful: 'He who has land should cultivate it. If he will not or cannot, he should give it free to a Muslim brother and not rent it to him' (1980, p. 9). Since 'having' land would imply having improved land, as plain land may not be 'had', this may be interpreted as a limitation on ownership of land beyond the amount one can cultivate and a justification for redistribution of large land holdings (Mannan, 1986, p. 80). Sheikh maintains that '[a] person can possess only that much land which he can himself cultivate' (1961, p. 181). The surplus land must be 'surrender[ed] to the State'.[27]

There are, however, other *hadiths* which explicitly allow land rent. Sa'd Ibn Waqqas, a Companion, is quoted to have said, 'We used to rent land and pay the owner as rent the produce grown on the banks of irrigation canals. The Prophet prohibited this and ordered us to pay rent in gold or silver' (Choudhury, 1986, p. 9). Clearly, it is not the rent but rent in kind that is prohibited here. The payment of rent is considered lawful by most Islamic economists as long as some improvements have been made on the land.[28] To Choudhury, rent on improved land is a rightful return to value created by work and capital (1986, p. 9). To Sadr, rent on improved land is legitimate since it is the cost of depreciation of work done and capital expended for its improvements (1978, p. 245). As Siddiqi points out, however, it is clear that rent on improved land is almost always higher than depreciation (1981, p. 15). If so, then the rent in excess of depreciation is *riba*. On this basis some Islamic economists (Mannan, 1986, p. 80 and Sheikh, 1961, p. 181) regard rent even on improved land unlawful, a position which others view as 'dogmatic' (Siddiqi, 1981, p. 15).

Sharecropping is considered as unlawful by a small number of Islamic economists, including Sheikh (1961), Yusuf (1957), and Abu Sulayman (1980), and unlawful by most others. Sheikh's argument against sharecropping is theoretical rather than jurisprudential. He argues that sharecropping and rent on land would hinder economic development and creation of employment in an Islamic society where the rate of interest 'is made to fall to zero by a religious ordinance or legislation' (1961, p. 180). Sheikh maintains that in such circumstances 'moneyed people would begin to buy land and live on its rent. . . .'.[29] Thus, in Sheikh's view, although profit sharing is permitted by Islam in industry and commerce, profit on land in the forms of rent or sharecropping is prohibited.

Yusuf's and Abu Sulayman's arguments are jurisprudential. Abu Sulayman relies on this *hadith* of Muhammad to support his position: 'Whoever would not abandon sharecropping he is at war with Allah and his Prophet' (1980, pp. 20–1). It is, however, well known that Muhammad himself engaged in sharecropping upon his victory in Khaybar, where he 'let the Jews to stay on the land, cultivate it and share one-half of the crops with the Muslims'. Abu Sulayman explains the contradiction between these two traditions by noting that in Khaybar, Muhammad engaged in sharecropping only with non-Muslims. It must, however, be noted that in the first statement that Abu Sulayman quotes, 'sharecropping' is the translation of the Arabic word *mukhabara*, meaning only land, and not seed, is provided by the owner of the land. The prevalent form of sharecropping sanctioned by Islamic law is *muzara'a*, when the owner of land provides seeds as well as land.[30] Abu Sulayman's objection to sharecropping is, therefore, relevant only to a special case and, as such, is not as significant as he makes it appear.

The restrictions suggested by various Islamic scholars on land utilisation, land rent and sharecropping are regarded by these scholars as the egalitarian dimension of Islam in preventing exploitation of the poor by the wealthy and arrogant. This view, the jurisprudential queries notwithstanding, must be evaluated in light of the relations of production in an Islamic economy. To Islam, wage labour is 'perfectly normal' (Rodinson, 1978, p. 16). Labour is hired by the employer under a contractual agreement with the worker. The only restriction is that wages must be specified in amount and not be subject to uncertainty (*gharar* or *maysir*) (Rodinson, 1978, p. 16). According to Muhammad, 'The wages of labourers must be paid to him before the sweat dries upon his body'. And, 'the best earning is that of labourer provided he does his job with care and regard for his employer' (Mannan, 1986, pp. 116–17). With the acceptance of wage labour there is no limitation on the extent that capital or land can be used in the production process. Even if the restriction that some Islamic economists suggest on the land utilisation, land rent and sharecropping were fully true from a jurisprudential view, their implications would be the encroachment of capitalist relations of production upon the pre-capitalist relations in the rural sector. Muhammad's prohibition of rent in kind instead of payment of cash (noted above) appears to point in the same direction. The effects of the capitalist transformation of the rural sector on the development of an underdeveloped economy, although an interesting theoretical issue, is not what Islamic economists have in mind when they insist on such restrictions. These restrictions would not reduce inequalities in a modern market economy, where such restrictions are mostly not relevant, in any case.

On Capital

Islamic economists face an apparent dilemma when they deal directly with capital. The authors are confronted with the problem of private enterprise *vs.* social justice, both of which have received particular attention in the Quran and tradition. All authors believe the explicit restrictions of Islam on the use of capital and on the conduct of business, plus the behavioural norms based on Islamic values, would resolve the problem. Prohibition of usury, monopoly, hoarding and speculation are the commonly accepted Islamic restrictions on business practices.[31] These restrictions, with the exception of the first, are not, however, clearly defined to have operational significance in modern economies. The existing limitations on the activity of capital in the advanced capitalist countries are more clearly defined and more effectively imposed than Islamic jurisprudence would allow. For example, labour laws dealing with the right to collective bargaining, minimum wage rate, child labour, and maximum hours of work would confront particular difficulties in Islamic jurisprudence.[32] The contractual agreement between an employer and a worker may not be constrained by a third party (the state) as long as the two parties fulfil their obligations. Similarly, some other forms of state intervention practiced in the developed and underdeveloped economies may not be legitimate according to Islamic jurisprudence. For example, many forms of industrial and trade regulations and licensing by the state may be challenged by Islamic laws.[33] At most, Islamic legal restrictions on business practices can amount to no more than the anti-trust regulations, enforced in the advanced capitalist economies for nearly a century.

The Islamic norms of conduct are, however, expected to limit profit to no more than 'normal', 'just', or 'fair' profit in a market structure that is purely competitive[34] (Mannan, 1986, p. 63 and Siddiqi, 1981, p. 59). For example, according to Siddiqi, Islamic enterpreneurs would maximise profit within the constraints set by Islamic justice (1981, p. 56). That is, entrepreneurs 'would not be maximising their profits if . . . by lowering their profit margins they can further the good of the society . . .'. To Naqvi (1981, p. 64), the ethical considerations in an Islamic market result in 'interdependence of utility functions and production functions'.[35] These views resemble those of the proponents of the 'social responsibility of business' in the capitalist economies. (See, for example, Almeder, 1980.) The paramount question is, then, to what extent the ethical or social responsibility of entrepreneurs can be left to their own conscience and how and to what extent the state can or should interfere in the market. In more realistic terms, the issue will centre upon the forms and extent of the state's intervention in market economy (see, for example, Chapra, 1980 and Naqvi, 1981) and as such capital may confront either more or less regulation in an economy which is capitalist in character.

Islam permits partnership (*musharaka*) and profit sharing (*mudaraba*). (See Saleh, 1986, pp. 91–4, 101, 114 and Siddiqi, 1985.) Profit sharing is encouraged, particularly as a means of channelling money capital into economic activities in the face of prohibition of interest payments. Interest-free Islamic banks[36] or individuals may enter a profit-sharing contract with a company or with individuals. Under a profit-sharing contract, the owner of money may receive a specific percentage (and not a specific amount, in which case it would be considered *riba*) of the profit that the 'borrower' will make during a given period. Since the profit of an enterprise is subject to risk, the 'lender' may receive profit or may incur a loss on the original capital. The arrangement is closely similar to a joint stock company where stockholders will receive dividend if the company makes profit and will lose all or part of their capital if the company incurs losses.

There is no specified limits in the *shari'a*, according to any school of Islamic jurisprudence, on the amount of capital that an individual or a company can possess or the amount of profit that may be earned. Even scholars like Sadr, who on an abstract level reject risk bearing as a justification for profit and see profit justifiable only if it is a return to entrepreneurial activity, stand to approve profit sharing under the *mudaraba* arrangement, even though the owner of capital has not done anything but take risk.

Mudaraba is seen by Islamic economists as a means for encouraging cooperative arrangements in an Islamic economy. Therefore, any 'misuse' of *mudaraba* as a way for 'excessive' accumulation of capital is regarded as *riba* by some Islamic economists. For example, Abu Sulayman maintains 'share holding could be understood as a means of encouraging movement of capital whenever there is a man without capital. . . .' (1980, p. 24). But even this principle, if upheld, does not prevent an owner of capital from providing capital to tens, of 'men' without capital to share the profit that results from their activities. Abu Sulayman, however, argues that share holding 'was not meant to open a side-door for exploitation and false private claims' (1980, p. 31). This position is similar to the objection to sharecropping or land rent. If there is no objection or limit to the use of capital in employing wage labour in market activities, one may say that Abu Sulayman is concerned with opening the side door when the front door is wide open.

JURISPRUDENTIAL REFORMISM, OR HERESY?

Abu Sulayman, and more generally the Islamic economists in the 'populist' tendency, confront a serious dilemma. That is, the strictest interpretation of Islamic *shari'a* would not prevent rapid accumulation and high concentration of capital in a market economy, even in an underdeveloped one. These reformer-scholars envision a market economy comprised of small farmers, merchants, and artisans, where those who are better off may give a hand to those who are less fortunate in the form *muzara'a, mudaraba* or even charity and alms. This is the utopian picture of a pre-capitalist society minus the landlord and all the other unpleasant features. In such an economy, business will be conducted in 'a well-maintained market' as in the time of Muhammad when 'no monopoly was allowed, no unfairness or cheating was permitted [and all] opportunistic speculation and ill-deals were ruled out'[37] (Abu Sulayman, 1980, p. 30).

The 'populist-state control' tendency goes one step beyond the latter position by prescribing a much larger role for the state. The extent to which a large state sector and an interventionist state would obstruct or facilitate private accumulation of capital in a market economy would depend on the class character of the state. That, of course, is a political question. The more interesting question in the study of the reformist tendency in Islamic economics is the legitimacy of these reforms in the context of Islamic jurisprudence. Islamic economists are well aware of the constraints they confront in acquiring jurisprudential sanction for their reforms to the extent that these reforms are in conflict with the traditional views of *mujtahids*. Medhat Hassanein in an opening statement to a conference of Islamic economists in April 1968 said:

> In any battlefield, seeking victory depends on three elements: the soldier, the officer and the armament. . . . In the first half of this century, substantial progress was made in preparing a truthful . . . soldier. . . . But [this soldier] has been fighting . . . with obsolete, 13th century-fashioned weapons. . . . The officers have lately realized the problem and are now pleading for building the modern equipment factory. . . . They possess the modern technique, but the tools are in the hands of *mashayekh* (the traditional religious leaders), and there exists a wide gap between the two. . . .
>
> The traditional *ulama* (the religiously-learned) for their part look upon the introduction of modern techniques with suspicious doubt. Their preferred ways of approaching problems are outmoded and no more effective (1980, p. 2).

The '13th-century fashioned weapon' is no less than Islamic jurisprudence, the guardian of which are *ulama* and *mashayekh*, or in correct terminology, *mujtahids* or *muftis*. What Hassanein and other Islamic scholar-reformers are suggesting is a reform in Islamic jurisprudence. But many elements of such reforms amount to abrogation of Muhammad's tradition and the consensus of great mujtahids of the past and will be regarded as *bid'a* (literally, 'innovation', and in this context, 'revisionism') which is heresy (Aghnides, 1969, pp. 30, 120). Such a reform would be possible in any one of the schools of Islamic jurisprudence only if a consensus is formed among the existing *mujtahids* of that school, agreeing upon the jurisprudential implications of the modern conditions of life in an Islamic society.

Sadr is the only prominent *mujtahid* who has stepped in this direction by challenging the established jurisprudential view about Muhammad's tradition.[38] Sadr maintains that the actions of Muhammad must be viewed in their historical context, and, as such, they may not be regarded as unchangeable (1978, pp. 34–5). This in itself is not new. What is new in Sadr's analysis is the application of this approach to the specific realm of economic activities, where he maintains the Islamic state has a 'free legislative realm' for achieving 'social balance'. According to Sadr, in Muhammad's time, the means of production were limited, and 'excessive' utilisation of natural resources was not possible; therefore, many economic activities of individuals were approved, or were not objected to, by Muhammad (1978, pp. 57–60). With the advance of technology, Sadr argues, owners of means of production in a capitalist economy can employ many workers and make extensive use of natural resources. According to Sadr, this cannot be sanctioned by Islam, since only 'utilisation [of natural resources] by direct labor is legitimate' in Islam. Therefore, Sadr argues that what may appear legitimate according to tradition is not in fact in accordance with Islam in the modern economic condition.

Sadr points out quickly here that his view should not be regarded as some form of Islamic socialism. He maintains that he is pointing to emergence of a 'third pole' by rejecting both socialism and capitalism. In fact his economic model suggests a capitalist market with an interventionist government which nationalises large enterprises and maintains a market composed of many small firms. These small firms, by acting in accordance with the Islamic principles of justice and compassion, will never grow in size. On the theoretical level, Sadr has made what one may call a Sismondian-Saint Simonian synthesis: a centrally planned welfare state with extensive government ownership in a market economy composed of many small private enterprises which would behave according to the idealised Islamic norms of conduct. To Sadr, capitalist relations of production – as long as they are within the confines of a market with small, non-oligopolistic enterprises and do not result in 'excessive' accumulation of profit – are legitimate. The state will complement and regulate the private sector. In this sense he is certainly correct when he claims he is not suggesting 'some form of socialism'. Sadr is merely suggesting an idealised market economy where the accumulation process in the private sector would be regulated and limited by the state.

Sadr's model of an Islamic economy is, of course, within the realm of possibilities *only* if the political obstacles in disarming the existing oligopolistic structure in the private sector of the economy and the emphasis on the practice of idealised Islamic behavioural norms are overlooked. These limitations are less serious in the economies which are still in their earlier stage of capitalist development, especially if, as in the oil exporting countries, the state has a major source of revenue other than taxation.[39] The Libyan, Algerian and Syrian economies resemble, to a great extent, the model of Sadr, except they (especially the latter two) lack the necessary 'Islamic spirit'. As the result of the 'un-Islamic' capitalist accumulation, the growing bourgeoisie in these economies (again, especially in the latter two economies which are more advanced in their capitalist development) is challenging the extensive role of the state in the economy. Whether, or how, the type of market structure suggested by Sadr may be sustained in the face of the ongoing capitalist accumulation in the private sector of the economy is an issue beyond the scope of the present analysis. What we are concerned with here is whether Sadr's economic model is consistent with Islamic jurisprudence.

The authority here is the existing community of Islamic jurists. Since Sadr is a *shi'i*, his views are ignored by the *sunni* schools of jurisprudence, who view *shi'ism* itself on the border line of Islamic heresy. Iran is the only Muslim country where *shi'ism* is the dominant sect.[40] In post-revolutionary Iran, when the restructuring of the economy became, and remains a heated issue, a strong faction in the Islamic Republic took on the 'populist-state control' approach of Sadr.[41] For the past ten years, the political debate has turned into a jurisprudential confrontation. The prominent Iranian *mujtahids* (including Ayatollah Kohii who resides in the Najaf *shi'i* center in Iraq), with the exception of Khomeini, have opposed the 'populist-state control' tendency on jurisprudential grounds. The main objection of these *mujtahids* is to the limitation of private property rights by the Islamic state. This position is supported by the propertied class, the most vocal elements of which are the bazaar merchants who traditionally have had close ties with the Islamic hierarchy. Although the 'populist-state control' tendency has been the dominant faction with the Islamic Republic of Iran, this faction has not succeeded in establishing the legal foundations for carrying out its policies. The charge of heresy by the community of prominent *mujtahids* is too serious to be ignored by a regime which seeks its legitimacy in the guardianship of the faith. The political-jurisprudential entanglement continues in Iran, while in the midst of the chaotic economic conditions a decentralised, yet lucrative, state clientalism is giving rise to a rapid accumulation of capital for those who have close ties with the regime. With the lost revolutionary momentum, and the growing political and economic power of the propertied class, the populist dimension of the 'populist-state control' tendency has abated, as this tendency has continually converged toward the *laissez faire* orientation (Behdad, 1988a). The Iranian experience should provide a sobering lesson to those Islamic social reformers who believe in a genuine struggle toward an egalitarian society.

CONCLUSION

I have shown in this paper that the root of the property rights controversy in the Islamic reformist movement is the Islamic notion of God's ultimate ownership. Some Islamic economists have found the notion of God's ultimate ownership and Islam's compassion for the poor and destitute as the ideological ground supporting their aim of establishing an egalitarian society under the Islamic banner. They regard the Islamic economic system as a just and humane alternative to socialism and capitalism. However, since in an Islamic society social relations, and from our perspective here, social relations of production, must be in accordance with Islamic law, the reformist view of an Islamic economy must be clearly within this confine. I have shown in this paper that the Islamic economic system proposed by these reformers is at most a capitalist economy with an interventionist-welfare state, where these reformers hope adherence to the Islamic spirit will bring about an Islamic 'social balance'. The blueprints of the proposed Islamic economy must, however, be sanctioned by the Islamic jurisprudential tradition. I have argued that even such a non-radical reform has not received, and it is doubtful that it will receive, approval from the community of *mujtahids*, who are the guardians of the Islamic law. The Islamic jurisprudential traditional is more forcefully explicit in the defence of private property rights than many Islamic social reformers are willing to realise. The Iranian experience is another concrete historical support of this claim.

NOTES

An earlier version of this paper was presented at a joint session of American Economic Association and Middle East Economic Association in the annual meeting of Allied Social Science Association, Chicago, 27-30 December 1987. I wish to express my gratitude to Bahram Tavakolian for his intellectual and moral support and for his many comments and corrections. I would also like to thank Warren J. Samuels, Paul King, Robin Bartlett, Cyrus Bina and Fatemeh Moghadam for their valuable comments. The opinions and remaining errors are mine. This study was supported by a Faculty Development Grant from Denison University.

1. Donohue and Esposito (1982) provide an anthology of works of Islamic political theorists and ideologues. For a review of Islamic political movements in various Muslim countries of Asia, see Esposito (1987).
2. For a survey of literature see Siddiqi (1981), and for a critical analysis see Kuran (1983 and 1986).
3. In 'Islamic Economics: A Utopian-Scholastic-Neoclassical-Keynesian Synthesis! (1992) I have examined the methodological eclecticism of Islamic economics.

4. For example: 'And we desired to show favour unto those were oppressed in the earth, and to make them examples and to make them inheritors'. (Quran, XVIII:5) The Quran is quoted from Pickthall's translation.
5. Most of the strong condemnations of the wealthy and arrogant are seen in the earlier chapters of the Quran revealed in Mecca, where Muhammad was engaged in direct confrontations with the powerful lords of the Quraysh tribe. For example: 'Nay, but ye (for your part) honor not the orphan; And urge not the feeding of the poor; And ye devour heritage with devouring greed; And love wealth with abounding love.' (Quran, LXXXIX:17–20) It is, however, explicitly clear in the Quran that it is not wealth but its accompanying arrogance that is condemned.
6. A parallel may be drawn between the issues raised by the contemporary Islamic political movements and those generated by the Christian Humanist and Christian Socialist movements in the 1920s and 1930s, and Liberation Theology in this decade. See Segundo (1984), Gutierrez (1983), Berryman (n.d.), and the collection of essays in Tabb (1986), among others.
7. The Iranian revolution is a case in point. Political groups ranging from the proponents of a *laissez faire* market economy to the supporters of 'state capitalism' and 'cooperative socialism' have sought to carry on their debate on the terrain of Islamic ideology, each claiming to long for 'true Islam'. The central issue in these debates has been the limits of private property rights (Bakhash, 1984 and Behdad, 1988a).
8. In this paper I use the term 'reform' to mean a change in social conditions without implying that such a change is necessarily progressive from a historical perspective.
9. I have made Arabic nouns plural by adding 's' to the singular, e.g., *faqihs* for *fuqaha*.
10. There are close similarities between Islam's notion of property rights and that of Medieval Christianity. The study of these similarities are beyond the scope of this paper. The readers may consult Spiegel's (1983, pp. 689, 695–9) extensive bibliography of the relevant works on property rights in Christianity.
11. Some of the arguments in this paragraph are from Behdad (1988a).
12. The economists who subscribed to this approach accept some government intervention in order to correct for 'market failures'.
13. It ranges between 2.5 and 10 per cent depending on the form of wealth. 'Unlike modern taxation, *zakat* is a flat rate and does not rise exuberantly on an ascending scale.' (Abdul-Rauf, 1979, p. 9). See also Kuran (1986, pp. 143–9).
14. The similarity of these thoughts with the conservative version of the post-Reformation Christian paternalistic ethic is striking. See Hunt (1979, pp. 21–3, 28).
15. Muhammad is quoted to have said: 'When one of you looks at someone who is superior to him in property or appearance, he should look at someone who is inferior to him.' (Mannan, 1986, p. 383).
16. Obviously, many Islamic economists disagree with this interpretation of *tawhid*. There are many explicit acknowledgements of inequality in the Quran and statements of Muhammad (see above).
17. Almost all Islamic economists interpret *tawhid* to mean brotherhood and

cooperation. See, for example, Choudhury (1986, p. 8) and Naqvi (1981, pp. 48–9). Abu Sulayman, however, is among the few Islamic economists who extend the interpretation of *tawhid* to equality in property rights.

18. In Sadr's view, state ownership in capitalist economies, and private ownership in socialist economies are deviations from the working principles of these systems.
19. MacPherson (1978, pp. 4–6) also classifies forms of ownership in a capitalist economy into similar categories: common, private and state.
20. Except in the long-run in the perfectly competitive and monopolistic competitive markets, where demand is tangent to the average cost curve. See Choudhury (1986, pp. 33–9) for a mathematical treatment of price and output determination of a firm, in the neoclassical tradition, in an Islamic economy. For the application of neoclassical analysis in Islamic economics, see Behdad (1989).
21. Here I have used *riba* as it appears in Arabic instead of usury which appears in translation.
22. For definition of *riba* and an extensive treatment of it in major schools of *sunni* jurisprudence see Saleh (1986, Chapters 2 and 3). On ambiguities about the definition of *riba* see Rodinson (1978, pp. 14–15).
23. Kahf (1973, p. 44) as quoted in Siddiqi (1981, p. 59) asserts that in an Islamic economy '[a]ll prices, whether of the factors of production or of products, stem out of this [market] mechanism, these prices are looked at as just or fair prices in this respect'.
24. Muhammad is quoted to have said: 'Merchants are the messengers of this world and God's faithful trustees on Earth'. From Rodinson (1978, pp. 16–17) where a number of similar statements of Muhammad are quoted.
25. Mannan (1986, pp. 123, 131–2), Siddiqi (1981, p. 59) and Ahmad (1977, p. 29). It is interesting to note that Ahmad claims since real interest earnings are subject to unpredictable fluctuations due to changes in the rate of inflation, such earnings are legitimate in Islam.
26. On the economic conditions under Islamic rule in the Middle Ages see Rodinson (1973 and 1978, Chapter 3).
27. In Sheik's view '[t]he State is the ultimate owner of all land . . . and the State would determine to allot [the surplus land] to other self-cultivators or to keep it as a State farm for grazing cattle' (1961, p. 181).
28. Then the return on land is not 'rent' but profit in a capitalist sense. See Marx (1959, Part VI).
29. It is interesting to note the rest of this sentence, keeping in mind that Sheikh is considered an 'extreme socialist' by M. N. Siddiqi (1981, 7). Sheikh continues ' . . . and the purpose which the society wants the moneyed people to serve, i.e., the purpose of creating employment, speed up economic development or tide over economic depression, will not be served'.
30. Sadr (1978, pp. 226–7) points to the differences between *mukhabara* and *muzara'a*.
31. These restrictions are enumerated in almost every treatise on Islamic economics. See, for example, Choudbury (1986, Chapter 1) and Mannan (1986, pp. 118–24, 150–4).

32. Labour law has been the issue of a heated jurisprudential debate in the Islamic Republic of Iran for seven years. Mannan (1986, 94), unable to find any support in Islamic jurisprudence for the right to collective bargaining, maintains that 'if both workers and employers are imbued with the values of Islam, the whole question of strikes and lockouts would be relatively unimportant'.
33. The Islamic Republic of Iran has not been able to resolve the jurisprudential issues related to the proposed Foreign Trade Bill in the past nine years. The Council of Islamic Guardians has rejected several versions of the Bill passed by the Parliament on jurisprudential grounds. The main objection of the Council is to the extensive role that the Bill provides for the state in the conduct of foreign trade. As the result of this and similar jurisprudential objections to the policies of the Islamic Republic, the formulation of the First Economic Plan of Iran has confronted a deadlock. See Behdad (1988a). Another interesting case is that the Central Bank of Iran was forced to liberalise its foreign exchange control policy under the pressure of export merchants who argued that according to Islam the state may not force merchants to surrender their exchange earnings to the Central Bank. See Behdad (1988b).
34. Some Islamic economists have, however, attempted to differentiate their ideal market conditions from the *laissez faire*, competitive model. For example, Naqvi (1981, pp. 66–7 and Chapter 9) argues that 'the model of competitive equilibrium may not be of much use' since external economies, and the social injustices resulting from the existing inequalities will require intervention of the government in an Islamic economy. Choudbury (1986, Chapter 3) in the neoclassical tradition regards the objective function of a firm to be cost minimisation subject to profit constraint.
35. For a critical study of the behavioural norms in an Islamic economy see Kuran (1983).
36. On the interest-free banks see Siddiqi (1983) and for a critique of it see Kuran (1986, pp. 149–58).
37. The idealised Islamic behaviour was hardly ever practiced in the fourteen centuries of Islam except, maybe, by Muhammad and his few Companions. See Rodinson (1978, Chapter 3).
38. Being a *shi'i*, Sadr has had a pronounced impact on the development of Islamic economic thought in Iran.
39. Mahdavy (1970) and Skocpol (1982) refer to the oil exporting countries as 'rentier states'.
40. In Iraq and Bahrain also, *shi'is* constitute the majority of population, but *shi'ism* is not the dominant sect. In Iran, however, even before the 1979 revolution, *shi'ism* was the official religion of the state.
41. Systematic efforts to formulate Islamic economics in Iran date back only to the recent revolutionary period. (See Behdad (1988a) and Katouzian (1983).) Bani Sadr's *Economics of Divine Unity* was first published abroad in 1978. This and later works on Islamic economics in Iran are deeply influenced by Sadr's book which was published in Iran in the 1970s. Earlier works by Taleqani, Shari'ati and Mutahhari (see Hosseini

(1987) lacked a systematic effort in dealing with Islamic economies or the Islamic economic system. The Constitution of the Islamic Republic of Iran provides a blueprint for the Iranian economy closely similar to Sadr's model. The debate about economic policies in the post-revolutionary period has been mainly around Sadr's interpretation of the role of the Islamic state in the economy.

REFERENCES

Abdul-Rauf, Muhammad, *The Islamic Doctrine of Economics and Contemporary Economic Thought: Highlight of a Conference on Theological Inquiry into Capitalism and Socialism* (Washington, D.C.: American Enterprise Institute, 1979).

Abdur Rauf [Abdul-Rauf], Muhammad, 'Islam and Contemporary Economic System', in *Contemporary Aspects of Economic Thinking in Islam, Proceedings of the Third East Coast Regional Conference of the Muslim Students' Association of the United States and Canada, April 1968* (Plainsfield, Indiana: American Trust, 1970) 1980, pp. 51-6.

Abu Sulayman, Abdul-Ilamid Ahmad, 'The Theory of the Economics of Islam: The Economics of Tawhid and Brotherhood', in *Contemporary Aspects of Economic Thinking in Islam* (1970) pp. 8-50.

Aghnides, Nicolas P., *Mohammedan Theories of Finance with an Introduction to Mohammedan Law and a Bibliography* (New York: AMS Press (1916) 1969).

Ahmad, Syed, 'Reflections on the Concept and the Law of Riba', in *Outlines of Islamic Economics, Proceedings of the First Symposium on the Economics of Islam in North America* (Indianapolis, Ind.: Association of Muslim Social Scientists, 1977) pp. 26-36.

Almeder, Robert, 'The Ethics of Profit: Reflections on Corporate Responsibility', *Business and Society*, 19 (2) Winter 1980, 7-14.

Bakhash, Shaul, *The Reign of Ayatollahs: Iran and the Islamic Revolution* (New York: Basic Books, 1984).

Bani Sadr, Abulhasan, *Eqtesad-e Tawhidi* (*Economics of Divine Unity*) (place and publisher not specified, 1978).

Behdad, Sohrab, 'Islamic Economics: A Utopian-Scholastic-Neoclassical-Keynesian Synthesis!' *Research in the History of Economic Thought and Methodology*, vol. 9, (1992).

Behdad, Sohrab, 'The Political Economy of the Islamic Planning in Iran', in H. Amirahmadi and M. Parvin (eds) *Post-Revolutionary Iran* (Boulder, Colorado: Westview Press, 1988a).

Behdad, Sohrab, 'Foreign Exchange Gap, Structural Constraints and the Political Economy of Exchange Rate Determination in Iran', *International Journal of Middle East Studies*, 20 (1), February 1988b.

Berryman, Phillip, *Liberation Theology* (Bloomington, Ind.: Meyer Stone and Company, n.d.).

Chapra, M. Umar, 'The Islamic Welfare State and its Role in the Economy', in Khurshid Ahmad (ed.), *Studies in Islamic Economics* (Leicester: The

Islamic Foundation, for the International Centre for Research in Islamic Economics, King Abdul Aziz University, Jeddah, 1980) pp. 143–69.

Choudhury, Masudul Alam, *Contributions to Islamic Economy Theory: A Study in Social Economics* (New York: St. Martin's Press, 1986).

Donohue, John J. and John L. Esposito (eds), *Islam in Transition: Muslim Perspectives* (New York: Oxford University Press, 1982).

Enayat, Hamid, *Modern Islamic Political Thought* (London: Macmillan, 1982).

Esposito, John L. (ed.), *Islam in Asia: Religion, Politics, and Society* (New York: Oxford University Press, 1987).

Faruqi, al-, Isma'il R. A., 'Foreword', to *Contemporary Aspects of Economic Thinking in Islam* (1980) pp. ix–xiii.

Gutierrez, Gustavo, *The Power of the Poor in History*, translated from *La fuerza historica de los pobres* (1979) (Maryknoll, NY: Orbis Books, 1983).

Hallaq, Wael B., 'Was the Gate of Ijtihad Closed?', *International Journal of Middle East Studies*, 16 (1), March 1984, pp. 3–41.

Hassanein, Medhat, 'Towards a Model of the Economics of Islam', in *Contemporary Aspects of Economic Thinking in Islam* (1980) pp. 1–7.

Hosseini, Hamid, 'Notion of Private Property in Islamic Economics in Iran: A Review of Literature', presented at a joint session of American Economic Association and Middle East Economic Association, Chicago, 27–30 December 1987.

Hunt, E. K., *History of Economic Thought: A Critical Perspective* (Belmont, CA: Wadsworth, 1979).

Ibn Taymiya, al-Shaykh al-Imam, *Public Duties in Islam: The Institution of the Hisba* (circa, 14th century), translated from the Arabic (Leicester: Islamic Foundation, 1982).

Kahf, Monzer, 'A Contribution to the Study of the Economics of Islam', University of Utah, 1973, mimeo.

Katouzian, Homa, 'Shi'ism and Islamic Economics: Sadr and Bani Sadr', in N. Keddie (ed.) *Religion and Politics in Iran: Shi'ism from Quietism to Revolution* (New Haven, Conn.: Yale University Press, 1983).

Koran, translated by Mohammad Mamaduke Pickthall (*The Meaning of the Glorious Koran*) (New York: Mentor Book, 1930).

Kuran, Timur, 'The Economic System in Contemporary Islamic Thought: Interpretation and Assessment', *International Journal of Middle East Studies*, 18 (2), May 1986, pp. 135–64.

Kuran, Timur, 'Behavioral Norms in the Islamic Doctrine of Economics: A Critique', *Journal of Economic Behavior and Organization*, 4 (4), December 1983, pp. 353–79,

Macdonald, Duncan B., *Development of Muslim Theology, Jurisprudence and Constitutional Theory* (London: Darf Publishers (1902) 1985).

MacPherson, C. B., 'The Meaning of Property', in C. B. MacPherson (ed.) *Property: Mainstream and Critical Positions* (Toronto: University of Toronto Press, 1978) pp. 1–13.

Mahdavy, H., 'The Patterns and Problems of Economic Development in Rentier States: The Case of Iran', in M. A. Cook (ed.), *Studies in the Economic History of the Middle East: From the Rise of Islam to the Present Day* (London, Oxford University Press, 1970).

Mannan, Muhammad Abdul, *Islamic Economics: Theory and Practice*

(Foundations of Islamic Economics), revised edition (Sevenoaks, Kent, U.K.: Hodder and Stoughton, 1986).
Marx, Karl, *Capital*, Volume III (Moscow: Progress Publishing, 1959).
Momen, Moojan, *An Introduction to Shi'i Islam* (New Haven: Yale University Press, 1985).
Mutahhari, Morteza, *Jurisprudence and its Principles (Fiqh and usul ul-fiqh)*, translated by Muhammad Salman Tawheedi (Albany, California: Moslem Student Association, n.d., circa 1983).
Naqvi, Syed Nawad Haider, *Ethics and Economics: An Islamic Synthesis* (Leicester: Islamic Foundation, 1981).
Nowaihi, al-, Muhammad, 'Fundamentals of Economic Justice in Islam', in *Contemporary Aspects of Economic Thinking in Islam* (1970) pp. 65–81.
O'Brien, George, *An Essay on Medieval Economic Teaching* (London: Longman Green, 1920).
Rodinson, Maxime, *Islam and Capitalism*, translated from *Islam et le capitalisme* (1966) (Austin: University of Texas Press, 1978).
Rodinson, Maxime, *Mohammed*, translated from *Mahomet* (1961) (Harmondsworth: Penguin Books, 1973).
Sadr, Muhammad Baqir, *Eqtesad-e ma*, a Persian translation of *Iqtisaduna* (1961) (Tehran: Entesharat-e Eslami, Volume I , 1971, Volume II, 1978).
Saleh, Nabil A., *Unlawful Gain and Legitimate Profit in Islamic Law: Riba, Gharar and Islamic Banking* (New York: Cambridge University Press, 1986).
Schacht, Joseph, *An Introduction to Islamic Law* (Oxford: Clarendon Press, (1964) 1982).
Schacht, Joseph, *The Origins of Muhammadan Jurisprudence* (Oxford: Claredon Press, (1950) 1985).
Segundo, Juan Luis, *Faith and Ideologies*, translated from *Fe e ideologia* (1982) (Maryknoll, NY: Orbis Books, 1984).
Sheikh, Nasir Ahmad, *Some Aspects of the Constitution and Economics of Islam* (Woking: The Woking Muslim Mission and Literary Trust, 1961).
Siddiqi, Muhammad Nejatullah, *Partnership and Profit-Sharing in Islamic Law* (Leicester: The Islamic Foundation, 1985).
Siddiqi, Muhammad Nejatullah, *Banking Without Interest* (Leicester: The Islamic Foundation, 1983).
Siddiqi, Muhammad Nejatullah, *Muslim Economic Thinking: A Survey of Contemporary Literature* (Leicester: The Islamic Foundation, for the International Centre for Research in Islamic Economics, King Abdul Aziz University, Jeddah, 1981).
Sivan, Emmanuel, *Radical Islam: Medieval Theology and Modern Politics* (New Haven, Conn.: Yale University Press, 1985).
Skocpol, Theda, 'Rentier State and Shi'a Islam in the Iranian Revolution', *Theory and Society*, 11, May 1982.
Spiegel, Henry William, *The Growth of Economic Thought*, revised edition (Durham, NC: Duke University Press, 1983).
Tabataba'i, Hossein Modarressi, *An Introduction to Shi'i Law: A Bibliographical Study* (London: Ithaca Press, 1984).
Tabb, William K. (ed.), *Churches in Struggle: Liberation Theology and*

Social Change in North America (New York: Monthly Review Press, 1986).
Yusuf, S. M., 'Land Agriculture and Rent in Islam', *Islamic Culture*, 31 (1) January 1957, pp. 27–39.

4 Islamic Perspectives And Class Interests [1]

Ziaul Haque

The problems of economic retardation, general poverty, and political instability in Muslim societies are exacerbated by the blatant manipulation of Islamic ideology. This ideology is based on vague notions and medieval categories of thought articulated in servile subservience to foreign capital. The basic aim of the 'Islamisation' process, as will be substantiated in the course of the following discussion, is to justify the existing economic relationships and the status quo by obfuscating the immediate socio-economic problems of the masses.

As this paper is an appraisal of the process of 'Islamisation' of society and economy, it would be appropriate to define more clearly what is meant by 'Islam'. The term has been grossly misunderstood and misused – sometimes tendentiously – by scholars, statesmen, politicians, and apologists of capitalism and even Islamic socialism. As every ruling class needs an ideology to perpetuate its rule, Islam has been variously interpreted throughout centuries in the Muslim world by different classes, political groups, autocratic rulers, fundamentalists, modernists and religious fanatics. Unless the concept of Islam is clearly defined, emotive and confusing terms like 'militant Islam', 'upsurge of Islam', 'renaissance of Islam', 'Islamic democracy', 'Islamic economics', 'Islamic science', etc., cannot be correctly understood. For simplicity's sake, all such interpretations in this chapter have been categorised into: 1) original or revolutionary Islam of the Quranic conception; 2) feudal or medieval Islam; and 3) capitalist or bourgeois Islam – the forms of interpretation which actually pertain to different historical periods, socio-economic formations and conditions of medieval and modern times.

The economies of developing societies today are, in the main, dependent on the advanced capitalist countries and form a part of the international capitalist system. The political independence of these former colonies and semi-colonies did not lead to economic independence because the colonial social and economic structures remained more or less intact. Hence, the larger economic decisions of what to produce, how to produce and for whom to produce in these economies, remained in the hands of indigenous ruling elites and foreign colonialists. As the modern world has come to be divided into two polarised economic systems of capitalism and socialism, with antagonistic models and world-views, the social and economic problems of Third World countries have been aggravated for lack of a coherent plan, purpose, direction and identity. They vacillate between the two poles. Economic chaos, social anarchy and intellectual confusion are the natural outcome of their general aimlessness.

The economy of the modern world is thus divided into a small number of advanced and rich countries, and a larger number of poor and developing countries. The poor countries of the Third World are internally divided into a tiny minority of rich people and a vast majority of working people.

REVOLUTIONARY ISLAM

The original or Quranic concept of Islam is essentially revolutionary. This statement needs explanation and qualification. The Quran is a holy book of revealed truths. It is a niche, a receptacle of truths, both natural and social, and the discovery of knowledge was condensed in a religious framework which was readily understood by the Arabs of a pre-feudal pastoral tribal society, since the Quran was revealed in the Arabic idiom. It comprises 114 *suras* or chapters. It was divinely revealed to the Holy Prophet Mohammad Ibn'Abd Allah Ibn'Abd al-Muttalib in Mecca and Medina in the years 610-32 – a period of almost twenty-three years. The verses of the Quran (ninety Meccan and twenty-four Medinan) relate in general to the social, political, economic, religious, spiritual and intellectual conditions of a community of revolutionaries headed by this great Prophet (570-632), who was born in Mecca in the tribe of Hashim of the merchant clan of Quraysh. He was a poor orphan and grew up as an extremely honest young man, whom even his enemies called *sadiq* (truthful) and *amin* (trustworthy).[2] He lived in a society which was riven with moral corruption, deep social inequality and religious and social decadence. It was a tribal society surrounded by the feudalist regimes of Byzantium, Persia and Ethiopia.

After his call to Prophethood in 610, the Prophet preached the divine message of the unity of God, unity of mankind (in place of the anarchic atomism of the tribal system), and human equality to the people of Mecca. The earliest converts were people of lowly social origins – slaves, artisans, blacksmiths, carpenters, masons, tribal outcastes, women and orphans – the pariah people who had no rights and no privileges.[3]

As this community of early revolutionaries gradually grew, so the opposition to it from the oligarchy of rich merchants of the *Quraysh*, the tribal chiefs and the privileged priestly class, whose social and economic power was now threatened, increased. The new converts were ridiculed, humiliated and persecuted. They were called *sabi'un*, the godless heretics, sorcerers and foreign agents. Their leader, the Prophet, was labelled a madman (*majnun*), a sorcerer-magician (*sahir*), a poet (*shair*) and a soothsayer (*kahin*), because the new movement had ripped society apart – alienating father from son, brother from brother, mother from child, and husband from wife, thus tearing the social fabric apart, uprooting the tribal structures and the vested interests attached to them.[4] The decadent social order was overthrown, privileges challenged, and autocrats and the mercantile oligarchy threatened. The entire structure of this unjust tribal society was thus menaced. The priests, the usurers, the merchants, the landlords of agricultural settlements and all the exploiters of the weak, saw in the new movement their ultimate ruin.[5] They formed a formidable alliance to kill the Prophet and crush the rising of slaves and workers. The Prophet and his followers left their hearths and homes, their wealth and families, in search of a new world and a new order of equality and justice which the Quran had promised them. This was the famous *Hijra*, or migration for their cause (622), when they left Mecca for Yathrib (afterwards Medina).

The Quran has termed this movement 'Islam' (literally, *aslama* means to surrender or submit to the will, cause or way of God).[6] This Quranic term actually means a prophet's submission or surrender to the way and laws of God to seek His countenance, His will, i.e. the divine cause, His unity, etc.[7] Translated from the religious to the social plane, the term means the establishment of a regime of social and economic equality, and the abolition of all injustices and inequalities of privileges and wealth which impede the fullest development of natural faculties and potentialities of all human beings. Religious rites such as prayers and fasting are a means to achieve these social ends. The Quran also uses the term 'Islam' in opposition to *kufr*. A *kafir* is a person who denies the truth of Islam. According to the Quran, although a *kafir* may believe in God (as a Christian or a Jew does) if he does not believe in the unity of God and the unity of mankind and its corollary, the social and economic equality of human beings, he is not a Muslim.

Kufr and *batil* (falsehood) both denote falsehood, and Islam and *haqq* are both truth.[8] Islam is therefore the establishment of truth in society, and as the Quran implies, the concept of this truth may vary from time to time. Under the specific pastoral conditions of biblical times, in the tribal milieu of *Hijaz*, and the industrial conditions of modern times, truth acquires different shapes. Consequently, conceptions of truth and falsehood change under different conditions. But ideally, says the Quran, Islam stands for truth (*haqq*) against the forces of *kufr* and *batil*. Islam is a way of life – *din* – based on social equality and justice (*'adl*); *kufr* is the way of life based on inequality and *zulm* (exploitation, transgression). According to the Quran, there are in general three broad social classes: *al-mustakbarun*, the rich who deny the truth of divine unity and social equality of mankind; *al-mustad'afun*, the poor who believe in this truth; and *al-munafiqun* the hypocrites who vacillate between these two classes. They belong neither to this nor to that, but waver between *haqq* and *batil* in the quagmire of opportunism.

'FEUDAL ISLAM'

The ideal of one God and one community exemplified in the perfect social equality of all the believers/revolutionaries in the classless egalitarian society was termed Islam by the Quran. Social equality was the *grundnorm*, the ideal and the cornerstone of early Muslim society. The subsequent abolition of ground-rent, usury/interest (*riba*), *muzara'a* and all speculative/exploitative economic practices, and the emancipation of the lower social classes, slaves, women and orphans, initiated by the Prophet were the beginnings of this revolution. But this social revolution was short-lived. It could not be consolidated. The Prophet died before he could finally abolish all the centuries-old exploitative institutions. The civil war after the death of 'Umar Ibn al-Khattab, 13-23 AH (633-44 AD), the second Caliph, gave the death blow to this Islamic regime of egalitarianism. The counter-revolution of the Umayyads, starting under the Caliph 'Uthman Ibn 'Affan, was the finale of this revolutionary ethos of Islam.

The emergence of the Umayyad autocratic regime was really the transformation of revolutionary Islam into a feudal dispensation. How this transformation took place and how the new interpretations of Islam in a feudal society were formulated are topics beyond the scope of this paper. Suffice it here to note that the social relationship of kings and subjects, landlords and serfs, masters and slaves were rationalised by the Muslim scholars, mainly the jurists (*fuqaha*), for the social stability of the feudal system. This feudal character is discernible in the social, legal and economic literature produced throughout medieval times. The pre-Quranic institutions of ground-rent, interest, usury, landlordism, slavery and hundreds of other exploitative practices, were justified by the majority of Muslim jurists through a legal and administrative apparatus erected by the autocrats and ruling classes on the foundations of the pre-Islamic regimes. The legal instruments and concepts elaborated by the jurists, like *qiyas* (analogical reasoning) and *ijmac* (consensus), were used to give sanctity to these institutions with a view to consolidating the Muslim community against its formidable enemies.

Let us see how pre-Quranic institutions and concepts were reinterpreted in the feudal/medieval period. It is an established fact that the Prophet, in addition to the Quranic ban on usury and interest, had abolished leasing of lands by declaring that lands belonged to those who cultivated them. This negates landlordism in all its forms. But the *fuqaha* rationalised the age-old institutions of ground-rent for the reason that the entire political superstructure of their times – the incomes of the ruling classes – were derived mainly from the revenues paid by the peasantry in the form of *kharaj* (taxes).[9]

As there were no financial institutions, like banks, joint-stock companies, industries and stock exchanges, etc., medieval jurists justified the ancient institution of *mudaraba*, a primitive form of business organisation suitable for distant journeys. It was a pre-Islamic commercial institution, in which a capital owner entrusted his capital to a worker for some business. They both shared the profit thus earned in pre-agreed proportions, as one-third, two-thirds, etc. All loss was borne by the capital owner. Such commercial transactions were carried on in medieval times under economic conditions when capital could be mobilised only as an usury or merchant capital. This has no basis in the Quran or *Hadith* of the Prophet.[10]

The *fiqh*, as interpreted by the *fuqaha* of the early and late medieval times, reflects the feudal mode of production and its related social, economic and political relationships based on autocratic monarchies, feudal estates and the existence of serfs and slaves, perpetually bound to the soil they tilled from generation to generation. The Quranic terms of *zakat*, *sadaqa* (alms) and others were also reinterpreted under feudalism. Private property had not developed under early Islam because of the clear abolition of landlordism, and because the objective pastoral and tribal conditions of the Arabian peninsula did not encourage it. Therefore, early Islam had enunciated that surplus over basic needs (*al-afw*) must be given to the poor in order to level all inequalities.[11] The early evidence shows that orchards and wells – the sources of scarce water and staple food (dates) of the common people – were given as common *waqf*, mortmains or trusts by Muslims for the use of all whenever the Prophet urged them to do so.[12] Even the Prophet (and his family) subsisted on water and dates throughout his life. Dates were the staple food of the poor.[13]

It has also been reported that no other community of any Prophet faced so large a number of orphans, abandoned women, widows and poor as that of Mohammad Ibn 'Abd Allah.[14] So private property in land was discouraged. *Zakat* was generally levied on cattle, agricultural produce, money (gold and silver), etc.[15] It appears that the jurists in their literal interpretation of *zakat* tended to confine its meaning to personal property. Land therefore came to be exempted, although conscientious people voluntarily continued to pay *zakat* on their land possessions.[16] Under the feudal conditions of society, *zakat* lost its real meaning and content. It was originally a concept which meant transfer of surplus wealth from the rich to the poor in order to level inequalities.

On the face of it, feudal Islam is a negation of Quranic Islam, which stands for social and economic equality. It does not, however, mean that all the great saints and scholars who were also great jurists, like Mohammad ibn Idris al-Shafi'i (d. 204 AH/819-20 AD), Abu Hanifa (d. 150 AH/767-8 AD), Malik ibn Anas (d. 179 AH/795-6 AD), Ahmed ibn Hanbal (d. 241 AH/855-6 AD) and others who justified a number of pre-Islamic social and economic institutions, did not understand the real message and ideal of Quranic Islam. With their intellect and knowledge of the sources of Islam, they made genuine efforts to apply the teachings of Islam to solve contemporary problems, but their efforts were circumscribed and limited by the social formations in which they lived. In their personal lives, early scholars like Ahmed ibn Hanbal, Malik and Abu Hanifa did not compromise with oppressive and exploitative regimes. But they could not go beyond the contemporary systems and their structures. Their remarkable and ingenious developments of Islamic legal principles and sciences to understand and apply the original revolutionary principles of the Quran and the Prophetic *hadith* must be evaluated and appreciated in this context.

'BOURGEOIS ISLAM'

In modern times, in particular after the sixteenth century, when European colonialism conquered Muslim societies, capitalism began to penetrate them. Its modern phase, imperialism or monopoly capitalism, has succeeded in reducing Muslim societies to dependent economies – mere appendages of more powerful advanced capitalist countries. These developing economies and societies of Muslim lands are ruled by the native upper classes of capitalists, businessmen, landlords and bureaucrats – both civil and military. These classes are generally in league with the foreign bourgeoisie, who supply them through aid and trade with capital goods and related advanced technology. The economies of Muslim lands have thus become a part of the international capitalist system, and the ruling elite forms a part of imperialist culture and civilisation.

Capitalism is based on the principles of private ownership of the basic means of production by a tiny minority of capitalists, free enterprise, the profit motive and exploitation of the working classes. Whereas the original Quranic Islam had abolished interest, usury, ground-rent and all speculative economic transactions, modern capitalism promotes private ownership of the means of production, like land and capital. It develops finance capital, joint-stock companies, stock exchanges and banks. It thrives on the earnings of profits, interest, ground-rent and the exploitation of the labour of the working classes. These are clearly antagonistic to the basic teachings of the Quran and the *hadith* of the holy Prophet, which consider all these earnings, incomes and profits *haram* (illicit).

In the wake of the European movements of the Renaissance and the Reformation after the decline of feudalism, the capitalist mode of production gradually emerged as the dominant form from the sixteenth century onwards. Subsequently, religion came to be separated not only from the natural and social sciences, but also from state structures. This new social order, liberated by the rising bourgeoisie, was based on reason, science and a democratic/pluralistic political dispensation. In advanced capitalist societies, with the progress of science and industry, religion receded from many areas of thought and action because man now began to control nature. Natural and social phenomena, so avers the modern scientific method, are ruled by laws which the human mind tries to discover. Modern capitalist (and socialist) societies are industrial societies, which have been competing with each other in the discovery of modern scientific knowledge, its application, and in its conquest of nature and the universe. The religious sensibilities of the static feudal ages have therefore given place to rational and scientific perceptions. This means that science and religion, as far as their concepts and historical developments are concerned, belong to two different epochs and milieux. Therefore, to term any science 'Islamic', 'Christian' or 'Hindu' would be meaningless because modern science has become universal, and modern society has become international in the sense that all societies share the heritage of science, knowledge and technologies.

ISLAMIC IDEOLOGY AND THE PROCESS OF 'ISLAMISATION'

Some Muslim ruling elites have ingeniously devised an 'Islamic' ideology to conserve and justify social and economic relationships based on a decadent status quo of feudalism and/or capitalism. Knowing that all Muslims have a great love for the Holy Prophet and Quranic Islam, the ruling classes are exploiting the fair name of Islam and have turned Quranic concepts into institutions which are in fact the citadels of vested interests.

Various 'ideological' institutions have been working in order to help the government (central and provincial) to 'reconstruct society on truly Islamic lines'. Councils of 'Islamic' ideology, 'Islamic' research institutes, 'Islamic' universities and scores of other 'Islamic' institutions are aiding the ruling classes in their efforts to 'Islamise' the present social and economic structures of moribund feudalism and capitalism. By 'Islamisation,' the present rulers mean the transformation of society according to the basic teachings of Quranic Islam. In actual practice, such ruling elites are usually appealing to the historical categories of feudal Islam, that is, pre-Quranic medieval forms of *riba*, *mudaraba*, *muzara'a*, *zakat*, *ushr*, etc., which originated and developed within different social contexts and which have not lost their original meaning and significance.[17] *Mudaraba* (profit-sharing), for example, is being reinterpreted and projected as a sacred religious principle to justify the maximisation of profits under capitalism. A new 'Islamic' enterprise, Islamic or interest-free banking, is being developed on the basis of the medieval concept of *mudaraba*.[18] The medieval concept of *muzara'a*, or sharecropping, is interpreted to justify the present system of absentee landlordism.[19]

Zakat has become an instrument to tax the personal savings of the lower middle classes and agricultural produce (*ushr*). Landed estates and capital gains have been exempted. *Riba* is interpreted sometimes as interest on loanable capital, and sometimes as usury or unearned income in a broad sense, as was done under the early revolutionary Islam.[20]

This means that the real purpose of this political process of 'Islamisation' is to develop a capitalist or bourgeois Islam in line with the principles of international capitalism. This process deliberately aims at consolidation of the propertied classes, encouragement of private ownership of the basic means of production, and the opening up of all sectors to powerful multinational corporations, at the expense of genuine industrialisation. The absence of capital goods industries and the retarded growth of the economy have arrested the further development of genuine industry, and a scientific and democratic culture, because the national bourgeoisie, in the face of powerful foreign capital, has remained feeble. All scientific processes have been subverted, and such terms as 'Islamic economics', 'Islamic education', 'Islamic science', 'Islamic banking', and 'Islamic democracy' have been coined in a purely tendentious way to serve the interests of international capitalism by interpreting Islam in bourgeois terms.[21] Some political parties and economic institutions which promote the interests of capitalist, both native and foreign, impudently exploit the fair name of Quranic Islam.

Real Quranic Islam has been discarded by these ruling elites for the reason that its application would do away with the institutions of feudalism and capitalism. The feudal/medieval form of *fiqh* Islam suits the interests of the ruling elite, because feudal Islam was, in the main, reactionary, medieval and dogmatic. It promoted the interests of feudal lords and *compradors*. However, this feudal and retrogressive superstructure of legal, political, social and intellectual ideas and notions does not accord with capitalism, industry, economic nationalism and modern technology.

To illustrate this point, let us examine the nature of 'Islamic economics', as developed by some 'Islamic economists', e.g. at the Islamic University in Islamabad, Pakistan, and the International Centre for Research on Islamic Economics in Jeddah. 'Islamic economics' has not been clearly defined by 'Islamic economists'.[22] The syllabi and courses of 'Islamic economics' comprise a smattering of old *fiqhi* treatises of the ninth century such as the *Kitab al-Kharaj* of

Abu Yusuf; knowledge of the Arabic language; modern econometrics; and a selected collection of commentaries on Quranic verses and Prophetic traditions. 'Islamic economists' are trying to develop a 'non-secular' religious economics loaded with metaphysical axioms and postulates which do not relate to living human beings, but instead deal with dead fossils, abstract dogmas, medieval categories and institutions, and vague notions leading to confusion and complexities. Such attempts at the Islamisation of knowledge often suppress the spirit of enquiry, investigation and scientific reasoning. Such institutions of medieval conception tend to become islands and monasteries cut off from international developments in science, scholarship and knowledge, and which will ultimately decay and die like plants without light and water.

CONCLUSION

The political use of religion and the suppression of scientific and democratic processes have generated acute tensions, aggravated social and economic disparities and led to general disequilibrium in many Muslim societies. This has strengthened reactionary and *comprador* elements and tendencies. The contradictions between uneven development and the related official process of 'Islamisation' under the aegis of international monopoly capitalism have resulted in a sharp and dangerous polarisation of society. It has also unleashed an accelerating proliferation of graft, greed, selfish profit motives, corruption, shallow religiosity, hypocrisy, moral decadence and degeneration of almost all civil institutions – economic, political, cultural, educational and religious.

Recent history suggests that if societies do not bring radical changes to their social structures, they may explode in violence and revolution. The effete upper classes cannot suppress the lower classes in the limbo of a decadent status quo, whether through authoritarianism or religious dogma. Societies which fail to develop their economies end up as adjuncts of international monopoly capitalism. Without economic independence, there cannot be any political, social, cultural and intellectual freedom. Without bringing profound changes in social and economic structures, the problems of the broad masses cannot be solved. This means that liberation from monopoly capitalism is a *sine qua non* of real and genuine independence and honourable existence for developing countries.

NOTES

1. Abridged and edited version of 'Islamisation of Society in Pakistan', in Asghar Khan (ed.) *Islam, Politics and the State: The Pakistan Experience* (London: Zed Press, 1985).
2. Ibn Hisham *Sirat al Nabi* (Cairo: Al-muktaba Al-tijariyya), I, p. 197.
3. See, for details, the following: Quran, Chapter 6, verses 52–63; Al-Wahidi, *Asbab al-Nuzul* (Cairo: Matba'a Hindiyya, 1315AH), pp. 162–3; Ibn Hisham, *Sirat al Nabi*, I, p. 420; Tabari, *Jami al-Bayan Tafsir al Quran* (Cairo: Dar al-Maarif, n.d.), XI, pp. 374–5.
4. See early Meccan *surahs*: 51, 54, 68, 69, 74, 81 etc. See also Ahmad Ibn Hanbal, *Musnad* (Beirut: Dar/Sadir, n.d.) IV, pp. 341–4.
5. Quran, 2: 275–81; 9: 34.
6. Quran, 3: 19–20, 83–5; 5: 111; 10: 90.
7. The socio-religious missions and ways of life of the prophets like Ibrahim, Ya'qub, Ishaq, Musa (Moses) and 'Isa (Christ) are also called Islam. See Quran, 3: 64–7. See also Ziaul Haque, *Revelation and Revolution in Islam* (Lahore: Vanguard Books, 1987).
8. Quran, *surah* 43, 98, 109 etc.
9. See Ziaul Haque, *Landlord and Peasant in Early Islam* (Islamabad: Islamic Research Institute, 1977), chs I, II, III and VII.
10. See, for details on the origin and development of the concept of *mudaraba* (profit-sharing) in medieval times, Ziaul Haque, *Islam and Feudalism* (Lahore: Vanguard Books, 1984).
11. Quran, 2: 219.
12. There is abundant evidence in the compilations of *Hadith* (by Bukhari, Muslim, Malik, Nasa'i, Tirmidhi, Ahmed Ibn Hanbal) under the chapters of *zakat* and *sadaqa*, which suggests that the Prophet used to persuade his companions to give their wells, orchards and other forms of wealth for common use by all the people. See, for example, Ahmed ibn Hanbal, *Musnad*, III, p. 115; VI, p. 7.
13. Ahmed ibn Hanbal, *Musnad* (Beirut: Dar/Sadir, n.d.) VI, pp. 71, 128.
14. Ahmed ibn Hanbal, *Musnad* (Cairo: Dar al-Maarif, 1950), I, 185.
15. Malik ibn Anas, *Kitab al-Muwatta'* (Cairo: Dar *Ihya' al-Kutab al 'Arabiyya*, 1351/1370), II, 244–5.
16. Hafiz Abu al-Faraj 'Abd al Rahman ibn al-Jawzi, *Manaqib al-Imam Ahmad ibn Hanbal* (Cairo: Matba'a al-Sa'adah, n.d.), pp. 223–4.
17. Hasan Gardezi et al. (eds), *Pakistan: Unstable State* (Lahore: Vanguard Books, 1983); see the chapter entitled 'Pakistan and Islamic Ideology'.
18. A type of literature on *mudaraba*, profit-sharing, and interest-free 'Islamic' banking has recently appeared. See, for example, Muazzam Ali (ed.), *Islamic Banks and Strategies of Economic Cooperation* (London: New Century Publishers, 1982); Zia ud Din Ahmad et al. (eds) *Money and Banking in Islam* (Islamabad: Institute of Policy Studies, 1983); Khurshid Ahmad (ed.), *Studies in Islamic Economics* (Leicester: The Islamic Foundation, 1981).
19. See Government of Pakistan, Council of Islamic Ideology, *The Consolidated Recommendations on the Islamic Economic System* (Islamabad: Government of Pakistan, December, 1983).

20. See, for details, Ziaul Haque, '*Riba*, Interest and Profit', in *Pakistan Economist*, 24 and 31 May 1980.
21. See, for details on the concept of Islamic education, S. N. Al-Attas, *Aims and Objectives of Islamic Education* (Jeddah: King Abdul Aziz University, 1979). The book develops the idea that the modern system of education (in universities and colleges) is secular in approach as basic assumptions behind natural, applied and social sciences are not drawn from religious sources.
22. See Ziaul Haque, review of Khurshid Ahmad (ed.), *Studies in Islamic Economics*, in *Hamdard Islamicus* (Karachi), V, No. 1 (Spring 1981), pp. 93–108.

5 Islamic Economics: a Progressive Perspective

Asghar Ali Engineer

We are living in an industrial society whose very foundation is economics, and no progress or development is possible without consideration of the economic situation and adopting appropriate economic policies. It is therefore very important to examine the Islamic prescriptions in this respect. We may have to creatively interpret certain principles and doctrines prescribed by Islam relating to socio-economic problems if it is to help us sort out our economic difficulties in the industrial age. However, one word of caution is in order here. The Quran, the principle source of Islamic teachings, is primarily a religious scripture, and not a book of any physical or social science. It provides broad guidelines concerning the spiritual and material aspects of life. It also gives us a concept of society. It is with the help of this concept of society and these broad guidelines that we can deduce divine guidance: by restructuring and reformulating, if necessary, certain concepts validly accepted by the well-meaning theologians of earlier ages.

Quranic teachings have both contextual as well as transcendental relevance. Islam originated in the commercial milieu of Mecca and hence, in this socio-economic context, it emphasised the virtues of commerce (*tijarah*) and put the honest merchant next to prophets and martyrs in the way of God. At the same time, it severely condemned those traders and merchants who resort to dishonest practices and try to earn wealth unjustly. The Quran says:

> Woe unto the defrauders: Those who, when they take the measure from mankind, demand it full. But if they measure unto them, or weigh for them, they cause them less. Do such [men] not consider that they will be raised again, unto an awful Day, the day when [all] mankind stands before the Lord of the Worlds?[1]

Thus we see that the Quran demands a rigorous honesty in dealing with others and condemns short-weighting as this involves exploitation of others. The Quran gives us the concept of a just society free of exploitation. From this comes the transcendental aspect of Islamic teachings as far as economic principles are concerned. Any transaction relating either to production or commerce should be just and free of exploitation. Like *'ilm* and *hikma*, the key words in economic matters are *al-'adl wal al-ehsan*' (justice and benevolence). The Quran says: 'Lo! Allah commands you to [dispense] justice and benevolence'.

Whatever the mode of production or commerce, the concepts of justice and benevolence remain operative and go a long way in reducing social tensions, and hence these teachings remain transcendent. The concept of *'adl* and *ehsan*, needless to say, have eternal validity. In an industrial economy, which involves an economic system which leads to the intensification of capitalist exploitation, these concepts acquire an added significance. It is a well-known fact that capitalism leads to the emergence of powerful monopoly groups, in the form of multinational corporations, cartels and trusts, which are powers unto themselves. We thus see that in this economic system, concentration of wealth reaches unprecedented proportions, leading to a diminishing degree of justice and benevolence and an increased degree of social tension and conflict. It also leads to a dichotomy between developed and under-developed nations causing international conflict. It is therefore interesting to examine the Islamic approach in this respect.

The concepts of *'adl* and *ehsan* cannot be realised if there is concentration of wealth. The Quran strongly condemns hoarding and concentration of wealth. It says, 'Woe to all back-biting slanderers who amass riches and sedulously hoard them, thinking that their treasure will render them immortal! By no means! They shall be flung to the destroying flame'. This is, of course, a Meccan verse. But there is equally strong denunciation of wealth accumulation in the verses revealed during the Medina period as well. One can mention here the famous *ayah-e-kanz*, often quoted by the eminent companion of the Prophet, Abu Dhar al-Ghifari. 'Those who hoard gold and silver and do not spend it in the way of God, warn them of painful punishment.' Also, the Quran exhorts believers to spend the surplus beyond their requirements. 'And they ask thee what they ought to spend. Say: That which is superfluous'.[2]

We thus see that the Quranic injunctions are against the concentration of wealth, which leads to an unbalanced social structure full of tension and conflict. It also makes the rich oblivious of the moral and spiritual urges which are so essential for the creative growth of society. 'The worldly affluence has made you oblivious [of moral and spiritual values]. Until you come to the grave.'[3] The consequences of excessive affluence leading to sheer consumerism is clear for anyone to see. It leads to what is termed the rat race, and alienates man from man, seriously impairing human relationships and corroding the moral fibre of society. In such a society, the economy has no goal except multiplying profit through high pressure sales and encouraging artificial needs. Man is driven to consume more and more, while the spiritual and moral quality of his life keeps on declining. The state of western society proves this beyond any doubt. The Quran has shown keen insight into human nature by prescribing a goal-directed economy, i.e. an economy wherein production and distribution are directed by moral goals leading to the harmonious growth of society. It is the essential function of *rububiyyah* (i.e. growth towards perfection).

Here, we are dealing with a capitalist economy. How are we to achieve the objectives of social justice and benevolence in this type of economy? We have to address ourselves very seriously to this problem in order to achieve this important objective. The industrial economy, as is well-known, is production-oriented. Hence, contemporary economists address themselves to the objectives of production. The problem of distribution is no less important since in Islamic economics, production has to have a moral goal, and the distribution of whatever is produced must also be just. The concept of distributive justice has primary importance in establishing a society free of exploitation.

The Islamic approach accords primary importance to the concept of human dignity. It is maintained by the Quran that even *sadaqah* (i.e. charity) should not injure human dignity. Such an injury militates against the concept of human equality, which is a central proposition of Islamic teaching. The Quran says very unequivocally,

> O you who believe! Render not in vain your almsgiving by reproach and injury like him who spends his wealth only for ostentation and believeth not in Allah and the last day. His likeness is as the likeness of the rock whereon is dust of earth, a rain-storm smiteth it, leaving it smooth and bare. They have no control of aught of that which they have gained. Allah guideth not the disbelieving folks.[4]

Charity, according to the Quranic approach, is in vain if it injures human dignity and if its purpose is ostentation, rather than the service of humanity. Such charity has no firm roots in the social structure. Though a very apt simile, the Quran makes it very clear that such charity is nothing more than dust on a rock, which is washed off by the first rains. The Quran, as pointed out earlier, imparts teachings which have contextual relevance as well as transcendental significance. The concept of charity had contextual relevance in the society with which the Prophet was immediately concerned. In the society with which he was dealing, charity could not have been ruled out. Yet, the Prophet recognised its possible effects on human dignity: the revealed Quranic text made it very clear that charity would defeat its very purpose if it injured human dignity.

Quranic teachings make it clear that while charity may serve certain purposes during a transitional period, it cannot become a permanent solution to economic problems because it may violate human dignity. Since Islam lays great emphasis on equality, begging as a form of giving or receiving charity is regarded with repugnance. The next alternative is institutionalised forms of charity. However, in the modern age, when human dignity has presumably acquired added importance, even institutionalised charity is no less repugnant, and militates against the concept of human dignity and equality so central to Islamic teachings. Such charities are often instituted by those who concentrate wealth unjustly in their own hands, and then seek to lessen social tensions through ostentatious charity.

The next verse is quite significant. It says, 'And the likeness of those who spend their wealth in search of Allah's pleasure, and for the strengthening of their souls, is as the likeness of a garden on a height. The rainstorm smiteth it and it brings forth its fruits twofold . . .'[5] According to the criteria laid down in this verse, wealth should be spent for 'Allah's pleasure and for the strengthening of their souls'. Obviously, these goals cannot be achieved through ostentatious charity. Neither can it be achieved by the consumerism associated with Western society as it cannot lead to the 'strengthening of souls'; instead, this would result in the corroding of souls. Therefore, in order to realise these goals, the production and distribution of commodities will have to be strictly controlled by society. Such vital economic functions cannot be left to the whims of free enterprise, which, as pointed out earlier, is only interested in profiteering and encouraging artificial needs. In order to strengthen and enrich souls, the drudgery and alienation of labour has to be brought to an end. Clearly, this cannot be achieved within the framework of so called free enterprise.

The Holy Quran repeatedly emphasises the fact that man's efforts should be justly rewarded. 'Man does not get except what he strives for', says the Quran categorically. It clearly means that man's labour must be fully rewarded and no-one else can be permitted to live off his labour. In other words, in an Islamic economic system, there is no place for exploitation of labour. In yet another verse, the Quran declares, 'They will not be wronged in the least'. Thus, we see that the very basis of the Islamic economic system is justice, benevolence and the complete abolition of exploitation, oppression and wrong-doing. The evils of the capitalist system must be totally eliminated in order to lay the foundations of an economic system consistent with Islam.

Since we are now dealing with contemporary economies, we must distinguish between commercial profit and industrial profit. As pointed out earlier, Islam originated in the commercial milieu of Mecca and legitimised many commercial practices which were not exploitative or unjust. It allowed commercial profit, while forbidding speculation, forward deals, hoarding, black marketing and other similar unfair practices. There are a number of Prophet's traditions to this effect: 'The Prophet (peace be upon him) prohibited purchase by means of [random selection done by] throwing a stone [to select the object it hit as the commodity purchased] and he prohibited all dubious transactions'. Similarly, the Prophet prohibited the sale and purchase of animals not yet born, or even conceived by the female. Ibn Hazm says:

> Sale of a thing whose particulars are not known to the seller is not allowed, even if they be known to the buyer; likewise – with the commodity about which the buyer is in the dark, though the seller is informed. And also, transactions of such commodities is disallowed of which both of them know not the particulars.

Thus, we see that Islam does not allow anyone to gain at the cost of others, much less at the cost of the whole of society. Abu Ishaq Shatibi maintains that the interests of society have priority over the interests of the individual. Looking at all this, it becomes obvious that Islam allows commercial profit only in its most legitimate and non-exploitative form, keeping the interests of society in view. Industrial profits cannot be viewed on a par with legitimate commercial profits. Industrial profit is to be derived not by mere exchange transactions as with commercial profit, but out of production by labour. Surplus value, which yields industrial profit, is hence exploitative in nature.

Therefore, in order to enforce the principles of Islamic economics, the means of production will have to be socially-owned. It is only through socialisation of the means of production that exploitation of labour can be ended, and the interests of society as a whole can be protected.

Here, it is necessary to discuss two key concepts of Islamic economics, namely *zakat* and *riba*. These, it must be noted, are very popular, but often misunderstood terms. First, we shall deal with *zakat*. It is often maintained that *zakat* paid at the rate of 2.5 per cent will result in the equitable distribution of wealth. Far from it. Those who maintain this do not understand the complexities of a modern economy. In a capitalistic industrial economy, income differentials between wage earners and capitalists tend to be so large that a tax paid at the rate of 2.5 per cent cannot substantially narrow it. *Zakat* is paid on the combination of wealth and income every year. Thus, at a 2.5 per cent rate, income differentials would increase at an accelerated rate, and would bring about a greater concentration of wealth leading to more social injustice. The Quran, however, does not specify any rate. The principle of *infaq* (spending), on the contrary, lays down that one should spend whatever is superfluous. 'And when they ask thee what they ought to spend, say: That which is superfluous.'[6] Thus, it would be necessary to decide from time to time how much the rich should be taxed in order to effect a transfer of wealth from them to the poor. It is a revolutionary principle, and can bring about a just redistribution of wealth in society. Thus, it is not the quantum of *zakat*, but its principle which is important.

Zakat funds must be used to provide interest-free loans to weaker sections of society in order to meet their requirements, like housing, etc. Debt relief, health care, unemployment allowance, release and rehabilitation of bonded labour, and other similar social welfare measures also fall within the ambit of *zakat* funds. In keeping with the requirements of industrial society, a network of new institutions for the effective utilisation of *zakat* funds, especially in underdeveloped countries, is highly necessary.

The concept of *riba* is equally important. However, it is no less misunderstood. It would not do to set up interest-free banks on a profit-sharing basis within the existing capitalist framework. As already pointed out, profit in a capitalist economy, derived from production, is highly exploitative. Prohibition of *riba* cannot be treated in isolation from the capitalist economy. Such an approach would lead to greater exploitation of the poor by the rich. Consumption, production and distribution form an integrated whole in the modern capitalist economy. *Riba* has to be viewed as a part of this complex whole. The essence of *riba* must be understood as exploitation, and not merely as a fixed rate of interest. The actual purpose of prohibiting *riba* cannot be realised without ending exploitation in all its forms.

In a modern capitalist economy, one also has to take cognisance of inflation. In an inflationary economy, those who save are the losers, while those who borrow for investment gain. Abolition of interest in such a situation would amount to *riba* in so far as the borrowers would benefit at the cost of those who save. It would be another form of exploitation. Thus, it can be seen that taking a simplistic view of the abolition of interest – while profit and other forms of exploitation in a capitalist economy remain – would not serve the ends of Islamic justice. Also, in a situation where capital is scarce, one cannot allow it to be invested only in the most profitable sectors, while starving the other less profitable but socially more useful sectors serving the needs of the weaker sections of society.

The Holy Quran has given us the vision of a society and laid down its chief characteristics. Keeping this vision and its characteristics in view, we will have to devise new institutions from time to time, and not treat as unalterable the institutions evolved by theologians during the medieval ages to suit their time and conditions. Institutions, it must be remembered, are only instruments, and not ends in themselves. Instruments should be changed if they become injurious to the values enshrined in the Quran.

One more point is in order here before we end. Private enterprise on a small scale in a commercial society like that of Mecca cannot be treated on a par with private enterprise in a capitalist society in the form of huge cartels, monopolies and multinational corporations. These corporations have become powers unto themselves. They injure the interests of society for their private gain, and thereby negate the principles laid down by Imam Shatibi, as mentioned above, i.e. that the interests of society are above those of individuals. In such a situation, a nationalised or socialised sector, serving the interests of society as a whole, would be more in keeping with the spirit and value system of Islam than private enterprise.

NOTES

1. Quran 83:1–6.
2. Quran 2:219.
3. Quran 102:1–2.
4. Quran 2:264.
5. Quran 2:265.
6. Quran 2:219.

6 Islam and Capitalist Development: A Critique of Rodinson and Weber

Jomo K. S.

Maxime Rodinson's *Islam and Capitalism* was first published in France in 1966 and translated into English in 1974. It seeks to examine whether or not Islamic tenets can explain why capitalism did not develop indigenously in Muslim countries but was introduced from outside. It also seeks to determine whether or not Islam is opposed to capitalist development, as is often claimed. In particular, Rodinson refutes the Weberian thesis that Islam lacks the rationalism necessary for the successful development of capitalism. He outlines the elements of economic doctrine present in the Quran and the Sunnah (Islamic tradition) and examines the relationship between doctrine and practice in both the medieval and contemporary Muslim world. He identifies certain areas of ambiguity and contradiction within the doctrine itself and reveals the divergence between doctrine and economic practice in the Islamic world. He examines Islamic ideology and questions whether it has hindered or favoured capitalist development, on the one hand, and whether it provides sufficient basis for an anti-capitalist struggle or for promoting socialism, on the other. His answer to both these questions is negative. He further argues that the economic paths followed by Muslim countries, historically and today, cannot be attributed to Islam, but rather are primarily the result of the social forces of production.

The economic doctrine of Islam is to be found in both the Quran and the Sunnah (Rodinson, 1974, p. 14). There is no passage in the Quran which opposes private property. According to Rodinson, inequalities go unchallenged, though wealth is held to be useless in the face of God's judgement and also provides temptation to neglect religion. Nothing is said about the ownership of the means of production, and wage labour is held to be a natural institution. In the realm of economic activity, the Quran appears to favour commerce, to condemn fraudulent practices, and to require abstention from trade during festivals. The clearest and strongest prohibition is on *riba*[1] ('increase'), and there is an obligation to pay *zakat* – alms for the needy, distributed through a welfare fund controlled by the state.

The Sunnah has little to add to Quranic doctrine. It seems to uphold the right to private ownership, subject to customary and state restrictions in some countries, and 'the right of everyone to life'. That is, a man dying of hunger is justified in taking the minimum amount of food necessary to keep himself alive – even at the expense of the 'legitimate' owner. The Sunnah favours the search for profit, trade, and production for the market to the same extent as the Quran. But any selling in which there is an element of uncertainty, such as sale by auction, is prohibited, as are aleatory contracts based on risk or chance. Some traditions advocate absolute honesty in trade, prescribing that one should not praise one's merchandise, but should point out any defects in it and so on. These may pose obstacles to commercial competition.

In his examination of economic practices in the Muslim world of the Middle Ages (Rodinson, 1974, p. 35), Rodinson shows that they generally conflicted with prescribed doctrine. He argues against those historians who try to show that the prohibition of *riba* prevented certain types of economic activity among Muslims. In fact, Muslim legalists found many ways to get around theoretical prohibitions. These methods were called *hiyal*, or ruses. The ease of borrowing from non-Muslims tended to encourage specialisation in usury by the latter in a society where trade specialisation was the norm among particular religious, ethnic or local groups. But where such non-Muslim groups did not exist or were insignificant, Muslims readily took on these tasks themselves; and even where non-Muslim money-lenders did exist, there was frequently thinly-disguised competition from Muslims. Thus, usury, practiced by both Muslims and non-Muslims, was rife throughout the Muslim world. Rodinson cites many examples of this in different periods and regions.

Rodinson also discusses the existence of a capitalistic sector in the Muslim world of the Middle Ages, i.e. a sector from which a capitalist socio-economic formation might have been able to develop, given certain conditions. But Rodinson does not elaborate systematically on what these other conditions might have been. There was substantial development of commercial and financial capital and less in productive capital (Rodinson, 1974, p. 53). This capitalistic sector was already extensive and highly-developed in the Muslim world before the domination of the world market by the Western European bourgeoisie. Its failure to develop indigenously into a full-blown capitalist system was not exceptional – this was experienced by many other civilisations – and, according to Rodinson, was due to factors other than Islam. It is possible, for example, that the existence within the Islamic world of various economic systems based on a variety of agrarian modes of production could have been an obstacle to the development of capitalism.

It seems that Islamic doctrine was not adhered to even in the limited field in which it prescribed a certain economic practice (Rodinson, 1974, p. 72). Reality fell consistently short of the ideal. Rodinson suggests that medieval Muslim society provided itself with ideological precepts which conflicted with practice as a means of dealing with social problems affecting some ideal doctrine which encompasses, or even anticipates, problems which might arise in society. Thus, Islam has an ideal of 'social justice'. But the welfare activities of Muslim governments and individuals usually did no more than mitigate the worst effects of unequal distribution for a small minority.

In spite of the divergences between economic doctrine and practice, Rodinson believes that the economic practices of the traditional Muslim world were not technically unfaithful to the theoretical precepts of the Quran since these precepts neither prescribed nor prohibited any particular economic activity (Rodinson, 1974, p. 74). Further, the calls for justice and charity in Islam were not realised since the divine precepts did not grant the majority any effective, popular political control over the ruling minority; nor apparently, did they undermine the basis of the minority's power by attacking private property.

In the ideological sphere, the Quran emphasises rationality (e.g. in the 'evidence' of God), the internal coherence and consistency of divine revelations, rational proof of Allah's omnipotence, and so on (Rodinson, 1974, p. 78). Faith in Islam is to be developed on the basis of reason. Rodinson thus disputes Weber's contention that Islamic ideology is inimical to capitalist development because of its alleged irrationality, in contrast with Calvinist Protestantism. He also argues that the idea of predestination in Islam is present to more or less the same degree as in the Christian scriptures, and does not imply encouragement to 'wait passively for Allah's help'. In fact, the Quran exhorts Muslims not to be passive.

Thus, in Rodinson's view, there is nothing in the Quran which inhibits the development of capitalism. The Sunnah includes numerous contradictory tendencies; e.g. passages can frequently be found which support conflicting views (Rodinson, 1974, p. 101). Rodinson argues that 'post-Quranic ideology is not an external force moulding society, but an expression of tendencies emanating from social life as a whole' (Rodinson, 1974, p. 102). This does not rule out a certain gap or distance between ideology and contemporary society. If Weber was correct in saying that Islamic ideology was inimical to the rationalism necessary for capitalist development, the cause would lie not in Islam itself, but in all factors which shaped this ideology – i.e., the social life of the Muslim world and the previously existing ideologies, including Christianity in its Eastern form. Unfortunately, Rodinson does not expound further on this proposition. He believes that post-Quranic ideology in the Middle Ages did not contrast with Christian ideology as much as Weber implies. The two religions diverged as the economic paths taken by the two worlds separated.

Rodinson also discusses specific elements of Islamic ideology which, in his view, do not constitute a barrier to capitalist development. Magic has historically 'never diverted men from activity in the technical sphere', and there is nothing else in Muslim doctrine which 'could have served as an obstacle to technical activity' (Rodinson, 1974, p. 107). He suggests that there was less resistance to the constant striving for profit, the driving force of capitalism, in Islam than in Christianity. Islam did not apparently hinder Muslim traders in their search for profit; thus from the standpoint of religious morality, it could hardly have stopped them, or other Muslims, from similar activities which could have led to further development along modern capitalist lines (Rodinson, 1974, p. 112). The mystical tendency and reliance on reason were generally synthesised. If peasants of the Muslim world are fatalistic, Rodinson argues, this is not an irrational attitude on their part, but a correct estimation of the discouraging conditions in which they function. Deductions taken by landlords and the state were often so exorbitant that work efforts were discouraged since any improvement would only benefit others. From all this, Rodinson deduces that the ideas of Islam on economic life and general conduct are not opposed to capitalist activity.

Rodinson then examines Islam and capitalism in contemporary Muslim societies (Rodinson, 1974, p. 119). None of these countries have developed a full-fledged indigenous capitalist system, despite the existence of a capitalistic sector in the economies. The development of native industrial capitalism was prevented by their subjection to European imperialism. Capitalist penetration into the dominant agricultural sector was not complete, and was in any case incapable of transforming society into a capitalist socio-economic formation. Capitalist manufacturing existed, but, as in many other societies, did not subsequently develop into a full-blown capitalism. Other features necessary for the transition to a capitalist formation existed, such as urban development, ground rent, and private property, but they were still not sufficient. Again, Rodinson fails to explain why capitalism failed to develop autochthonously. Rodinson concludes that it is not possible to prove that, had it not been for colonialism, Muslim societies would have developed along European capitalist lines; but neither can the contrary be proved.

Rodinson argues that Islam has not been an obstacle to the development of the capitalist mode of production in contemporary Muslim countries as well. At the theoretical level, Islam presents no serious objections to capitalist practices. Islamic injunctions against certain economic practices necessary for the formation of a capitalist economic system – e.g. usury and contracts based on risk or chance – have constituted a hindrance to capitalist development. But such prohibitions have almost always been circumvented; hence, the only practical consequence has been to encourage economic specialisation along religious or ethnic lines and to sanctify the unwillingness to invest, which was common in these societies. Virtually all Muslim governments today officially tolerate the earning of interest. Unwillingness to invest, especially in productive activities, has historically been a feature of many societies, not only Muslim ones. This is usually the result of socioeconomic factors such as uncertainty, risk, low returns, more attractive alternative investment outlets in land, usury, trade, etc., rather than religious invocation.

Rodinson also argues that the specific form of capitalist development in Muslim countries is not fundamentally determined by Islamic influences. Diverse cultural styles of economic behaviour may be found within capitalism. Islam and the cultural factors associated with it may contribute to particular cultural styles. But, for example, no one has dared to claim that the behaviour of Muslim capitalists generally reflects the justice and compassion that Islam preaches. Islam has not significantly influenced the functioning of capitalist sectors in Muslim societies, for example, in the treatment of workers. The weak development and dynamism of the capitalist sector, the important role played by the state in the economy from the outset, the trend towards more pronounced forms of state-managed economies, etc., have all been attributed by some writers to Islamic influence. Rodinson denies this, arguing that it is futile to seek the basis for social conduct in the temporal world in the Quran and Sunnah, which mainly provide the religious veneer for behaviour conditioned by other factors. In his opinion, ideology shows itself to be less powerful in the long run than the requirements of social conditions and struggles for power and privilege.

What about the relevance of Islam to anti-capitalist struggles and socialism? Rodinson believes that the ideal of 'social justice' in the Quran is not a socialist concept, and that Islamic precepts alone cannot be used to advocate socialism, though the prestige of Islam may support socialist programmes originating outside the religious sphere. However, reactionary Muslims can also use Islam to combat proposed socialist solutions; in fact, they have certain advantages over the more progressive interpreters. The Islamic texts evolved in an era when the right to property was not seriously challenged; centuries of traditional interpretation have considerable weight and prestige; and teachers of religion are often inclined to support traditionalist interpretations.

Can Islamic teachings bring about a minimisation of class differences and the construction of an ideal society? Concepts such as solidarity, mutual aid, and a communal way of life, that some Muslims claim are inherent in Islam, can be found in almost all types of societies and tend to disappear under the impact and spread of capitalist relations and ideology. Certain noble principles do exist in Islam, but their practical applicability has been overlooked for centuries. Rodinson comments:

> It is not clear why that Muslim solidarity, which did not prevent the landlords from sucking the blood of the peasants, the owners of houses from bleeding their tenants white, the usurers from reducing their debtors to poverty, should prevent the owners of capital from applying to their wage-workers the (often gentler) laws of capitalist exploitation (Rodinson, 1974, p. 180).

Rodinson claims that these principles have not prevented – but rather camouflaged, to the benefit of the exploiters – the existence of two classes, one rich and one poor. Alms-giving merely serves to clear the conscience of the rich for the small price of relieving a few poor people from the worst consequences of poverty. The only way that the welfare of underprivileged sections of society can be ensured is by obtaining political power, abolishing privileges, and establishing an adequate and solid framework to safeguard and promote their own interests. Islamic principles, like those of other religions, may serve to give religious blessing to a society without privilege. But up to now, these same principles have been used to legitimise societies based upon privilege and have weakened the ability to mobilise people to seek redress for their grievances. In any case, one cannot rely on these religious principles alone to transform the world; they have as yet hardly played any role in checking capitalist forces or in orienting countries towards socialism.

Rodinson's thesis, then, is this: there is no justifiable correlation between Islam, or for that matter, any other religion with any particular economic activity or system. The precepts of Islam have not seriously hindered capitalist tendencies in the Muslim world, nor are they opposed to socialism. They have not brought about a radically new social or economic structure anywhere in the world. In the past, Islam has not mobilised the masses for economic ends. Yet, the masses are attached to Islam for cultural (national), class, as well as spiritual reasons. Under colonialism, Islam provided them with a cultural identity against European imperialism. Since independence, some local ruling classes have proclaimed their commitment to Islam in their search for an ideological guarantee for their own social and material advantage. To this end, they have often been supported by much of the Islamic *ulama*, who led the oppressed masses under colonialism, but have since risen in status and power after independence, and have become defenders of the status quo in alliance with the local elite! Some reactionaries use Islam to give religious endorsement to conservative attitudes, using appeals to Allah, tradition, and traditional morality, to disguise their exploitative relationship with the masses. Yet, they will be the first ones to resist the abolition of exploitation. The radical overturning of old structures requires a struggle for emancipation, but it is difficult for the devoted masses to oppose oppressors of the same faith, especially when the latter pretend to be defenders of that faith and of the nation. The attractions of socialism are limited by the fact that the highest religious ideals are other-worldly. Progressives have to apply themselves to drawing values applicable to the modern world from the Quran and Muslim tradition, which call for the abolition of privilege and exploitation. But such economic and social precepts as are found in the Islamic scriptures need to be developed for, and adapted to, contemporary conditions.

The economic doctrine of Islam originally developed partly as a critique of the social and economic practices of the time. It was progressive within that specific historical context, with an ideal of social justice and ethical concerns directed against some forms of exploitation which prevailed then. However, as times and the forms of exploitation in society change, the critique of society must also follow suit. In the environment Muslims face today, this should translate itself into a critique of capitalism and its contemporary manifestations.

Certain omissions in Rodinson's work need to be pointed out. For example, Rodinson asserts that the capitalist mode of production and productive capital 'was known to the Muslim world of the Middle Ages', but does not demonstrate this convincingly. He suggests that the wage-labour relationship existed in a primitive form in the medieval Muslim world, but fails to suggest why it did not develop further into a full-fledged capitalist system. Throughout his book, there is no discussion of what really hampered the development of capitalism in the Muslim world, if, as he convincingly argues, it was not the Islamic religion. Granted that what Rodinson attempts is largely but a critique of the Weberian view of Islam and economic development, a critique also needs to offer an alternative in order to be persuasive.

Rodinson also tends to underestimate and be too pessimistic about the revolutionary potential of Islam and its possible compatibility with socialism. In fact, he has elsewhere characterised the Quran as 'the message of an oppressed man who, at a given moment, had turned against injustice and oppression. It carried . . . much invective and defiance of the mighty, and many appeals for justice and the equality of man' (Rodinson, 1971, p. 296). The rapid spread and early popularity of Islam was, to a considerable extent, due to its dynamic evolution in opposition to the oppressive social conditions of the time. However, subsequent generations of Muslims – like the followers of most other religions – inherited their religion without struggle, and so it tended to become identified with the status quo. Thus, the dominant societal role of religion became the legitimisation of the status quo, rather than the motivation for, and initiation of, social change.

However, as Rodinson has also pointed out, under European colonialism, which most Muslim societies have experienced, Islam offered the potential for anti-imperialist struggle (Hodgkin, 1972; Keddie, 1968). In fact, Islamic-socialist alliances were born in the anti-imperialist struggles for national liberation by the peoples of the Third World. One of the most eloquent advocates of such convergence, Sukarno of Indonesia, even advocated Muslim cooperation with Marxists.

> The Muslim with a broad outlook, the Muslim who understands the needs of our fight, will certainly agree to friendship with the Marxists, because he will realize that consuming profits and imposing interest are acts prohibited by his religion, that they are forbidden things; he will realize that it is in this way that Islam wages war on capitalism down to its roots and right to its seeds, because, as I have already explained above, profit is the same thing as surplus value which is the very breath of capitalism. He realizes that, like Marxism, so Islam too, 'with faith in Allah, acknowledging the Kingdom of God', is a protest against the wickedness of capitalism. (Sukarno, 1971, p. 152).

Historically, there have been several attempts to establish Muslim communities based on egalitarian ideas, with an equitable division of the social product and well-developed mutual aid arrangements. One such period was that idealised by the Sunni, during the first twenty-nine years of Islam itself, between the Prophet's death and the ascendance of the Omayyad dynasty, as an attempt at creating a 'just society'.

Does Rodinson's thesis that Islam is not the reason for the economic backwardness of Muslim countries and their failure to become fully capitalistic hold when applied to an Islamic country outside his main area of interest, the Middle East? Looking at Peninsular Malaysia,[2] which received the first Islamic influences from Muslim traders who came to Southeast Asia before the fifteenth century, it seems to hold. Pre-colonial indigenous Malay peasant society was a class society in which wealth accumulation by the ruling class did exist. The distribution of the social product was determined by class relations and by different forms of exploitation. Usury was practised in various forms by Muslims in both pre-colonial and colonial Malaya and continues until the present day despite the presence in later periods of other ethnic and religious immigrants who also performed this function. Mokhzani (Mokhzani, 1973), for example, has detailed the different credit mechanisms existing in the Malay peasant economy.[3]

Thus, according to certain interpretations, some specific economic doctrines of Islam were generally not observed in Malay peasant society. In fact, some writers suggest that Islam has not deeply penetrated the social fabric of the economic organisation of Malay society; rather, traditional custom, or *adat*, appears to have been a stronger force than Islam.[4] This was because *adat* itself was conditioned by the prevailing social forces of production determined by the historical and environmental circumstances of Malay society. Thus, for example, certain cooperative tendencies, e.g. *gotong-royong*, *tolong-menolong*, are more correctly attributed to the traditional organisation of Malay production than to the influence of the Islamic ideal of fraternity.

Nevertheless, some Western social scientists still insist that the influence of Islam, particularly the attitude of 'fatalism', is responsible for the economic retardation of rural Malays.[5] They hold that the customs and religious beliefs strongly held by the Malays make them resistant to change through the adoption of an attitude of resignation – since 'all things come from Allah' – rather than the acceptance of human innovation and enterprise. This is seen to be a barrier to capitalist economic development. As in many other societies subordinated by imperialism, this has been shown to be an understandable response to British colonialism, and has also been true of other non-Muslim communities.

The ostensibly 'passive reaction' of Malays to British colonialism is also attributed to their racial and cultural personality, which is allegedly strongly influenced by the Muslim religion. Few of these scholars even allow that Islam was adapted by its local adherents to the historical environment and cultural practices of indigenous societies, or that it is usually of a syncretic nature. Acknowledgement that there is often a difference between what the Quran preaches and actual practices, is rare, though this is implied by recognition of the tension between religion (*ugama*) and custom (*adat*) in Malay peasant life.

Generally, these writers have uncritically adopted the Weberian view of Islam's supposed discouragement of capitalism.[6] Proceeding on this assumption, they attribute what they see as peasant fatalism to the Muslim religion, often ignoring other factors. While this argument can be quite elegantly formulated, Rodinson has persuasively demonstrated the fallacy of its basic assumption that Islamic ideology opposes capitalist socio-economic change. Therefore, it is necessary to look at factors other than Islam for an explanation of the economic 'inertia' supposedly found in rural Malay society. Such behaviour, where it actually exists, may well be a rational response to the peasantry's condition.

If Islam has not been antagonistic to capitalism in Malaysia, what is its relationship to the various political tendencies in the country? The current government of Malaysia, constitutionally committed to Islam as the state's official religion, proclaims its adherence to Islamic principles, while endeavouring to control Muslim religious interpretation and practice. On the other hand, the then Chairman of the Malaysian Peoples Socialist Party (PSRM) claimed that his organisation represented the left-wing political tendency within Islam in the country, while asserting that the Pan-Malayan Islamic Party (PMIP)[7] – which joined the ruling government coalition in the mid-1970s – embodied Islam's right wing. Certain other Muslim groupings, such as ABIM, the Malaysian Islamic Youth Movement, also professed an antipathy to certain aspects of capitalist development in the nation. Even the underground pro-communist movement includes an Islamic Brotherhood Party. This wide variety of political tendencies which aspires to the Islamic mantle in the Malaysian context, as in other Muslim countries, appears to validate Rodinson's claim that Islam is not obviously identifiable with any particular economic system or political tendency.

> Islam has served as a means and justification for both liberation and suppression. . . . Religion has been 'the opium of the people,' but it has equally been, to quote at greater length from the text in which Marx's famous sentence is found, 'the sigh of the oppressed creature, the kindliness of a heartless world, the spirit of unspiritual condition' (Rodinson, 1971, pp. 120–1).

NOTES

1. *Riba*: Used generally to refer to the practice of usury, the earning of interest and profit on credit, more rarely used to refer to a surplus derived from exploitation.
2. Also known as Malaya, referring to the geo-political unit spanning the Malay Peninsula. Since 1963, it has been incorporated into the political entity of Malaysia and is now referred to as Peninsular Malaysia.
3. Mokhzani states: 'The central position of Islam, which prohibits usury, in the Malay self-definition, and the existence of Malay Reservations, which legally limits such lands to Malays, leads to the formation of a special idiom of Malay moneylending in which there is a need to ignore and often deny interest taking between Malays. This adds to the high cost and onerous terms in Malay moneylending'. Also see S. Gordon (n.d.)

Gordon has shown that the system of *jual janji* is an effective disguise for usury. *Jual janji*, loosely translated as conditional sale, resembles mortgage, with the important exception that the proprietary rights are transferred to the creditor, to be returned to the debtor only if and when the debt is repaid in time.

> *Riba* was taken to mean only interest which was undisguised, and a disguise evolved which took the *apparent form of a sale*, the transaction being really usurious. Such an apparent form of sale is the *jual janji* system, a system of 'conditional sale'. . . . This vicious form of gaining *riba*, an 'excess' or 'addition', is not categorised as *riba* in Malaya where *riba* has been watered down to mean undisguised 'interest' only . . . We must remember that the money involved in the *jual janji* does not represent the actual value of the property, demonstrating that there is *no* real intention to sell – the *intention is to borrow and the gain* is an 'excess' or 'addition'.

Arguing that though the Islamic institution of *zakat* is intended to redistribute income by the taxation of wealth accumulated, Gordon shows that the main burden of *zakat* has fallen on the most impoverished sector of the Malayan peasantry – the rice cultivators – and not on the wealthier classes (nor even upon other relatively less-impoverished peasants). Further, the *zakat* burden is mainly borne by the tenants and owner-operator cultivators, and not by landlords. 'Thus, the contradiction that it is not he who is most able or most liable who pays the *zakat* but he who is least able and possibly not liable according to Islam itself.'

4. For example, with regard to early colonial Malaya, a contemporary observer remarked that:

> There is a never-ending struggle between the *hukum adat*, the 'customary law' of the Malays, and the *hukum shara* or 'religious law' of the Quran. Muhammadan priest [sic], who would sometimes seek, if they could, to enforce the latter, are met by the plea that the practice denounced is lawful by Malay custom, and it is thus that debt-bondage, like opium smoking, gambling, etc. is always defended . . . This institution of debt-bondage is a native Malay custom, and is wholly opposed to Muhammadan law, which is most lenient to debtors. . . . In the district of Kinta, ... debts were swelled in amount by a species of compound interest hardly conceivable among a people who profess to regard usury as sinful. (Maxwell, 1890, pp. 247–8, 251).

5. Parkinson, 1975. See also the critique by G. Sivalingam (1975).
6. See Alatas, 1972, for a different critical perspective on Weber. Alatas criticises Weber's attribution of the 'capitalist spirit' to Calvinist Protestantism. Alternatively, he suggests that 'what is decisive here is not religious but other factors'. He suggests that for communities in Malaya and Indonesia, the decisive factors 'which released the capitalist spirit' were 'their emigrant spirit and their position outside government service'. Apparently, Alatas does not break with Weber's central proposition that it is 'this spirit that released the tremendous energy characterizing modern

capitalism'. Thus, according to Alatas, the dynamic emergence and development of capitalism is, therefore, still primarily explained by ideology, despite his differences with Weber's particular formulation. For a similar, but less explicit argument, see W. Wilder, 1975.

7. In two articles (Kessler, 1972, 1974) Kessler argues that the PMIP embodied the interests of the rural Malay lower strata, especially those of the independent, but hard-pressed yeoman peasantry involved in intra-Malay political conflicts in the state of Kelantan. The PMIP and its brand of religious politics were, according to him, the behavioural expression of oppressed peasant class interests. With the benefit of hindsight – after the PMIP joined the ruling government coalition in late 1972 – Kessler amended his argument (Kessler, 1974). This time, he acknowledged the limitations of an opposition which employs such a medium to express discontent. Rodinson, approaching the matter more generally, had anticipated PMIP-type 'betrayals':

> The Muslim 'clergy', largely poor, and treated without respect by the occupying power, faithful to the values of the traditional society in which they lived, were their own people, providing them with leadership and speaking to them in their own language, a language at their own level. With the coming independence, however, the 'clergy' gradually rises in the social scale. The (more or less exploiting) upper strata increasingly proclaim their attachment to Islam, in a frenzied search for an ideological guarantee for their social and material advantages. The more successful the 'clergy' become in raising their standard of living, or even merely in becoming integrated in the nation, the less will Islam serve as an exclusive slogan for the disinherited (Rodinson, 1974, p. 22).

REFERENCES

Alatas, S. H. (1972) 'The Weber Thesis and Southeast Asia', in *Modernisation and Social Change* (London and Sydney: Angus and Robertson).

Coury, R. (1975) 'Why Can't They Be Like Us?', *Review of Middle East Studies*, 1.

Gordon, S. (n.d.) 'Contradictions in the Malay Economic Structure', *Intisari*, 1 (2).

Hodgkin, T. (1972) 'Some African and Third World Theories of Imperialism', in *Studies in the Theory of Imperialism*, ed. Roger Own and Bob Sutcliffe (London: Longman).

Keddie, N. R. (ed.) (1968) *An Islamic Response to Imperialism* (Berkeley and Los Angeles: University of California Press).

Kessler, C. S. (1972) 'Islam, Society and Political Behaviour: Some Comparative Implications of the Malay Case', *British Journal of Sociology*, 23.

Kessler, C. S. (1974) 'Muslim Identity and Political Behaviour in Kelantan', in *Kelantan: Religion, Society and Politics in a Malay State*, ed. W. R. Roff (Kuala Lumpur: Oxford University Press).

Kessler, C. S. (1978) *Islam and Politics in a Malay Society: Kelantan State 1838–1969* (Ithaca and London: Cornell University Press).

Maxwell, W. E. (1890) 'The Law Relating to Slavery among the Malays', *Journal of the Straits Branch of the Royal Asiatic Society*, 22.

Mokhzani, A. R. (1973) 'Credit in the Malay Peasant Economy' (Ph.D. thesis, University of London).

Parkinson, B. K. (1975) 'Non-economic Factors in the Economic Retardation of the Rural Malays', in *Readings on Malaysian Economic Development*, ed. David Lim (Kuala Lumpur: Oxford University Press).

Rodinson, M. (1971) *Mohammed* (London: Allen Lane).

Rodinson, M. (1974) *Islam and Capitalism*, trans. Brian Pearce (London: Allen Lane).

Sivalingam, G. (1975) 'Non-Economic Factors in the Economic Retardation of the Malays – An Empirical Refutation', *Development Forum*, 5, (1) (June).

Sukarno, I. R. (1971) 'Nationalism, Islamism and Marxism' (first published in 1929), reprinted in *Religion, Politics, and Social Change in the Third World*, ed. D. E. Smith (New York: Free Press).

Wilder, W. (1975) 'Islam, Other Factors and Malay Backwardness: Comments on an Argument', in *Readings on Malaysian Economic Development*, ed. David Lim (Kuala Lumpur: Oxford University Press).

7 Economic Aspects of Islamisation in Pakistan

Omar Asghar Khan

In the economic sphere, the Pakistani military regime, with the support of feudal and big business interests, claimed to have embarked upon Islamising the economy by introducing profit and loss counters in banks on one hand, and imposing *zakat* (poor tax) and *ushr* (tax on agricultural produce) on the other. If the objective of Islamisation is to abolish an exploitative socio-economic system, then the introduction of profit and loss counters has not achieved this, nor has the imposition of *zakat* reduced the level of poverty in the country. In fact, the system became more exploitative and oppressive in the late 1970s. While 35 per cent of the rural population were living in abject poverty in 1977, the percentage of poor people in the rural areas had increased to 37 per cent in 1979 (Asian Regional Team for Employment Promotion, 1983, p. 239).

While the introduction of profit and loss counters in banks was acclaimed by government circles as a 'great leap forward' towards the elimination of *riba* (increase in capital on loans or sales) from the economy, the entire socio-economic system has become more exploitative.[1] The introduction of interest-free banking in an essentially capitalistic economy, where a fairly large proportion of deposits belongs to the lower middle class, discriminates against the poorer depositors. These depositors, theoretically speaking, will be paid no profit in the event of a loss. In such a system, the investor can receive loans from banks at zero interest with a nominal service charge, and thus make a large profit, while the profit to be paid to depositors is determined by the banks' operations. In fact, investors borrowing from banks may well be earning much larger profits than the depositors receive under the PLS system. The depositor may thus receive only a nominal profit. Thus, within a capitalist economy, the replacement of the principle of limited liability by a system of sharing profit and loss would tend to result in the exploitation of the depositors, who have limited information regarding the inner functionings of a corporation.

In a country like Pakistan, where in order to avoid taxes, businessmen can get away with maintaining 'multiple account books', the profit and loss system, if generalised, is likely to result in fraud on a large scale. As happened in the case of the large number of financial houses that sprang up in the country a few years ago, large amounts of money were embezzled and could not be retrieved by ignorant depositors. However, so long as the profit and loss system is confined to the nationalised banks and a couple of *mudaraba* (profit-sharing) companies, as at present, there is little danger of the depositors suffering a major loss. If this were to happen, the acquisitive spirit that has come to permeate a large section of society would compel people to think twice before entrusting their savings to the banks. It is probably because of the government's awareness of the possibility of widespread fraud, as well as the structural constraints imposed by the present structure of a dependent economy, that it has adopted a rather cautious approach to the introduction of the profit and loss system of banking. It is evident that the profit and loss system has been introduced more as an eye-wash rather than as an overall system aimed at the abolition of exploitation and speculation.

Although the Pakistani government announced in June 1984 that all interest-bearing financial instruments would be replaced by the profit and loss sharing system, a substantial proportion of the banking sector will continue to operate under the interest-based system. The federal Finance Minister, while asserting that the interest-free system would supplant the existing system was, however, quick to state that 'all the pledges made under the existing system would be honoured, and dealings with foreign governments and international finance institutions will continue unchanged' (*Karachi Dawn*, 15 June 1984). The interest-based system would thus continue to be operative in the case of the large amounts of foreign exchange being lent to the industrial sector by state-controlled financial institutions, such as the Pakistan Industrial Credit and Investment Corporation (PICIC), the Industrial Development Bank of Pakistan (IDBP) and the National Development Finance Corporation (NDFC). They are, in turn, financed by foreign countries and international finance institutions. As a senior development banker remarked, 'these institutions are not willing to experiment with the Islamic system. Interest is equally a "theological" issue with them' (Ayaz, 1984).

The profit and loss sharing system of banking can be expected to be used by the bureaucracy within the present socio-economic framework to further its own interests at the expense of others. Such fears have been expressed by sections of the business community. They are of the view that the public sector-controlled nationalised banks would tend to keep a close watch on them after advancing credit on a profit and loss sharing basis. They would tend to interfere in the management of projects, since the nationalised banks would, under the profit and loss sharing system, be partners in loss as well as gain. These fears of the private sector have been confirmed by public sector bank officials when one of them remarked, 'banks would be justified in keeping an eye on the projects and advise the borrowers because the banks will be partners in loss as well'. While such a system of lending would increase the already ubiquitous control of the bureaucracy over the economy, it would make a mockery of the much-publicised 'liberalisation' of the economy, to which the government claims to be committed. It is not by introducing profit and loss accounts in the organised financial sector that exploitation and extortion can be checked. Interest is functional to the capitalist economic system, a system in which the decisions to save and invest are taken by independent parties in response to signals given by the market. Exploitation in such a system takes place at the level of profit-making. Therefore, to make the elimination of interest alone the focus of attention is to adopt a superficial view of capitalist exploitation. Interest paid by the corporation to the banks is merely the sharing of profit among various capitalist interests.

From the Islamisation policies followed by the military regime, as well as the recommendations of the Islamic Ideology Council, it appears that the purpose of the government is not so much to abolish the institution of interest as to make it appear to the public that interest has been eliminated from financial transactions. The Islamic Ideology Council, in its report on the elimination of interest, has suggested ways of getting round the theoretical prohibition of *riba* while retaining the essential characteristics of a capitalist economy (Ayaz, 1984). The report rather ingeniously suggests that the nomenclature of the price of, and return on capital, which has come to be known as interest, be altered to 'profit' in the case of *mudaraba* companies, and 'service charges' in the case of banks.

It may be relevant to point out that the concept of profit-sharing is not a system confined to Islamic theological opinion. The principle of investing on a profit and loss sharing basis was also prevalent in pre-industrial Europe, a period noted for the severest forms of exploitation. The concept of investment on a profit and loss sharing basis was elaborated at a time when financial institutions, banks and large industrial concerns had not yet developed:

> *Mudaraba* was an ancient type of commercial capital; it existed before Islam in Arabia and southern Europe. It was a sort of primitive commercial organisation in which the capital-owner entrusted his capital to an agent/worker on the basis of profit sharing in a pre-arranged proportion. . . . All risk was borne by the owner. . . . This institution is not based on any explicit text (*nass*) of the Quran or the Hadith (Council of Islamic Ideology, 1980, passim).

Later, with the expansion of markets, as the prospects of making a profit, either through trade or manufacturing, became more widespread, it became difficult for shareholders to monitor the profits of companies whose size had increased. As a result, profit and loss sharing as an investment technique was gradually supplanted in Europe by a fixed predetermined rate of return called interest.

In Pakistan, there have been a large number of cases where the interest-free system has been exploited by feudal and capitalist interests to their own advantage. A large number of interest-free or low interest loans earmarked for small farmers have been advanced to large and influential farmers with contacts with the ruling hierarchy. Moreover, in a capital-scarce economy like Pakistan's, with a highly inequitable pattern of income distribution, the availability of zero-interest loans would, by making the use of capital profitable, further displace labour. In such a situation, since demand for credit would be greater than its supply, credit would have to be rationed. This, in turn, would tend to increase the possibility of a select few with contacts with the regime pre-empting credit facilities.

LANDLORDISM AND *RIBA*

If the purpose of the abolition of *riba* is to eliminate all forms of extortion in financial transactions as well as unearned income, the measures taken by the military regime have been most unsatisfactory. Even if the abolition of *riba* is taken in the narrow sense to mean elimination of extortion from financial transactions, the regime has not taken any concrete measures to prohibit the extortionate interest rates charged from small farmers and landless peasants by money-lender landlords in the rural area. This however, would only have been possible if far-reaching land reforms had been carried out and alternative political institutions created. Given the reliance of the military regime for political support on rich landlords, it cannot implement a meaningful land reform. It should also be noted that those political parties whose leadership is predominantly feudal cannot be expected either to redistribute land in favour of the landless and small farmers or to set up the necessary institutions to give them a share in political power. There is a fundamental difference between reforms introduced from above and those brought about by the active participation of the oppressed whom the reforms are meant to benefit.

It is within the rural social structure that *riba* and the institution of *muzara'a* (sharecropping, ground rent) need to be eliminated in their various forms, whether in the form of extortionate interest rates or the feudal system of sharecropping. Due to the prevailing system of sharecropping practised on tenant-operated farms, a large number of tenants have to give half the produce to the landlords (Haque, 1982, p. 105). The elimination of *riba* in rural areas would put an end to the exploitation of millions of poor peasants at the hands of feudal lords who thrive on extortion and unearned income.

As in the case of Europe, where in the Middle Ages, sections of the clergy invoked religious injunctions to justify an iniquitous status quo, in Pakistan, the ruling classes and sections of the *ulama*, devoid of a popular mandate, interpreted Islam so as to uphold an exploitative social order. The exploitative nature of the Pakistani social formation is brought out by an examination of the structure of rural society and economy. Here the government's so-called 'Islamisation' policies have done nothing to alter the exploitative social and economic structure, in which a small elite, by virtue of its loyalty to successive governments, owns and controls a large proportion of land. According to the agriculture census of 1980, large farmers (fifty acres and above), who owned only 2 per cent of total holdings, controlled 24 per cent of farm land. On the other hand, small farms (twenty-five acres and less), which constituted 92 per cent of total holdings, had only 60 per cent of the total farm land.[2] A comparison of the 1980 and 1972 censuses shows that the distribution of land between small and large farmers has become more unequal (Agricultural Census Organisation, 1983, p. 3).

To justify the highly inequitable system of land ownership, sections of the *ulama* do not hesitate to refer to parts of *fiqih* on the one hand, and to the prevalence of a system of sharecropping and absentee landlordism during Islamic history on the other. Conversely, there are those who, in building up a case against the feudal order, refer to the egalitarianism of the Prophet's practice (Mahmood, 1984). These contrasting interpretations of Islamic history and injunctions relating to the question of landlordism are understandable, for the social structure of Muslim society underwent major changes between the early period of the Prophet and that of the conquests, when new lands and a feudal agrarian system were incorporated into the caliphate. It was during the later period, after the conquests, that the codification of *fiqih* took place. Notwithstanding the condemnation of *muzara'a* by *fuqaha* (Islamic jurists) like Abu Hanifa (d. 767–8), Ahmed ibn Hanbal (d. 891–2), and Mohammadd ibn Idris al-Shafi'i (d. 795–6), *fiqih*, as codified did not prohibit sharecropping or landlordism. The practice of sharecropping was thus legalised in actual practice in the interest of expediency. This was in spite of the fact that the Prophet disapproved of the institution of sharecropping, as has been pointed out by an Islamic scholar:

> According to evidence which remains unimpeached, the Prophet expressly disapproved of the landowner sharing with the actual worker the products of agriculture, though some thought it was only in the nature of an informal rebuke rather than a formal ban (Haque, 1977).

After the Prophet's death, successful attempts were made in the reign of the Caliph Umar to prevent the institution of sharecropping from establishing itself. But later, with the expansion of the caliphate and the incorporation of new lands with strongly entrenched feudal structures, the social structure of the Muslim community underwent a transformation. From one based on collectivism with a strong egalitarian spirit, the agrarian social order began to rest upon power being derived from control over land. Even *fiqih*, which was codified within a feudal milieu, did not place any restriction on the transfer of land from self-cultivating farmers to non-cultivating owners (Yusuf, 1970, pp. 198–9). Thus, the widespread transfer of land resulted in the gradual dispossession of the peasantry and the emergence of a landowning class with strong links to the ruling hierarchy. It was in the post-Prophetic period that the democratic spirit of Islam was replaced by the dynastic rule of the Umayyads, and a feudal-monarchical structure came to dominate most of the Muslim world.

Why is it that discussion of the Islamisation of the economy in

Pakistan has concentrated on the elimination of interest from only the organised financial sector, and has not focussed attention on the widespread prevalence of *riba* and *muzara'a* in the economy? There are a number of reasons for this. First, the main theoreticians of the concept of an 'Islamic economy' have elaborated it to be based principally on an interest-free system and *zakat*. Second, popular discussion and elaboration of the concept of an Islamic economy have been restricted mainly to the propertied classes. It is not in their interest to elaborate the true meaning and significance of the elimination of *riba* and *muzara'a*, as it would threaten their interests. Thus, a static and politically expedient interpretation has been given to Islamic injunctions, including the elimination of *riba*.

Throughout Muslim history, ways and means have been found to avoid the prohibition of *riba* and *muzara'a*. *Hiyal* (ruses avoiding prohibitions) have been a common device whereby, in the face of Islamic injunctions prohibiting *riba* and *muzara'a*, these practices have been permitted in various forms in different times and places in the Muslim world. Scholars of various legal schools have found ways to getting round theoretical prohibitions of *riba*. Out of the four Sunni schools of Islamic jurisprudence, the Hanafi school applies the principle of 'practical necessity' to overcome the theoretical prohibition of *riba*. Similarly, the Maliki and the Shafi'i schools of Islamic jurisprudence, to get round the injunctions prohibiting *riba*, have permitted *hiyal* in a limited number of cases. Various books were devoted by Muslims scholars of law, mainly of the Hanafi school, such as Abu Bakr Ahmad al Khassaf (d. 874) and Abu Hatim Mahmaud al Qazwini (d. 1050), to expounding the forms in which interest was permitted. Similarly, certain *fuqaha* of the Maliki and Shafi'i schools have justified the institution of *muzara'a* on the basis of actual practice.

DEVELOPMENT OF CAPITALISM IN MUSLIM SOCIETIES

By the time of the Abbasid revolution in 750, vast areas had been brought under the control of a central authority. Meanwhile, the Arabisation of the caliphate, which had been initiated by the Umayyad ruler Abdul Malik (685–705), helped to create the conditions for widespread commercial activity (Yusuf, 1970, p. 26). Arabic replaced Greek and Persian as the state language, and Arabs took over the civil administration. The caliphate expanded rapidly following the classical pattern of conquests and conversions on the one hand, and commercialisation of production and expansion of trade on the other. With the centralisation of authority and the development of communication networks, the opportunities for production for the market increased greatly.[3] The growth of industries producing for export was rapid in areas such as Khazistan (south-eastern Iraq), Syria, Bokhara and Baghdad. As a result of the increased demand for goods, the need for finance, both for investment and trade, increased. The Muslims, however, preferred to retain the more prestigious positions in the bureaucracy and military, while allowing other religious groups, especially Jews, to indulge in finance and trade.[4] However, in areas where other religious groups were not significant, Muslims themselves undertook commercial and financial activity. Where there were possibilities of making a profit through trade, credit was made available, and interest was charged by both Muslims and non-Muslims so that capital could fructify. The observant eye of Ibn Khaldun, probably the greatest of Muslim historians, was able to grasp the nature of commercial practices of an important section of Muslim society in the Middle Ages, notwithstanding the injunctions prohibiting *riba*:

> Commerce means increasing one's capital by buying merchandise and attempting to sell it for a price higher than its purchase price, either by waiting for market fluctuations or by transporting the merchandise to a country where that particular merchandise is more in demand and brings higher prices, or by selling it for a high price to be paid at a future date. . . . Now traders are few. It is unavoidable that there should be cheating, tampering with the merchandise (Rodinson, 1974, pp. 37–8).

Regarding financial practices which were based on interest, Ibn Khaldun was of the view that delay in repayment of debt is harmful to the creditor as it does not allow his capital to fructify (Ibn Khaldun, 1967, p. 312). Besides the observations of Ibn Khaldun, historical records covering different periods and regions of the Muslim world, for instance trade and commercial manuals, indicate that lending and borrowing on interest, practised in different forms, had been fairly widespread, despite Islamic injunctions to the contrary (Rodinson, 1974, p. 31). Wherever the Muslims themselves indulged in the financial practice of money-lending or borrowing from other communities or religious groups, they depended on the institution of *riba* for the accumulation of capital.

It seems therefore that the economic imperatives of commercialism and profit took precedence over the textual rendering of Quranic injunctions prohibiting interest. With the expansion of the Muslim community, the socio-economic structure of the areas that came to make up the Muslim world bore little resemblance to the tribal society and economy that had characterised the city-state of Medina at the time of the Prophet. As these communities and classes started developing close ties with the ruling hierarchy on the one hand, and sections of the *ulama* on the other, they were able to get round Islamic injunctions which threatened their material interests. Not only were they able to prevent the application of Quranic injunctions prohibiting *riba*, but they were also successful in influencing the thinking of certain legal schools of thought.

Changes in theological opinion, represented by the emergence of different schools of thought, which in turn reflected structural changes at the social, economic and political levels, have not been confined to Muslim society alone. They were a feature of medieval European society as well. In the case of Europe, religious thinking and popular opinion, which had hitherto been hostile to the practice of lending and borrowing on interest, which was termed usury, were gradually reconciled to the rising tide of capitalist practices and institutions. The popular thinking in Europe that led to the acceptance of interest towards the end of the Middle Ages may be summed up as follows: 'why should a creditor, who may himself be poor, make a loan *gratis*, in order to put money into the pockets of a wealthy capitalist who uses the advance to corner the wool crop or to speculate on the exchange?' (Tawney, 1977, p. 185).

Changes at the institutional level have therefore been accompanied by changes in popular and theological opinion. At the theological level, the reconciliation of secular and religious opinion was undertaken in Europe by John Calvin towards the end of the sixteenth century. It was not only Calvin's condonation of lending and borrowing on interest, but also his overall world-view that broke through the stagnant intellectual milieu of feudal-dominated medieval Europe:

> It is not wholly fanciful to say that on a narrower stage, but with not less formidable weapons, Calvin did for the bourgeoisie of the sixteenth century what Marx did for the proletariat of the nineteenth, or that the doctrine of predestination satisfied the same hunger for an assurance that the forces of the universe are on the side of the elect as was to be assuaged in a different age by the theory of historical materialism (Tawney, 1977, p. 120).

At a general level, be it Buddhism, Christianity or Islam, usury in particular, and the exploitation of man by man in general, have been denounced on moral grounds and because of their adverse economic consequences. The excessive concentration of wealth in the hands of the few is considered to breed arrogance and selfishness on the one hand and poverty and deprivation on the other. A society with a large number of poor and underfed persons, it is argued, can neither be economically healthy nor socially stable. One reason for the general consensus of opinion regarding the prohibition of usury among the various religious and early philosophical schools of thought has been the exploitative nature of most borrowing and lending in largely subsistence economies.

In societies where production is largely by subsistence, it is only in times of dire need that borrowing is resorted to. Taking advantage of the weak bargaining position of persons in need, the well-to-do classes with a surplus, advance commodities or money on credit. Such advances are made on the condition that within a specified period, the borrower returns not only the amount advanced, but a certain percentage of the principal as interest. The rate of interest on the loan advanced depends on a number of factors, such as the degree of competition between the lenders and borrowers, the accessibility to credit markets and the bargaining position of the borrower.

Lending and borrowing in various forms have been practised ever since society was divided into the two main classes of surplus producers and appropriators. The propertied classes, who have traditionally controlled the surplus, have barely permitted the direct producers to exist at a subsistence level. When, due to an increase in the rate of exploitation or to unpredictable natural factors, the level of existence of the direct producers falls below the subsistence level, they are forced to borrow to keep themselves alive. It is such borrowing, which is still prevalent in large parts of the rural areas of Pakistan, that is highly exploitative.

Usury or *riba* has derived its exploitative nature in the popular mind from the highly unequal relationship between the moneylenders (who in a large number of cases have been owners of large estates) and weak and poor borrowers. This was the case in Western Europe prior to the development of modern capitalism, and is still so in the Indo-Pakistan subcontinent and many other Third-World countries. It is the reaction among the poorer sections, who in times of need are forced to seek subsistence loans, that has been articulated by sections of religious opinion as a vehement attack on the institution of money-lending. When we find reference to the prohibition of *riba* in Islamic thought, or usury in Christian religious opinion of the Middle Ages, we must bear in mind that

> like the modern profiteer, the usurer was a character so unpopular that most unpopular characters could be called usurers, and by the average practical man almost any form of bargain which he thought oppressive would be classed as usurious (Tawney, 1977, p. 157).

Although the above observations of Professor Tawney, describing the popular perception of usury, relate to feudal Europe during the Middle Ages, the description of both usurers and usurious loans could very easily be applied to Muslim societies past and present. Complaints about usurers that appear in Islamic literature of the medieval period not only point towards the prevalence of the institution of money-lending, but the contempt in which the usurer was held. In a poem attributed to the eleventh-century Ismaili propagandist Nasir-i-Khosraw, usurers are defined as 'contemptible creatures who drink the blood of the poor and are destined to end up in eternal fire' (Rodinson, 1974, p. 40). Notwithstanding the aversion to money-lending at the popular level, the position of the money-lender, who in a number of cases was also the owner of large estates, was protected in the case of medieval Europe by sections of the clergy and, in Muslim societies, by sections of the *ulama*.

In countries like Pakistan, where feudalism still persists alongside a modern capitalist sector, the concept of *riba* should encompass the whole gambit of oppressive and exploitative relations between the exploiter and the exploited: the feudal lord and the landless tenants, the capitalist owner and the worker, the extortionate merchant and the consumer. All these exploitative relations stem from a social structure that gives rise to the division of society into the exploiter and the exploited, and the oppressor and the oppressed. The concentration of economic wealth and power in the hands of a privileged few implies the denial of economic opportunities and well-being of the majority of the population. Unless the social, economic and political structures that perpetuate the exploitation of the many by the few are changed by the organised strength of the oppressed classes, mere moral exhortations in the name of Islam will not put an end to the pressing problems of poverty, deprivation and socio economic backwardness. Instead of making the elimination of interest and the institution of *zakat* and *ushr* the cornerstones of a so-called Islamic economy, the propagators of such an economy should concentrate on the establishment of a society where true egalitarianism exists. This, however, they will not do. Paradoxically, whereas the exploiting classes see in the feudal and oppressive practices of the Muslim ruling classes a justification for the status quo, the oppressed classes see in Islam a panacea for their sufferings.

So-called Islamic governments may claim that *riba* has been prohibited, but in fact, exploitative socio-economic structures are still prevalent. This is because the socio-economic structures of most countries which claim to be Islamic are actually distorted extensions of those in developed capitalist countries. Parts of these societies are backward, with semi-feudal or tribal structures interacting with the more developed centres of finance, commerce and industry. Since capitalism is the more developed mode of production, capitalist relations tend to dominate those social formations where capitalist and semi-feudal relations coexist. The so-called Islamic policies adopted by a state representing both capitalist and feudal interests are aimed generally at appeasing conservative and well-to-do sections of society, rather than at achieving objectives such as the elimination of *riba*. It is not possible to eliminate *riba* without first demolishing the exploitative socio economic edifice on which society and economy are based. Whereas Pakistan's rural society is yet to free itself from the stranglehold of feudal interests and values, the urban areas have a long way to go before they experience meaningful industrialisation from which workers and ordinary people can benefit.

CONCLUSION

Why is it that the Muslim world, which some ten centuries ago was one of the leading civilisations in the world, is today underdeveloped, and dependent economically, militarily and technologically on foreign powers? It has become convenient to invoke modern theories of imperialism to explain the cultural and economic backwardness of the Third World, of which most Muslim countries are a part. In emphasising the effects on the colonies of developments in the centres of Western imperialism, such explanations, however, do not give sufficient weight to indigenous social and cultural factors. While interacting with external factors, indigenous factors have given rise to underdevelopment in its various dimensions.

Broadly speaking, the intellectual reaction to imperialist domination in the Muslim world has taken two forms – doctrinaire and institutionalised Marxism on the one hand and Islamic fundamentalism on the other. Both these responses have, however, not been able to strike deep enough roots among the masses to be able to create the conditions for the social transformation of Muslim communities in the present stage of social evolution. Whatever the official ideology adopted by the ruling classes, the basic structure of most Muslim countries remains exploitative and authoritarian, and feudal and capitalist modes of production coexist in varying degrees. Even if, under pressure from the oppresed classes, the egalitarian message of Islam is emphasised in official ideology; the ruling elites try to prevent the participation of the masses in political power by not allowing the establishment of effective political, economic and social institutions.

In the case of Pakistan, we have seen the manner in which the ruling elites have, while accepting Islam as the official ideology, given it a reactionary interpretation. Institutions which could revolutionise the lives of the downtrodden and oppressed (for whose sake Islam was popularised by the Prophet) have not been allowed to develop. On the other hand, fundamentalist Islamic groups such as the Jama'at-i-Islami, which enjoys the support of the establishment, present an authoritarian and reactionary interpretation of Islam. The objective of the ruling hierarchy and the Jama'at appears to be to retard social progress by not allowing the emancipation of the masses. Their interpretation of Islam regards the social order as something static and unalterable. Their concern with economic issues is not caused by anxiety for reform, but by concern with the maintenance of an idealistic moral code, of which economic conduct forms an essential part. Their idealistic moral code, based on the appealing universal values of brotherhood, egalitarianism and justice, is essentially bound up with the economic and social structures of the past, canonised during a period of history when societies and economies were not as complex as today. Such concepts of morality in the present era of modern capitalism are incapable of eliminating exploitation and oppression on their own.

NOTES

1. Broadly defined, *riba* is an increase in income earned without expending labour. It therefore covers the capitalists' income as well as that of landlords, earned through renting out land to sharecroppers.
2. According to the 1980 agricultural census of Pakistan, close to 36 per cent of the total farm area in Pakistan was tenant-operated. See Agricultural Census Organisation, 1983, p. 5.
3. For a discussion of the Arabisation of the caliphate under Abdul Malik (685–705), see Mahmud, 1960, pp. 74 and 77.
4. For a discussion of expansion in trade and growth of production for the market in the early Abbadid period, see Mahmud, 1960, pp. 130–2, and Rodinson, 1974, pp. 28–75.

REFERENCES

Agricultural Census Organisation (1983) *Pakistan Census of Agriculture 1980* (Islamabad: Government of Pakistan).

Asian Regional Team for Employment Promotion (ILO-ARTEP) (1983), *Employment and Structural Change – Issue for the Eighties* (Bangkok, January 1983), p. 239.

Ayaz, Babar (1984) 'Islamic Banking: Island in Capitalist Ocean', *Karachi Dawn, Economic and Business Review*, 17 June.

Council of Islamic Ideology (1980) *The Elimination of Interest from the Economy* (Karachi: Government of Pakistan).

Haque, Ziaul (1977) *Landlord and Peasant in Early Islam* (Islamabad: Islamic Research Institute).

Haque, Ziaul (1982) 'Book Review: *Studies in Islamic Economics*, ed. by Khurshid Ahmad', *Hamdard Islamicus*, 5 (1) (Spring).

Ibn Khaldun (1967) *An Introduction to History: The Muqaddimah* trans. F. Rosenthal, abridged and ed. N. J. Dawood (London: Routledge and Kegan Paul).

Mahmood, M. (1984) 'Changes in the Agrarian Structure of Pakistan', *Islamabad Daily Muslim*, Friday Magazine, 6 July.

Mahmud, S. F. (1960) *A Short History of Islam* (Karachi: Oxford University Press).

Rodinson, M. (1974) *Islam and Capitalism* (Harmondsworth: 1974).

Tawney, R. H. (1977) *Religion and the Rise of Capitalism* (Harmondsworth: 1977).

Yusuf, S. M. (1970) *Studies in Islamic History and Culture* (Karachi: Islamic Book Service).

8 Principles of Islamic Economic Reform

S. N. H. Naqvi, H. U. Beg, Rafiq Ahmed, Mian M. Nazeer

That Islam's is a 'complete' system is axiomatic, at least for Muslims, in view of the categorical Quranic declaration; 'This day have I perfected your religion for you and completed My favour unto you . . .' (5:3). An unambiguous perception of the Unity of all life processes – social, economic and religious – is Islam's original contribution to civilisation, and offers the best hope to Muslims for reordering their socio-economic affairs according to the tenets of Islam. All this is clear enough. However, the full implications of the unitary Islamic philosophy are not always fully understood. Specific recommendations are made by many Muslim economists to 'Islamise' the existing economic systems by foisting into them elements of the Islamic economic system without any idea of the 'priority' of those elements for attaining the avowed policy objectives. A syncretism of this kind is both illogical and counter-productive because it ignores the inherent incompatibilities between the Islamic and other economic systems. Such a transplantation may produce a 'mixed economy', but not necessarily an Islamised economy. Indeed, the mixture may be positively un-Islamic if it aggravates the worst characteristic of the existing economic systems – viz. economic exploitation of the poor by the rich. In that case, such efforts get no support from the Holy Quran, which prohibits such dressing up: 'Confound not truth with falsehood . . .' (2:42).

Economic systems or regimes are complete and internally consistent social entities, with a set of distinctive value premises and the logical consequences of those premises. It is, therefore, essential that the internal consistency of the Islamic system is respected when introducing specific elements of the system which should always be related to its totality. It should be noted that when the totality of the Islamic system is emphasised, it does not necessarily follow that the elements of the system cannot fruitfully be introduced sequentially into an existing non-Islamic economic system to initiate the Islamisation process. However, what it does mean is that:

(i) Elements of the Islamic reform should add up to an Islamic system, which should be clearly 'recognisable' as a totality;
(ii) These elements should be appropriately 'ordered', singling out those which contribute the most to achieving the basic objectives of the Islamic economy;
(iii) In determining the order of priorities, the pre-existing societal context must be kept in view.

The Islamic economic system should be clearly defined to spell out its basic 'structure', policy objectives and the necessary policy instruments for achieving those objectives. Furthermore, in implementing the Islamisation programme, the priority list of the elements of the Islamic reform should be drawn up with a view to minimising the evils of the existing economic system. For instance, a highly skewed distribution of income and wealth, high levels of open and disguised unemployment, socially unacceptable levels of literacy rates, allocative inefficiency, low level of business and public morality, etc., are the major 'pollutants' of the economic and social environment in Pakistan. Any meaningful programme of Islamisation must, therefore, face up to these problems with the help of distinctive Islamic solutions. True, public policy under any economic system must squarely meet these problems, but that does not mean that the Islamic system should walk away from them. In fact, the presumption is that the Islamic economic system will succeed where other systems may have failed, because they do not *explicitly* make moral and ethical values the guiding principles of man's economic behaviour.

The distinctive character of the Islamic economic system which sets it apart from existing non-Islamic economic systems lies in the high priority it accords to the needs of 'the needy and the deprived' at all levels of economic development, making explicit recommendations to end the exploitation of man by man and insisting on preserving *al-'adl*, which literally means social balance or equilibrium, in social and economic relations. To achieve these objectives, Islam prescribes a unified framework within which the successful pursuit of the above-mentioned objectives *must* contribute to spiritual ascent. There is no place in the Islamic perspective for an economic order which is *exclusively* devoted to the attainment of material plenitude. The Holy Quran clearly prescribes:

> But of mankind is he who saith: 'Our Lord! Give unto us in the world', and he hath no portion in the Hereafter. And of them (also) is he who saith: 'Our Lord! Give unto us in the world that which is good and in the Hereafter that which is good, and guard us from the doom of Fire' (2:201).

THE CHARACTER OF AN ISLAMIC ECONOMIC SYSTEM

Having emphasised that the Islamic system should be seen in its 'totality', we pass on to a more difficult question on which there is more room for an honest difference of opinion. What are the 'dimensions' of this totality which sets an Islamic economic system apart from other economic systems? An answer to the question requires that the Islamic economic *system* be clearly defined. Unless this is done, no meaningful discussion of the Islamisation process can be conducted. This is because there would then be no reference point to determine the Islamic nature of a particular reform, which may have been introduced in the name of Islam; nor would there be any consistent set of criteria for rejecting any specific 'statement' as un-Islamic.

Exact definitions of systems are quite often treacherous territories: such definitions can be made broad enough to accommodate 'everything under the sun', or they may be made too restrictive to capture the essential features of these systems. Definitions of the former type are meaningless as analytical devices, while those of the latter type have little explanatory power. However, economic systems can be identified and compared in terms of their basic properties. As recent works on comparative-systems analysis have shown, the attitude on the following matters locates the distinctive character of an economic system fairly accurately: (i) property relations; (ii) kinds of economic freedom; (iii) the character of the incentive system; (iv) the character of the coordinating or resource-allocating mechanism; and (v) location and system of decision-making.

Property Relations

The basic characteristic of an Islamic system is its attitude towards private property. In the Islamic perspective, all wealth belongs to Allah: 'Unto Allah belongeth whatsoever is in the heavens and whatsoever is in the earth' (3:129). While absolute ownership of all wealth is Allah's, man is only a trustee of whatever he has and not its absolute owner: '. . . . and spend of that whereof He hath made you trustees . . .' (57:7). This Islamic position is unique and can easily be distinguished from the position of capitalism, where the private ownership of wealth is a sacred institution to be preserved at all cost, and from the position of socialism (communism) where all wealth belongs to the state, which is considered a separate entity as opposed to the individual. One logical consequence of the concept of trusteeship is that the right to own private property, though recognised, is severely limited because in the Islamic perspective, man's freedom to own property is only relative to the needs of the society. There is unanimity among Muslim scholars that such things as grazing lands, natural forests and water resources, mines, roads, graveyards and places of congregational prayers cannot be privately owned. As for land, ownership rights are liable to be lost if the land lies unreclaimed or is not used for three consecutive years.

A more difficult question to settle in this context is that of *inherited* wealth. There is a view that since the individual is the legal owner of inherited property, the state cannot impose death duties, nor can it take away any part of it. This may be so, but it does not follow that the Islamic law of inheritance pre-empts all distributive initiatives of the state. That would be to miss the whole point about the heavily egalitarian Islamic economic philosophy underlying the Islamic law of inheritance, which derives its distinctive character from its insistence on a social balance or equilibrium so 'that mankind may observe right measure' (57:25). The Islamic law, while prescribing the rights of heirs in given ratios, gives man the freedom to pass on a part of his wealth for the welfare of the society. This is precisely the spirit of the provision that a *maximum* of one-third of man's total *inheritable* wealth can be willed for the welfare of the non-family members of the society.

A careful reading of the Quranic commandments should make it clear that even though, to begin with, there may be such a thing as coexistence of the rich and the poor, it need not persist – at least the gulf between the two should not widen over time – after the redistribution of wealth ordained by Islam has taken hold. It is inevitable that with the implementation of Islamic reform, there will occur a general rise in the average income levels and wealth of the 'needy and the deprived' and a corresponding fall in the wealth of the privileged minority, who, because of the workings of an unjust economic system, got more than what was rightfully theirs in the first place. At any rate, the 'distance' between the rich and the poor will have to be greatly reduced once the Islamic state goes about the task of restoring the 'rights' (*haqq*) of the 'deprived' and the 'oppressed'.

The argument for adopting measures to redistribute private property more widely gains further strength from the fact that we are living in an economic system which is not consistent with Islamic economic philosophy and which is marked by gross inequities in the ownership of wealth, of which land is a very substantial element. To maintain that nothing can be done about redistributing private property more widely in society, so that it remains locked within certain families through customary inheritance, would really amount to taking the absurd position that the existing distribution of wealth is in accordance with the Islamic precepts! It is an absurd position because it would be tantamount to acceptance of pre-existing social inequities as Islamically permissible.

Kinds of Economic Freedoms

The principle of consumer sovereignty, held so dear in capitalistic societies, and its total suppression, as practised in socialistic societies, are both anathematical to the 'balanced' Islamic economic philosophy. In Islam, individual freedom has been appropriately checked by social responsibility, as contained in its ethical principles. The Islamic view is founded on an explicit realisation of the 'fact' that, as a general rule, man is greedy and selfish by nature. If left to himself, he would not do much for others in society. The Holy Quran attests to this aspect of man's nature: 'Say: "If you possessed the treasures of the mercy of my Lord, you would surely hold them back for fear of spending, for man is ever grudging"' (17:100). However, it is the 'intention' of Allah that everybody should be provided with a minimum of sustenance: 'There is no moving creature on earth but its sustenance dependeth upon Allah' (11:6). Thus the existence of hunger and abject poverty is entirely man-made and a direct result of an unjust economic system. The Holy Quran is absolutely clear on this point: 'And if the people of the townships had believed and kept from evil, surely We would have opened for them blessings from the sky and from the earth' (7:96). The Islamic system, with its heavy emphasis on the act of 'giving' as the essence of a just socio-economic ordering, reflecting Allah's intention, must devise ways and means of checking individual greed, and lay out a framework wherein all members of society get a minimum of sustenance.[1]

Hence, to introduce Islamic reform in a society like Pakistan, the structure of which has been raised on feudalistic-capitalistic principles, it will be essential for the state to take up increasing responsibilities to ensure satisfaction of society's demand for such basic requirements as health, education and housing. In doing so, consumer sovereignty will have to be appropriately curtailed, though not eliminated, so that enough resources are released for financing an elaborate public-sector programme to fight poverty, hunger and economic deprivation.

The Character of the Incentive System

Another important factor distinguishing one economic system from another is the kind of economic incentives that keep the system going. In particular, the place accorded to price incentives – viz. profits, interest, rents and wages as sources of income – in a given economic system determines its character. In a 'pure' capitalistic setting, profits (and rents) tend to grow at a rate faster than that of wages to allow the investible surplus to accumulate.[2] Such a strategy is based on an acceptance of income and wealth differentials, which are allowed to grow even further as a means of achieving rapid growth rates. In socialistic societies, where profits accrue to the state, disproportionate amounts are reinvested into the production of capital-goods industries. Thus, consumption is unduly restrained to accelerate capital formation, causing severe economic hardships to the common man. Islam would reject both of these extremist economic strategies. It would not – as it cannot – use widening income differentials as a policy instrument on the pretext of promoting capital formation and economic growth, whether the economic agent implementing such a policy is the individual or the state. This is because of the simple reason that in an Islamic society, neither the individual nor the state can perpetuate or strengthen the pre-existing socio-economic structures that have not been raised on the teachings of Islam.

The Resource-Allocating Mechanism and the Location of Decision-Making

The observations just made have a direct bearing on the character of the resource-allocating mechanism and the economic decision-making process in an Islamic economy. As pointed out above, while the private sector will have a due place in it, the public sector will be called upon in an Islamic economy to assume, among other things, the predominant role as a producer of 'wage goods'. For social welfare requires not only a transfer of financial resources from the rich to the poor, but a diversion of *real* resources to the production of the basic necessities of life – and away from non-essential production. In other words, the fact that the composition of the consumer-goods basket must change drastically in an Islamic economy will require the state to play a predominant role in it, because the production of such a 'basket' may not maximise private profits. The matter is too important to be left to the 'invisible hand' of market forces, which respond to a specific distribution of economic power – or rather the purchasing power, in technical parlance – which in turn is determined by the structure of wealth-holding in the society.

The predominant, but not arbitrary and oppressive, role of the state in an Islamic economy follows logically from Islam's explicit recognition of the limits to what individuals will voluntarily do for the betterment of society. As such, man is not allowed to become an independent entity apart from society, of which he is an integral part and to the betterment of which he must *commit* himself: '. . . man doth transgress all bounds, in that he looketh upon himself as self-sufficient' (96:6–7). In the 'unified' programme of thought and action, issuing forth directly from the Divine principles of *tauheed* (unity) and *'adl* (equilibrium), everything has been assigned a proper place for maintaining and promoting social equilibrium. The ideal social behaviour is not egoistic self-glorification, but a *commitment* to ameliorating the lot of the least-privileged in society. If it takes frequent, even large-scale, state intervention to restrain individual greed so that social welfare is maximised, then this is no occasion to prevent, on false doctrinaire grounds, an Islamic state from doing its social duty by employing legitimate Islamic policy instruments. However, in doing its duty, the Islamic state, being representative of the collective will, cannot extend protection to those forces which obfuscate social change.

OBJECTIVES OF AN ISLAMIC ECONOMY

All the indicators of the Islamic economic system specified above unmistakably point to the humane economic philosophy of Islam, whose kingpin is *al-'adl wal-ihsan*. The Holy Quran is explicit on what the individual and the society should be doing: 'Lo! Allah enjoineth *al-'adl wal-ihsan*' (16:90). By the same token, Islam rejects an economic order which is *not* based on these divine principles. These related attributes of the Islamic system are eternal: 'The Word changes not before Me, and I do no injustice to My servants' (50:29). The Islamic economic system explicitly aims at re-establishing a delicate balance between social and economic forces, with a clear 'bias' in favour of the poor and the economically weak. According to the Holy Quran: 'And in whose wealth there is a right acknowledged for the needy and the deprived' (70:24–5). This is indeed a revolutionary principle: what the poor must get from the wealth of the rich is not charity, but their *haqq* (right), of which someone, including a particular social system, may have 'deprived' them.[3]

The implementation of this divine commandment on the economic plane would require a heavy redistribution of income and wealth to redress the gross social and moral disequilibrium created by the present economic system. The rich must part with excess wealth *because* they are not its absolute owner, but only trustees so that its disposal is subject to the divine law: 'And what aileth you that ye spend not in the way of Allah, when unto Allah belongeth the inheritance of the heavens and the earth?' (57:10). And those who do not fulfil the obligations of a trustee will be punished by Allah: 'And leave Me (alone to deal with) those in possession of the good things of life, who (yet) deny the Truth . . .' (73:11). Thus, *not* giving to fulfil one's social obligation is a denial of Truth. The Islamic state *must* ensure that man attains success by being saved from his innate greed because in the Islamic perspective, 'And whoso is saved from his own avarice – such are they who are successful' (59:9).

Three points should, therefore, be crystal-clear about an Islamic economic system:

(i) It must enforce an 'equilibrium' among the consumption, production and distribution relations in the society, while keeping a delicate balance between individual freedom and social responsibility. This must come about by virtue of Allah's commandment to establish *al-'adl*. As man is only a trustee, not an absolute owner of wealth, his right to spend is regulated.

(ii) The second part of Allah's commmandment – i.e. *al-ihsan* – requires that economic policies in an Islamic economy have a distinct tilt towards the poor. Not only that. The process of pushing up the poor along the scale of social hierarchy must continue until the 'deprived' in the society receive their 'due share'.

(iii) There is a clear 'separation' in Islam between a poor man's needs and his ability to earn through his own labour.

These over-riding Islamic requirements can be met if economic policy is geared to the attainment of the following objectives: social justice; universal education; economic growth; maximum employment generation; and improving the quality of life.

True, these are the objectives of any economic system, but that does not disqualify them from being the objectives of the Islamic system as well, particularly because they follow directly from Islam's own distinctive economic philosophy, and the reasons for the avowal of these policy objectives are not the same as in other economic systems.

Social Justice

Social justice follows from *al-'adl*, since there can be no justice without a delicate balance obtaining among the many social and economic forces that shape the basic structure of the society. One of the most important elements of this structure is the pattern of asset ownership. It is for this reason that man has been warned against concentration of wealth: '[Let] it [i.e. wealth] become not a commodity between the rich among you' (59:7). Thus, *al-'adl* requires that social justice must obtain in every walk of life so that the divine principle of unity is reflected on the plane of social existence. Man has been commanded again and again to realise and maintain the quality of justice under all circumstances. In financial transactions, the observance of this principle is absolutely essential for an orderly society: 'Give full measure and full weight in justice, and wrong not people in respect of their goods' (11:85).

Universal Education

Universal education is a very strong means of establishing *al-'adl* in the society. It is not only a powerful redistributive mechanism which equalises opportunities in order to bring out the best in man, it is also the only means of securing the technological advance required for a dynamic economy. It is for this reason that Islam declares the acquisition of knowledge to be the most sacred pursuit of man, who has been advised to pray constantly: 'My Lord! Increase me in knowledge' (20:114).

Economic Growth

Economic growth in the Islamic perspective is required to attain social justice inter-generationally; for equity must hold not only within a generation, but between generations as well. As such, economic growth cannot violate the requirement of *al-'adl*: the scarce resources of the society can neither be squandered away for the consumption of the present generation, nor stored away for posterity beyond a certain point: 'Make not thy hands tied (like a niggard's) to thy neck, nor stretch it forth to its utmost reach . . .' (17:29). In other words, the flow of consumption must be optimised not only at a given point in time, but also over time. Such a strategy will rule out both profligate spending behaviour, which lowers domestic savings below the optimal level, and excessive abstention from present consumption, which forces saving to above this level. It should, therefore, be obvious that *al-'adl* defines both the lower and the upper limits of the socially desirable rate of economic growth. Even more, divine law also regulates the *quality* of economic growth by requiring that the flow of essential goods and services consumed by the poor is at all times kept at an adequate level. What is an 'adequate' level will be decided in the societal context.

Maximum Employment Generation

Economic growth must also maximise employment generation in order to make the greatest contribution to human happiness. However, for this to be an economically efficient and socially just process, it is essential that capital/labour ratios correspond to the resource endowment of the country. In a labour-abundant economy like Pakistan's, the capital/labour ratio must be such that economic growth remains consistent with the generation of maximum employment opportunities. This would, in turn, require an appropriate choice of techniques, which, in the long run, can be promoted only by making a heavy investment in human capital formation.

Improving the Quality of Life

The requirement of *al-ihsan* as a rule reinforces the process of securing *al-'adl* by ensuring that the 'needy and the deprived' are moved up the social hierarchy scale through a series of redistributive measures. In the context of an economy like Pakistan's, it will take considerable effort to improve the quality of life, not only in financial terms, but in real terms as well. A diversion of resources, financial and real, will be necessary if abject poverty is to be eradicated and the opportunities for social advancement are to be made accessible to all, irrespective of the circumstances of their birth.

AN APPROPRIATE POLICY PACKAGE

The choice of an appropriate policy package aiming at the Islamic ideal must be governed by a clear realisation of the fact that its immediate 'point of contact' will be the existing economic system, which is *not* based on the Islamic principles of *al-'adl* and *al-ihsan*. Hence, the success or otherwise of the Islamic reform will be judged by its success in handling the problems of ensuring social justice *and* economic growth, in particular those relating to absolute and relative poverty, low literacy levels, high levels of open and disguised unemployment, and technological backwardness.

To make the Islamic reform effective, it will be essential to move towards the Islamic ideal by gradually, though consciously, encompassing all or most of the essential aspects of social and economic life. However, the requirement that Islamic reform be carried out in its multi-dimensionality will slow down considerably the pace of the Islamisation process, for the experience at each step of the implementation of the Islamic reform will have to be carefully analysed to permit a maximum of 'feedback effect'. It is only through the process of a prolonged two-way interaction, between the theory of Islamic economic philosophy, and its empirical verification in real-life situations, that a systematic body of scientific knowledge will emerge to provide reliable guidelines to Muslim economists and policy-makers and to lay the foundations of an economic science raised entirely on Islamic principles.

What at present passes under the grandiose title of Islamic economics is nothing more than a smattering of broad and vague ideas about the introduction of *zakat* and the abolition of interest, giving the impression that Islamic economics – assuming for the sake of argument that it already exists – can be reduced to just these two elements. Such a claim is logically fallacious because no complete economic system, such as Islam's, can be described merely in terms of one or two of its policy instruments. Furthermore, the real meaning of these two important elements of Islamic reform must be understood. The Islamic rejection of interest is, in fact, a rejection of the entire feudalistic-capitalistic system, which condones the exploitation of the poor by the rich to achieve high rates of economic growth; and *zakat* is symptomatic of Islam's highly egalitarian economic philosophy. However, to maintain that interest can fully account for capitalistic exploitation, or that proceeds from *zakat* alone will be sufficient to solve the problems of want and poverty, and to bridge the yawning gap between the rich and the poor is to oversimplify what in fact is a more complicated problem.

There is a real danger that if the abolition of interest and the introduction of *zakat* are overemphasised as *initiators* of the process of Islamisation, then policy-making will concentrate on just these two elements to the *exclusion* of the fundamental structural elements of Islamic reform. Attempts will then be made to achieve these 'targets' by one means or another, irrespective of their effects on the economy. And once they are achieved, it may give everybody a false sense of accomplishment, as if all that was needed to be done had been done! Nothing could be more dangerous. After all, it is not difficult to envisage situations where gross social injustice prevails in violation of the requirement of *al-'adl wal-ihsan* even though *zakat* may be the only form of taxation and interest may have been abolished. In capital-scarce poor societies, where economic exploitation is rife, such tendencies will be still greater. In particular, the profit-sharing system, which is advocated as the sole replacement of the interest-based system, may lead to gross exploitation of the poor by the rich; and *zakat*, if interpreted only as a limited means of resource mobilisation, may prove to be insufficient to end economic injustices in society. What is worse, nothing can be done about this state of affairs when the failure to end exploitation results from the reforms introduced in the name of Islam (see the final section below). The process of Islamisation will, therefore, have received a permanent setback because of its association with an Islamically unjust state of affairs. The elements of Islamic economic reform cannot violate the basic conditions that define the totality of the Islamic economic system: the perpetuation and accentuation of the gross exploitation of man by man is incompatible with Islamic ideals.

Another important point which has a direct bearing on the choice of an appropriate Islamic policy package is that specific elements of the package cannot be rejected just because they bear superficial resemblance to policies pursued in non-Islamic economic systems. For instance, if Islam's emphasis on man's (limited) economic freedom translates into a definite, though limited, role for private enterprise, then this is not capitalism. By the same token, if Islam's commitment to *al-'adl wal-ihsan* requires far-reaching land reforms and nationalisation of banks and public-goods industries, then such recommendations cannot be rejected simply because they look superficially like a communistic collectivising philosophy. These are just two examples of a general principle, that formal similarities among some elements of different economic systems will always exist, because all economic systems directly or indirectly grapple with the problems of scarcity, want and poverty. However, these similarities do not deprive any economic system of its originality or distinctive character. The important thing is that in each economic system, given its ideological framework, policy instruments should bear a direct relationship to basic policy objectives and the former should follow from the latter.

Lastly, it must be borne in mind that the success of any economic system in achieving its objectives depends crucially on the availability of a sufficiently large number of policy instruments. It would, therefore, greatly compromise the potential possibilities of the Islamic economic system if the set of policy instruments were kept very small. From this point of view also, an undue emphasis on just two policy instruments – (i.e. the abolition of interest and the introduction of *zakat*) – to the exclusion of all else – will severely limit the avenues for fulfilling Islamic policy objectives. Unfortunately, as things are, we tend to spend much more time specifying what is *not*, than on what *is* Islamically permissible.

THE ISLAMIC POLICY PACKAGE – I

The implementation of a programme of Islamic reform will, depending on the magnitude and intensity of existing socio economic injustices, inevitably involve a corrective transfer of real and financial resources from the rich to the poor. This follows logically because if the distribution of income and wealth had been just to begin with, there would have no injustice in the initial situation and no need for replacing the pre-existing system by an Islamic economic system, based on *al-'adl wal-ihsan*! To achieve such a transfer of resources, the existing institution of private property, which rests on feudalistic-capitalistic foundations, will have to be reformed in accordance with the Islamic ideal.[4] Other elements of the Islamic policy package are: launching a vigorous programme of universal education, particularly at the primary level, and providing social security in order to relieve absolute poverty and social deprivation. Measures designed to increase the employment impact of the economic development process and to ensure technological progress with an appropriate choice of techniques, and those meant to regulate the rate, form and quality of economic growth to preserve inter-generational equity should also compete for the attention of the policy-makers. A brief explanation of each of these proposals is given below.

Private Property

Private property accounts for about one-third of the GNP in most capitalistic countries. Similar estimates are not available for Pakistan, but it can be safely asserted that privately-held wealth – urban and rural property, including land, houses, jewellery, etc. – accounts for a large part of inter-class income differentials. It follows that no programme of income redistribution can make much sense unless the distribution of wealth in the society is made equitable to begin with. The most important element of wealth is landed property, which, if not equitably distributed, not only becomes the most important source of economic injustice, but also leads to social tensions and moral degeneration in the society.[5] It is, therefore, essential that steps be taken to regulate and dilute this institution in a manner which conforms to the Islamic concept of trusteeship rather than to the capitalistic notion of *absolute* ownership, which is alien to Islam.

The crucial question is: what steps should be taken to translate the idea of trusteeship into a set of meaningful socio-economic relationships? It is clear that leaving the matter to individual initiative alone will at best, be a naive, if not hypocritical, prescription. While every effort should be made to nurse the altruistic instinct in man, the state will have to intervene where private initiative fails. And in view of man's instinctive greed, to which the Holy Quran testifies, the role of the state will have to be quite large in order to effect a substantial transfer of privately-held property to 'the needy and the deprived'.

The invisible hand of the market, which helps vested interests and the 'haves', as opposed to the 'have-nots', when purchasing power is unequally distributed, cannot be relied upon for ushering in an Islamic dispensation based on the divine principles of *al-'adl wal-ihsan*. This is because without drastically reducing the initial wealth differentials between rich and poor, and making the relative share of the latter gradually rise, the inequalities of income and wealth will continue to widen with the passage of time.

As pointed out earlier, contrary to popular misconceptions, the Islamic law of inheritance does allow a wider distribution of landed property outside the small circle of legal heirs to prevent inter-generational snowballing of wealth – i.e. each generation adding to the inherited wealth, which keeps on growing within the same family. With wealth, comes political power, privilege and social influence. It should clearly be the concern of the state to prevent the emergence of family oligarchies, which tend to be the strongest anti-reform, reactionary force in society. Hence, for anyone to take the extreme position that the Islamic law of inheritance effectively pre-empts any redistributive initiative of the state is really to condone a highly exploitative economic system. Such a position, whatever the cover of legality it may claim, clearly contradicts the divine principle of *al-'adl wal-ihsan*: indeed, it is also against both the letter and the spirit of the Islamic law of inheritance.

Such a narrow view of the matter must be rejected. On the other hand, it should be accepted that substantial reforms will be required in this vital area. While legal heirs of the deceased should be protected against any arbitrary state action tending to deprive them of their rightful share of the wealth of their parents, the inter-generational snowballing of wealth must effectively be checked, to redistribute wealth among needy non-family members of society, for which the Islamic law of inheritance makes an explicit provision. One possible way of effecting this provision of Islamic law is that every time wealth passes from one generation to another when its legal owner dies, the legal heirs pay a registration fee *up to a maximum* of 30 per cent of the total value of the wealth inherited by them. This percentage can be varied with the financial condition of the heirs, the value of the inheritance and the extent of the encumbrances on the inherited property.

In addition to this, land reforms should be introduced to confer ownership rights on tenants and to reduce the size of *family* land holdings. Steps should also be taken to reform the existing unjust system of partnership tenancy along Islamic lines, and to abolish altogether the widespread practice of hiring out bare land for fixed rent, which – according to acknowledged *fuqaha* (jurists) – is formally equivalent to interest. Furthermore, there is the explicit Islamic injunction that land not cultivated for three consecutive years should be taken away by the state, and that such land should be given to those who would cultivate it. These measures would also be economically beneficial because they would lead to a more intensive and economical cultivation of land. It will also be essential to take similar steps to regulate the size of urban land holdings and other property. And in line with clear Islamic injunctions, all grazing lands, mines, natural springs and forests must be owned by the state.[6] Also, the existing un-Islamic practice of granting lands reclaimed through state-financed irrigation works to individuals, without any charge, must be discontinued.

Universal Education

As pointed out above (pp. 161–2), universal education, at least at the primary level, must form an integral part of the Islamic policy package, both as a mechanism for redistributing income equitably and as a measure for improving the quality of life. However, it should be kept in mind that education can have a maximum equalising effect *only* within the matrix of an economic system which distributes opportunities *and* wealth more equitably. It is not enough that opportunities for education are made available. The financial capacity of all members of society must also be improved enough to allow them access to those opportunities. If these steps are not taken, there is a danger that education may itself perpetuate, even exacerbate, existing inequities of the economic system.

Employment Generation and Economic Growth

There can be no doubt about the highly positive attitude of Islamic society towards economic growth. However, it places certain restrictions on the rate, form and quality of economic growth, as well as on the policy mix designed to achieve pre-assigned social objectives. First, the aim of public policy in an Islamic economy is to ensure that the *rate* of economic growth is consistent with the maintenance of *al-'adl* inter-generationally: the cost of economic growth borne by each generation should have some relationship to the benefits accruing to that generation. It follows that public policy must aim at optimal saving to satisfy the divine law of *al-'adl*. Such a 'balanced' growth policy will also require a proper mix of consumer goods, particularly wage goods, and capital goods obtained through domestic production and/or foreign trade.

Secondly, public policy must also be sensitive to the *form* of economic growth. It is common knowledge that economic growth in many developing countries, including Pakistan, has not made a significant difference to the economic misery of the poorer strata of the society, mainly because of a capital/labour ratio that is far too high in relation to their resource endowments. In labour-abundant countries, unduly high capital/labour ratios, symptomatic of an inappropriate choice of techniques, cause growing unemployment to accompany economic growth. The basic problem here is one of promoting appropriate technological change, which in turn depends on the supply of the relevant technical education.

Thirdly, the *quality* of economic growth needs to be regulated to reflect Islamic intentions. In 'mixed' capitalist economies, such as Pakistan's, economic growth has often been promoted by exacerbating pre-existing inequities in the distribution of income and wealth. It should be clear that such a strategy must be rejected, as it is contrary to the Islamic commitment to *al-'adl wal-ihsan*. In this context the role of the public sector must also increase in an Islamic economy to promote capital accumulation. Not only that: the public sector must also be called upon to produce, through state enterprises, wage goods for consumption by the poorer sections of society. Also, the production of those goods which have been explicitly prohibited by Islam should be banned, even if it is profitable to produce them.

Social Security and Anti-Poverty Programmes

It should be clearly understood that no anti-poverty programme can ever succeed while economic power is unjustly distributed among various classes of the society. This is because, as recent studies have shown, acute poverty and hunger depend crucially on who *owns* the real resources. Thus, poverty can, as it does, coexist with great material prosperity. The Quranic verse, 'In their wealth, the needy and the deprived have due share' (51:19), clearly points to the need for an economic system in which economic power is justly distributed and wherein an individual's consumption level may not necessarily be proportional to his capacity to earn. The difference between these two magnitudes – viz. the individual's earning capacity and his level of consumption – has to be made up by a social security programme which guarantees a minimum consumption level to the poor, the sick and the old in society. The programme will also provide general medicare and 'rehabilitative medicine' – i.e. artificial limbs, hearing aids, etc. The institutionalisation of such a programme, along with universal education, must be the most 'visible' elements of the Islamisation programme for the simple reason that it translates into a specific set of policies the Islamic emphasis on *al-ihsan*, and makes clear to the common man, as nothing else does, the blessings of an Islamic economic dispensation.

THE ISLAMIC POLICY PACKAGE – II

The Islamisation process has generally been considered synonymous with the abolition of interest from banking operations and the introduction of *zakat*. This is too restrictive a view of what Islamisation stands for and how we can best establish a truly Islamic system. Although there is no denying the fact that in an Islamic economic system there is no place for interest and that *zakat* will be an essential element of the Islamic fiscal policy, it is crucial to understand that these elements of an Islamic regime may not necessarily be consistent with a capitalistic economy. The focus of Islamic reform should more appropriately be on replacing the capitalistic system by an Islamic economic system. It is only within the framework of such a system that its elements can bear fruit. We do not accept the popular view that capitalism itself will be 'purified' and work more efficiently if only interest were abolished from the banking transactions and replaced by the not-so-Divine principle of profit-sharing. Islam does not offer any such guarantees for an automatic fulfilment of the Divine Plan without man *first* making all efforts, physical and intellectual, to realise it. The Holy Quran is explicit on this point: 'Lo! Allah changeth not the condition of a folk until they (first) change that which is in their hearts . . .' (13:11).

The Islamic injunction against interest is, in fact, a signal for a complete restructuring of the entire economic system along Islamic lines: the Islamic principle of *al-'adl wal-ihsan* must be reflected in basic consumption, production and distribution relationships. The abolition of interest will come about only as part of this fundamental restructuring of the economy. To think of abolishing interest without reference to the totality of the Islamic economic system is to put the cart before the horse! In fact, there is a real danger that the replacement of interest by the profit-sharing system may increase the level of economic exploitation of the poor by the rich, thereby negating the basic Islamic principle of *al-'adl wal-ihsan*. As pointed out above p. 170), an Islamisation process confined mainly to the replacement of interest by the profit-sharing system without regulating profits according to the tenets of Islam, will provide a perfectly safe subterfuge for reinstating capitalism in the name of Islam. It would not be doing any service to the cause of Islam if its welfare-raising possibilities are compromised in any way.

The following paragraphs will clarify our standpoint, both on the question of *zakat* and on the replacement of interest by an alternative policy instrument. A few proposals will be given on how to deal with the latter problem.

The Introduction of Zakat

It will be grossly confusing to consider the introduction of *zakat* sufficient to provide enough resources to the Islamic state to solve the many grave economic and social problems the country is faced with. Such emotionalism must be avoided. Things must be seen in their proper perspective and not exaggerated out of proportion. It is important to look at *zakat* as a limited step towards financing elaborate social security and anti-poverty programmes, which are essential elements of a fruitful Islamisation process. The real thing is to offer an *Islamic solution* to the problems of poverty and the grossly uneven distribution of income and wealth in society.

It should be borne in mind that *zakat*, as a tax, is only one of the policy instruments available to achieve the objective of an Islamic economy. In particular, its imposition does *not* preclude the imposition of other taxes – not only on income, but also on wealth. Furthermore, the mode of spending *zakat* proceeds is at least as important an issue as that of raising it. *Zakat* and other public revenues must be used productively to alleviate poverty and to finance a wide-ranging social security programme (see pp. 169–70 above). The comprehensive and revolutionary Islamic conception of *infaq* – 'And they ask thee what they ought to spend. Say: that which is superfluous' (2:219) – should be the focal point of our thinking. It was this divine commandment which led Hazrat Abu Dharr, the distinguished companion of the Holy Prophet (peace be upon him), to insist on a heavy redistribution of all kinds of wealth in society in favour of the 'needy and the deprived'.

Abolition of Interest

The popular discussion of the problem of abolition of interest does not show full understanding of the complex nature of the problem.

Firstly, in a capital-scarce economy like Pakistan's, it is meaningless even to talk of a zero rate of interest. The real question is not how to abolish the interest rate, or even how to lower it: the problem is how to *replace* it by a system which reflects the opportunity cost of capital in accordance with Islamic principles. Equally important in this context is the problem of how to institute a mechanism which ensures a reasonable return on money lent by individuals or by the State.

Secondly, it would be an exaggeration to maintain that social injustice in society can be entirely explained in terms of the existence of a positive rate of interest in banking operations. In fact, speaking generally, profits and rents are by far the most important sources of economic exploitation in present-day feudalistic-capitalistic society.

Thirdly, as noted above, an economy-wide replacement of interest by profits can only be beneficial, if at all, within the context of far-reaching readjustments in the pattern of asset holdings, in the 'real' sector – consumption, production and distribution relations – and in the financial sector of the economy. Indeed, without such structural adjustments occurring, any mechanical shift of the financial system from interest to profits (or profit-and-loss-sharing) is most likely to increase the production and consumption of those 'goods' which are consumed by the rich even more. The mode of generation of profits, their size, and the market structure that generates them are matters of crucial importance for ensuring that capitalistic exploitation due to the existing institution of interest is not replaced by an equally exploitative, or even more exploitative system based on profits.

In Search of Viable Alternatives to Interest

The search for a viable Islamic financial system should be guided by five related considerations. Firstly, the risk liability of the individual investor must be related to his capacity to bear risk. This capacity will be a function of his financial standing. Secondly, there will be a majority of individuals in society who are perfect risk-averters because their financial circumstances do not permit them to take *any* risk at all. No Islamic financial system should force them to take risks when they cannot afford to do so. It should rather provide them with some protection against the steady erosion of their purchasing power by inflation. Thirdly, these should be financial institutions whose main function should be to *minimise* the element of risk and uncertainty in financial transactions for investors. Fourthly, banks and financial institutions should be constrained to invest mainly in industries which produce essential goods, particularly wage goods and investment goods, rather than those which produce luxury goods. This restriction – the form and intensity of which will vary with distortions in the pre-existing production structure that mostly reflects the tastes and preferences of the *rentier* class – is crucial to making sure that a financial system introduced in the name of Islam does not exacerbate such 'distortions'. Fifthly, the credit needs of the low-income groups in society should be adequately met to promote individual initiative among those whose only problem is a shortage of capital funds.

To achieve these objectives, a policy *package*, and not just one policy instrument, is required. The elements of this policy package are:

(i) A limited scheme for giving interest-free loans as subsidies;
(ii) For the banking sector, a comprehensive, non-automatic system of indexing which will be symmetrical with respect to bank deposits and bank advances;
(iii) A system of investment auctioning for long-run advances by financial institutions, including banks;
(iv) An investment company which invests in risky ventures on behalf of banks on the basis of profit-sharing, subject to the condition that these ventures do not produce wasteful luxury consumption goods irrespective of profitability; and
(v) A long-run solution to the problem which relates the abolition of the institution of interest *directly* to the process of restructuring the financial and real sectors of the economy along Islamic lines.

Interest-Free Loans

Since capital commands a scarcity price in a capital-scarce country like Pakistan, interest-free loans constitute a net subsidy to the borrower, the size of the subsidy depending on the rate of interest in the economy. As noted above (pp. 158–9), the government may have to subsidise the production of wage goods by extending interest-free loans to the producers of such goods. However, the subsidy given in this form would partly or wholly replace the fiscal subsidies normally given to the private sector. It should be noted that the subsidy given in this form will be in the nature of a *permanent subsidy* – i.e. once it is extended as part of the Islamisation package, it cannot be withdrawn. Hence, it will be essential to impose countervailing taxes on those industries where a subsidy is no longer needed to maximise investment.

Interest-free loans may also be given to those sectors which require permanent subsidisation by the government. The construction of small houses, particularly those built in rural areas or urban slums, needs to be subsidised. Furthermore, local initiative in the construction of hospitals, nursing homes, modest schools and small-scale industries in the rural areas should be encouraged through this policy. In this connection, special mention must be made of small farmers, who should be provided with subsidies on essential inputs like seeds, fertiliser and other implements to enable them to be more effective producers.

Indexing Time Deposits and Bank Advances

In the persistent inflationary situation that the world (and Pakistan) will have to live with for quite some time in the future, it is essential that steps be taken to encourage saving and to promote an economical use of investment resources. Inflation cuts both ways – it discourages savings and favours borrowing for investment. The longer the period for which savings are kept or borrowing sought for, given the rate of inflation and given the period for which saving and borrowing are done, the greater will be the disequilibrium between investment and saving. It is for this reason that periods of high inflation are associated with rising rates of interest. Any proposals to replace the institution of interest in the banking system must keep these considerations in view together with the fact that the return on saving, or the cost of borrowing, may not be fixed in advance.

The proposal to index time deposits and bank advances to changes in the price level satisfies all requirements of Islamic legitimacy. Each year, the state bank may decide the percentage by which the nominal values of bank deposits (i.e. time deposits) and bank advances are to be escalated. The indexing need not be automatic; nor does it have to be 100 per cent. All that is being proposed is that the indexing be some multiple of the rate of inflation: it could be less or more than, or equal to, 100 per cent, depending on the size of the required return (cost) of saving (borrowing). The rate of indexing can also vary with the period for which saving (borrowing) is done.

The proposed system is Islamically legitimate because indexing will involve some percentage of the rate of change of the price level and the length of the period for which borrowing (lending) is made. Both are variable quantities which cannot always be foreseen with perfect certainty. It will also be economically viable and a perfect alternative to the interest-bearing option. In fact, there is a decisive advantage in the proposed system over the existing interest-based system: it makes all those who stand to gain most by inflation, namely the bankers and the borrowers, inflation-conscious. Since there is a definite cost attached to it, everyone will have a 'vested interest' in controlling the rate of inflation. The proposal is also administratively simple – a decisive advantage over the administrative nightmare that the proposed profit-and-loss-sharing system will be for policy-makers.

Investment-Auctioning System

The proposal to institute an investment-auctioning system is designed to provide a mechanism to regulate the terms on which long-term lending is done by financial institutions. It takes into account considerations of social profitability in private investment decision as far as possible. The proposed system can be operated as an alternative to, or in conjunction with the system of indexing loans to changes in the price level. Under this system, the financing institutions will periodically auction investment authorisations to investors through the market mechanism. This procedure will make it possible for the investors to take into account the scarcity price of capital, which will be high and positive in a capital-scarce economy, in making investment decisions. To prevent unnecessary 'cornering' of investment authorisations by a few bidders and also to reflect social investment priorities, the auctions will take place periodically according to the following scheme.

The government, in consultation with the planning commission and other responsible authorities, will parcel out investment resources into several categories of investment to be specified in an investment schedule. Each broad category of investment in the investment schedule would be assigned a maximum monetary limit. Auctioning will stop in a particular category once the monetary limit assigned to it is reached. This system will achieve both of the objectives stated above and will ensure that investment resources are not all forced into uses considered most profitable from the point of view of individual investors. It will also prevent over-capitalisation and excess capacity, and will not allow the capital/labour ratio to go too far out of line with the resource-endowment pattern of the country.

It may be asked whether this system has an element of interest built into it. The answer is in the negative. All that is envisaged in the scheme is that the investors be allowed possession of scarce investment resources, only at a price which corresponds to the prevailing scarcity of capital resources. The scarcity price will not be fixed in advance; instead, it will be determined by the supply of and demand for investible funds.

Investment Companies

The profit-sharing arrangement can be usefully employed to promote interest-free investment on a limited scale. However, as noted above, to create a production structure in keeping with the tenets of Islam, which prohibit wasteful consumption, investment options will have to be constrained and regulated. It is not a question of generating large profits, but profits which are Islamically acceptable. Furthermore, to be viable, the profit-sharing system must somehow incorporate the principle of limited liability without which no economic system that envisages an important role for the private sector can work. This general principle can be incorporated in the financial system through investment companies, which, being more knowledgeable about the working of the system, can minimise risk under conditions of uncertainty. Since they will be managing an investment portfolio, they will not bear any loss, but will charge a commission for their services. Under this system, banks will be investing – through these companies – funds made available to them by those depositors who wish to take risks. This is not only Islamically legitimate, but makes economic sense because the risk will be borne by those who are not risk-averters, with this latter group still having the option of risk-free investment.

It may be objected that the proposed arrangement is not Islamically legitimate because according to it, the individual risk liability is limited. This may be so, but as pointed out above, the profit-sharing system can work within a mixed economy only on the basis of limited liability. And in making a transition to the Islamic system, there is no option available to the policy-maker but to accept the present financial structure as the natural *starting*-point for introducing bits and pieces of Islamic reform. At any rate, it is entirely reasonable to stipulate that the incidence of risk on investors should bear some relation to their financial capacity, and that they should not be made to take any risks at all if they cannot afford to take it.

The Long-Term Solution

How far can we go down the road leading to the economy-wide abolition of interest with the help of the above-mentioned measures? We are afraid, not very far. As far as the banking sector is concerned, the proposals will 'cover' only time deposits on the liabilities side, and bank advances on the assets side of commercial banks' 'T-Accounts'. These proposals will not, in any way, change the status of interest-bearing securities. This is because interest-bearing government securities in Pakistan account for almost all the 'secondary reserves' of the commercial banks and are a very high proportion of their total reserves, which form the basis of money creation through the banking system. Hence, if these are abolished, the 'monetary base' will shrink sharply, causing a steep fall in the money supply. These securities also offer an outlet for short-term, riskless investment of their 'excess reserves' by commercial banks because the risk of loss on sale is zero on securities – a feature that makes them both highly liquid and marketable. It is for this reason that the money market, of which the banking system is an important part, uses interest-bearing government securities to effectively perform their risk-minimisation function – i.e. the function of keeping a proper balance between securities and equities, and among equities of differing maturities.

The spread of risk, ranging between zero-risk and high-risk investment options, is called the interest-rate structure. This range is the continuum through which monetary policy makes an impact on the 'real sector' of the economy. This holds not only for those policy instruments which formally involve manipulation of the interest rate – e.g. the bank rate and open market operations – but also for those which do not carry a similar involvement, e.g. variations in cash-reserve requirements. In terms of their effect on the financial and real sectors of the economy, all these instruments are equivalent because they all operate on the same interest-rate structure. Interest-bearing government securities also form the most important source of non-inflationary finance to the government. By issuing long-term securities, the government raises non-inflationary loans from the public, while inflationary finance requires issuance of short-term deposit receipts, against which the state bank prints new money. It is thus clear that interest-bearing securities form the hub of the present monetary structure, which would collapse if they are abolished: monetary policy, in the traditional sense, will cease to be operational, while government will have no way of raising non-inflationary, non-tax finance.[7]

It follows that as long as the capitalistic structure of the economy continues unchanged and the traditional banking system remains intact, there is a definite limit beyond which the process of abolishing interest cannot go. What should then be done? Can't we ever abolish interest on an economy-wide basis? We can; but *not* if we persist, for whatever reasons, with the capitalistic economic system, where the financial and real sectors of the economy are linked together through the modern money market and where investment and saving decisions are made independently by atomistic 'economic agents', and small savers, in view of their precarious liquidity position, are risk-averters. This consideration brings us back to the point already made: in implementing its elements, we must never lose sight of the totality of the Islamic system, which must replace capitalism to make way for a society based on Islamic principles.

There is no way to replace interest on an economy-wide basis unless the process of monetary creation is directly linked to the process of production, and both saving and investment activities are coordinated. This means that to create the necessary, though not necessarily sufficient, conditions for replacing the interest-based system, the public sector must become not only saver and investor, but also the producer of public goods and wage goods. Furthermore, the entire banking system will have to be effectively controlled, even nationalised (as has already been done in Pakistan), and then operated only as a means of financing the liquidity requirements of the real sector of the economy, where the Islamic 'priorities' must be clearly reflected.

SUMMARY AND CONCLUSIONS

The *leitmotiv* of this essay has been the delineation of the basic features of the Islamic economic system, with emphasis on its totality. An important implication of this 'fact', not always clearly recognised in popular discussions, is that bits and pieces of Islamic reform are meaningful only within the matrix of the Islamic economic system, which should be clearly 'recognisable'. However, this does not mean that there is no other way to Islamise the economy than to introduce the Islamic economic system *in toto*. That would not be a helpful statement because no blueprint yet exists of a total Islamic economic system, and also because social dynamics are subject to societal constraints. It does mean, however, that when charting the direction of Islamic reform, certain 'initial conditions' are fulfilled to ensure that we move decisively and visibly towards the Islamic ideal. What we should be aiming at is not just some sort of a 'mixed economy', with a thin Islamic whitewash, but a genuine Islamized economy.

In spelling out the central features of the Islamic economic system, we have been guided by the unambiguous Quranic commandment: 'Lo! Allah enjoineth *al-'adl wal-ihsan*' (16:90). Translated onto the economic plane, while *'adl* requires a delicate and just balance among production, consumption and distribution relationships in the basic structure of the economy, *ihsan* enjoins a special concern for the economically downtrodden in the society. To maintain intergenerational equity, such a philosophy also dictates a specific policy to regulate the rate, form and quality of economic growth. The measures favouring 'the needy and the deprived' in society will have to take precedence over everything else for implementing the Divine Purpose. That this is what Allah requires us to do is made quite explicit in the Holy Quran: 'And We desire to show favour unto those who are oppressed in the earth, and to make them examples and make them the inheritors, and to establish them on earth . . .' (28:5–6). According to the Holy Quran, the poor in the land have a right to the wealth of the rich – 'And in their wealth the needy and the deprived have due share' (51:19). Hence, to provide a firm basis for a complete societal re-ordering according to the precepts of Islam, the socially unacceptable gap prevailing between rich and poor must be minimised.

It follows that economic policy should *first* concentrate on ensuring an equitable redistribution of all kinds of wealth among the members of society. In particular, land must be equitably distributed among those who cultivate it. That this should be the linchpin of a fruitful Islamic reform follows from the unambiguous Islamic position that all wealth belongs to Allah, Who has conferred it on mankind as a whole. Hence, any institutions that set up or support the monopoly of a few on Allah's bounties are un-Islamic. The Holy Quran holds out a warning against such tendencies: '[Let] it [i.e. wealth] become not a commodity between the rich among you' (59:7). The logic of the argument is impeccable because *not* doing so would amount to accepting the present non-Islamic economic structure as Islamically just. If that were so, there would have been no point in initiating Islamic reform in the first place.

An equitable distribution of wealth will lead to a just distribution of economic and social power without which all social reconstruction programmes will come to naught. In this connection, the present essay accords special attention to the phenomenon of inter-generational snowballing of wealth within the same families. Contrary to widespread misconceptions, the Islamic law of inheritance does permit a wider distribution of wealth of the deceased outside the closed circle of a few families to meet the needs of the society. Such a redistribution of wealth, rural and urban, will provide the basic force for social change. To reinforce this process, and to add to the quality of life, the need for universal education, particularly at the primary level, has also been emphasized as an essential building-block of an Islamic society. Furthermore, to highlight the quality of *ihsan*, which is an integral part of an Islamic economic dispensation, ambitious social security and anti-poverty programmes must be instituted so that 'the needy and the deprived' get their 'acknowledged right' to a respectable social life.

It is from the vantage-point of such a comprehensive framework that the existing Islamisation attempts, concentrating exclusively on the abolition of interest and the introduction of *zakat* as a limited tax on wealth, must be evaluated. While according general support to such measures, we have forcefully argued against taking a narrow view of them. The Islamic rejection of interest is, in effect, a rejection of the entire capitalistic system: an interest-free economy is in fact an exploitation-free economy. There is absolutely no doubt in our minds that a full-fledged Islamic economic system will have no use for interest, and that in it, *zakat* will be one of the elements of fiscal policy. However, it is essential to understand that the elements of the

Islamic system cannot always be foisted to non-Islamic economic systems with impunity. For instance, an unqualified recommendation to replace an interest-based economy with a profit-based economy within the capitalistic framework may result in some kind of a 'mixed' economy, which need not even be Islamically legitimate *if* the result of such a 'reform' is to raise the overall level of economic exploitation of the poor by the rich. And the grail may recede even further from the grasp of those who choose this route to the Islamic ideal.

In the same vein, while supporting the introduction of *zakat* into Pakistan's fiscal system, in principle, we believe that the objectives for which *zakat* is levied, and the egalitarian economic philosophy that it represents, should receive the primary emphasis and *zakat* should not be construed as just another revenue-raising device. This is because, according to the Holy Quran, *zakat* is one of the means to enforce the comprehensive and revolutionary Islamic concept of *infaq*. That being the case, the primary objective of the Islamic reform should be to aim at changing the basic structure of the present feudalistic-capitalistic economy. It would not do to strike quixotically at windmills, while leaving capitalism intact. If we confined our Islamisation efforts only to cosmetic changes, then we would belong to the class of men, 'whose efforts', according to the Holy Quran, 'have been wasted in this life, while they thought they were acquiring good by their works' (18:104).

This then is the basic message of the present essay: the totality of the Islamic system is what should count most with the policy-makers; and its elements must be seen in relation to this totality. Since the point of departure of Islamic reform in Pakistan will inevitably be the existing feudalistic-capitalistic system, this fact cannot be ignored in formulating an Islamic policy package and in fixing the order of priority in the package. Interest is an integral part of a financial system in which saving and investment decisions are made independently by economic agents, whose behaviour is controlled indirectly through monetary (and fiscal) policy. As long as the financial and the real sectors are interconnected through the money market in this fashion, not much progress can be made towards evolving an interest-free economy. We take the view that the abolition of interest should be part of a fundamental restructuring of the entire spectrum of production, consumption and distribution relationships on Islamic lines. However, the search for such a system must be gradual, though decisive, to let the interaction between the theory and practice of

Islamic economic philosophy produce an economic system and a body of economic thought which correspond to the overall vision of an Islamic economic system – a system based on *al-adl wal-ihsan*.

The emphasis on the totality of the Islamic economic system *plus* the need for 'escaping' from the gravitational pull of existing exploitative non-Islamic economic systems leads to a predominant role of the state both as the initiator of Islamic reform and as its sustainer and promoter. Even standard economic theory tells us that in the presence of market imperfections and 'externalities' in production and consumption, state intervention becomes necessary to optimise production and consumption. The exact 'form' of state intervention is, however, a matter of detail to be decided in the actual societal context. What is clear is that an Islamic state cannot lend support to forces which perpetuate social injustices in society. Indeed, an economy raised on the basis of *al-adl wal-ihsan* will require considerable state intervention to eliminate all sources of economic exploitation by establishing a just balance between individual freedom and social responsibility. To think that market forces, guided by the invisible hand of vested interests, will yield an Islamic solution is exceedingly naive, if not hypocritical.

The question can be raised at this point: Is it not socialism that we are advocating? Not at all! As has been shown, the suggestions noted above follow from Islamic economic philosophy. As pointed out above, p. 165, we do not reject a solution just because it *resembles* the one offered by socialism. For if we were to use this logic consistently, we will also not be able to advocate an economy run mainly on the basis of profits, which are central to capitalism. If we can't have a private sector because it reminds us of capitalism, and a public sector because it smacks of socialism, then what else shall we have for the Islamic economic system? Such reasoning generates neither heat nor light. It is patently false.

Till such time as an Islamic economy, based on *al-adl wal-ihsan*, becomes fully operational, we should move decisively towards the ultimate goal, concentrating *first* on those aspects of the Islamic solution which *directly* come to grips with the problems of poverty, want and economic deprivation, and then moving gradually to a reform of the financial system, which supports the 'real' system. If the real system continues to be non-Islamic, financial reforms along presumably Islamic lines will remain merely cosmetic and may indeed turn out to be counter-productive. Furthermore, even if such reforms make the financial system more *efficient*, there is no guarantee that it will also make it more *just*. In that case, these reforms will not qualify as *initiators* of an Islamic economic system.

Another possible criticism against the thesis of the present essay may be: what is *new* about these proposals? This is no objection at all. The fact that an equitable distribution of wealth, universal education, social security and anti-poverty programmes are an integral part of any just economic system does not disqualify these aspects of social reform from being a part of the Islamic policy package. Formal similarities among economic systems are inevitable because they all face common problems of want, poverty, disease and economic deprivation. The basic contribution of the present essay is that it demonstrates that such a social reform follows directly from Islam's distinctive economic philosophy, which makes ethical constraints binding on man's economic behaviour.

The main merit of an approach that focuses on the 'totality' of the Islamic system is that it draws attention to the political aspects of the Islamisation process as well. This is important because no attempts at Islamisation can strike roots unless people feel the beneficial effects of such a fundamental social transformation in their daily lives. The squalor, hunger, disease and abject poverty still prevailing violate the basic principles of Islam's economic philosophy. In such a milieu, people should be convinced that the Islamic system, once enforced, will not tolerate this state of affairs for the simple reason that it is contrary to its absolute commitment to *al-adl wal-ihsan*, which implies an integrated programme of social amelioration. Indeed, it will be 'rational' for the individual and the state not to tolerate such a state of affairs because, within the unitary perspective of Islamic economic philosophy, steps taken to relieve human misery also point the way to man's spiritual salvation. The act of 'giving', being the quintessence of a societal ordering enjoined by Islam, achieves both these aspects of man's life, the material and the spiritual, within the framework of a comprehensive philosophy of life processes.

A message so humane, and yet so revolutionary, touches the human heart and arouses the deepest emotions in man. A system which can offer so much more than the existing non-Islamic systems is bound to command the support of the people. This is because by enlisting the active, *voluntary* cooperation of the common man, the Islamic economic system will become for them the medium through which they can channel their longing for social change.

It must be clearly realised that a society based on exploitation and given to misappropriation by a few of what Allah has conferred on mankind as a whole is doomed: 'When We decide to destroy a population We [first] send a definite order to those among them who lead easy lives and yet transgress; so that the word is proved true against them: then [it is that] We destroy them utterly' (17:16). The social injustices are all man-made and must be rectified by man, who, as Allah's vicegerent on earth, must implement the divine plan through Islamically-legitimate means, with a clear understanding that Allah sees all our actions: 'And say (unto them): Act! Allah will behold your actions' (9:105). With the freedom that Allah has conferred on man, both individually and collectively, he is responsible for his actions. And these actions must be such as translate Allah's favours to man into a set of effective institutions which do not tolerate social and economic exploitation in any guise, least of all in an Islamic guise. A failure to do so will invite Allah's displeasure: 'He who altereth the grace of Allah after it hath come unto him [for him], lo! Allah is severe in punishment' (2:211). Thus, in search of the Islamic ideal, man must strive constantly through a process of trial and error. It is only when his striving for Allah's cause is both sincere and intense that man will qualify for Allah's help. Such efforts cannot stop short of complete societal transformation, guided by the divine principles of *al-'adl wal-ihsan*, when the 'oppressed in the earth' become the 'inheritors' of Allah's bounties.

NOTES

The *Agenda for Islamic Economic Reform* appeared in May 1980 in the form of the Report of the Committee on Islamisation appointed by the Federal Finance Minister, Mr Ghulam Ishaq Khan. As expected, the Report drew both appreciation and criticism. It is our good fortune that appreciation has dwarfed the criticism. Since its publication, the main thesis of the *Agenda* – that the Islamic economic system is based on the Divine Law of *al-'Adl wal-Ihsan* – has received 'universal' acclaim. Indeed, this thesis has now become a household word, so much so that those who make assertions to this effect do not always remember to acknowledge the *Agenda*.

Since the publication of the *Agenda*, we have done some more thinking on the subject and have felt that at several places the argument needed a more cogent and clearer articulation. Accordingly, we decided to bring out this version not merely as a second edition of the *Agenda* but as a different work. As such, a large number of substantial changes have been made and at places the argument has been completely recast and the presentation changed so that the present version is not merely recommendatory and exhortative but is more carefully worded and logically consistent. However, to enable the interested reader to compare the *Agenda* with the present work, we have retained the original headings and subheadings. We hope that the end-product of our joint labour of love is a much-improved representation of our ideas, even though they remain controversial, and that it makes a contribution to the growing literature on the subject. The main thrust of the basic argument of the *Agenda* has remained intact; indeed it has become even more pointed because its underlying logic has been more clearly and cogently spelt out.

Now that the Islamisation process appears to be well-nigh irreversible in Pakistan, it has become essential that we move in the 'right' direction. However, to make any progress at all, we must 'recognise' what an Islamic economic system is and what it stands for. The present essay states a point of view which offers plenty of grist to the Muslim economist's mill. Its basic premise is that, within the framework of universally-accepted Islamic ethical principles, there is much room for debate and honest difference of opinion on how best the Islamic ideal can be achieved. We take the view that there is no such thing as Islamisation without tears. The Islamic system is by no means synonymous with the maximisation of the exploitative largesse that the feudalistic-capitalistic system confers on the 'haves' at the expense of the 'have nots' in the form of rent, profit and interest. In Islam, the emphasis is on altruism and commitment rather than on egoism as the ideal form of economic behaviour. The 'way of Allah' is not a primrose path, but one requiring abnegation and sacrifice. The Holy Quran has promised: 'And surely We shall try you with something of fear and hunger, and loss of wealth and lives and crops . . .' (2:155). Accordingly, we have endeavoured to chart out a route which requires changes in the basic structure of the economy. This route, even though it may be more thorny, is, in our opinion, the shortest one to get 'there', with the Divine assurance that 'Allah increaseth in right guidance those who walk aright . . .' (19:76).

We have built our argument on the universally-accepted view among Muslim scholars that Islam's is a complete system. As such, phrases like Islamic capitalism and Islamic socialism are unacceptable syncretisms, and, therefore find no place in the present essay. However, the 'completeness' of the Islamic system does *not* preclude inter-system 'borrowings'; nor does it prevent even apparent similarities of policy objectives or specific policy instruments with other economic systems. This is because all social and economic systems address themselves to practically the same economic problems facing man. The distinction of the Islamic economic system is that it rejects a total separation between ethics and economics. Accordingly, it makes economic pursuits of man subservient to ethical constraints, accords highest priority to the needs of the 'needy and the deprived' and de-emphasises the quest for material plenitude that greed and avarice sustain: 'And who is saved from his own avarice – such are they who are successful' (59:9).

The present essay lays special emphasis on the need for implementing both the structural and financial aspects of the Islamisation process within a unified framework. It is essential that, by employing the Islamic revolutionary concept of *infaq*, the vast income and wealth differences between various classes of the society are minimised to sharply decrease the 'weight' of *rentier* consumption in the economy. Correspondingly, the production structure must be reorganised to ensure an adequate flow of wage goods and investment goods. Without such fundamental changes, a mere shifting of the financial system from 'interest' to 'profit' will exacerbate the existing socially undesirable trends in the production, consumption and distribution structure. As we chart out the Islamisation strategy, we must not lose sight of what the entire purpose of the Islamisation process is: it is to usher in a society based on *al-'adl* and *al-ihsan*. This is the reference point from which to 'measure' the distance of an Islamised economy from the existing feudalistic-capitalistic socio-economic system in Pakistan.

It may be noted that this essay, unlike the *Agenda*, is not a government report. It is an essay in persuasion by the authors who are represented here in their individual capacities. The views expressed by them do not necessarily reflect the position of the government of Pakistan or of the respective institutions to which they belong. It is hoped that, regardless of who has said it, the present essay will be read for what it says.

1. It should be noted that the argument in the text is not inconsistent with the fact that Islam assigns the highest importance to man's altruistic behaviour, where the act of giving is guided solely by the desire to gain Allah's pleasure: 'We feed you for the sake of Allah only. We wish for no reward nor thanks from you' (76:9). While the virtues of giving are extolled, man's innate selfishness and greed are also recognised, *though not justified*. There must, therefore, be explicit provisions for handling an unjust situation, which man's egoistic behaviour gives birth to.
2. In Pakistan, following the prevalent development theory at the time, such a strategy did, in fact, operate during the 1960s, when government policies consciously let profits multiply while increase in wages were restricted to maximise the flow of investible surplus in the corporate sector.
3. The same theme recurs in the Holy Quran even more pointedly: 'And We desire to show favour unto those who are oppressed in the earth, and to make them examples and make them the inheritors, and to establish them on the earth . . .' (28:5–6). When it is read along with the Quranic verse given in the text, it should be clear that any effort to 'deprive' the 'inheritors' of what properly belongs to them is against the Divine design.

   Those who object to our interpretation of this verse because, according to them, it refers to a historical incident in the time of Moses, ignore the timelessness of the Divine vision. The Holy Quran emphasises the intertemporal continuity of the Divine message: '(This was Our) way with the apostles We sent before thee: thou wilt find no change in Our ways' (17:77). (*Note*: In Pickthall's translation the verses (28:5–6) are translated in the past tense which reflects the necessity of the English language. However, the relevant Quranic verse employs the present continuous tense.)
4. Nothing that is said in the text implies a recommendation for an abolition of private property. Indeed, among other things, what distinguishes an Islamic economy from both capitalism and socialism is its position on private property, with ownership rights sharply limited in such a way as to

make them consistent with the Islamic concept of trusteeship.

5. According to an econometric study being done at the Pakistan Institute Development Institute (PIDE), land rent accounts for more than 50 per cent of value added in the agriculture sector in Pakistan.
6. However, to repeat ourselves, both the individual and the state must act as trustee and not as absolute owner of the property owned. There should be institutional safeguards to ensure that neither of them uses the property for any purposes that are not Islamically legitimate.
7. It is true that it is not necessary that monetary policy must work in the 'traditional sense' in an Islamic economy. The rules of the game will change and so will the 'composition' of monetary policy. However, it is essential that the new rules of the game are laid down by those who offer interest-free banking as a panacea for all economic ills.

Appendix: Fundamentals of Islamic Jurisprudence

Sohrab Behdad

Specific acts of Muslims must be in accordance with the Islamic rules of conduct. These rules of conduct are called *shari'a*. The primary source of the *shari'a* is the Quran. The Quran, however, as a book of religious teachings contains many ambiguities and conflicting statements. The believers sought Muhammad's interpretation of the Quran during his lifetime. Soon after the death of Muhammad (AD 632), however, controversies arose on interpretation of the Quran, which gave rise to development of various schools of Islamic jurisprudence. The history of development of these schools has been studied elsewhere (Schacht, 1950, 1982, and Macdonald, 1975). Here we are concerned with the fundamentals of jurisprudence in the major *sunni* and *shi'i* schools.[1]

The process of deducing specific rules of conduct from the *shari'a* is called *fiqih* (jurisprudence). The person who makes these deductions is a *faqih* (jurist). *A faqih* must be a *mujtahid*, that is a Muslim whose intellectual capacity and integrity has been recognised by the established *mujtahids*. (For attributes of *mujtahid* see Aghnides, 1969, pp. 117–224.) The act of deducing a specific rule of conduct from the *shari'a* is *ijtihad*.

The bases of jurisprudence in the *sunni* schools of *fiqh* are the Quran, Tradition (*sunna*), Consensus (*ijma*) and Analogy (*qiyas*). The ambiguities and conflicts in the Quran are to be resolved by the wisdom of *mujtahid* in the light of the philosophy of Islam and through the rules of jurisprudence established for utilising the other sources. The most important source of the *shari'a* after the Quran is Tradition. That is the conduct of affairs by Muhammad, statements attributed to him (*hadiths*) and the customs of the community where Muhammad and his Companions lived (Aghnides, 1969, pp. 35–5). The problem of application of the authority of Tradition stems not only from conflicting acts or statements of Muhammad but also from the existence of many false *hadiths* that have been circulated and transmitted. Therefore, Science of the Hadith (*ilm-al-hadith*) has become an element of Islamic jurisprudence. Complex rules of logical and historical scrutiny have been established to recognise the genuine from false *hadiths* and to interpret Tradition for deducing Islamic rules of conduct (Aghnides, 1969, 31 *et seq.*). This interpretation falls clearly in the domain of authority of *mujtahids*.

Thus, neither the Quran nor Tradition may be used by lay persons for advocating a position. The reaction of the *faqihs* to the layman's application of the authority of the Quran and Tradition has been, historically, nothing short of condemnation. This condemnation has been particularly strong if the Quran or Tradition were relied upon to advocate a social or political action or change.

The other two bases of Islamic *fiqih*, Consensus and Analogy, are methods of interpreting *shari'a* from the Quran and Tradition. According to Muhammad, Consensus among Muslims is the guarantee that the laws of God have been understood correctly. (Aghnides, 1969, p. 61). In the later periods, Consensus has been considered to be the agreement among the *mujtahids* of the past (Schacht, 1982, p. 30).

Analogy is 'the extension of the *shari'a* . . . from the original case . . . to a new case, because the latter has the same cause as the former' (Aghnides, 1969, p. 77). The complexity of making Analogy is in determination of the cause when the divine prescription has different attributes. Obviously, Analogy is a study in epistemology and logic. The complexity of Analogy is further expanded with possibility of abrogations in the divine prescriptions.

Within this jurisprudential framework, the new questions that may arise in the society of Muslims must be resolved by *ijtihad*. By the fourth century of Islam (tenth century AD), the view gained dominance, however, that all the essential questions have been clearly dealt with by the great *mujtahids* of the past (Schacht, 1982, pp. 69–75). According to this view, there would not be any need for independent reasoning in the *shari'a*, and the duty of the future *faqih* would be limited to the interpretation of 'the doctrine as it had been laid down once and for all' (Schacht, 1982, p. 71). This is referred to as 'closing of the gate of *ijtihad*' and is accepted in practice, if not in theory, by all major schools of *sunni fiqih*.[2] The *muftis* who issue religious rulings *(fatwa)* must rely upon the *ijtihad* of the great *mujtahids* of the past in a way not unlike judges in a system of common law.

Shi'i jurisprudence (Mutahhari, n.d.) provides a somewhat wider scope for interpretation of the divine prescription. Similar to *sunnis*, *Shi'is* accept the Quran, Tradition and Consensus. *Shi'is*, however, rely not only on the Tradition of Muhammad but also of the Imams (Tabataba'i, 1984, p. 3). This provides a longer period (lasting to the third century of Islam) and also a more varied socio-political context for Tradition. This is especially important since with the exception of the first Imam, Ali, all other Imams considered the Islamic state illegitimate. (For a brief history of the life of shi'i Imams see Momem, 1985, pp. 23–60.)

The most significant difference between *shi'i* and *sunni* jurisprudence is acceptance of Reason *(aql)*, instead of Analogy, as a basis of *fiqih* in *shi'ism*. *Shi'ism* maintains that Analogy 'is possible only where there is a basic common denominator between . . . two cases inasmuch as one can be certain that the same reason which is behind the precept in the original case, covers the other case as well' (Tabataba'i, 1984, p. 3). 'Reason', however, is 'categorical judgments drawn from pure and practical reason [and] whatever is ordered by reason is ordered by religion' (Tabataba'i, 1984, pp. 3–4).

Unlike *sunnis*, *shi'is* consider 'the gate of *ijtihad*' open. Every *shi'i mujtahid must* make his view by personal investigation of the sources of *shari'a* and may not imitate the opinion of another *mujtahid* (Tabataba'i, 1984, p. 16). Thus, *shi'is* may have, in theory, a wider latitude of interpretation of the *shari'a* than *sunnis*. In practice, however, this latitude is significantly limited by the jurisprudential tradition of the great *mujtahids* of the past. Deviation from this tradition is heresy and is condemned by *shari'a* (Aghnides, 1969, p. 30).

NOTES

1. The *sunnis* and *shiis* differ on the issue of the succession to Muhammad (Momen, 1985, pp. 11–22). The major *sunni* schools of jurisprudence are Hanafi, Shafi'i, Maliki, Hanbali and Zahiri. For a review of some differences among these schools see Aghnides (1969, pp. 133–47). The main schools of *shii* jurisprudence are Jafari, Zaidi and Ismaili. See Momen (1985) for detailed elaborations.
2. Aghnides who considers the closing of the gate of *ijtihad* a fiction quotes a modern Turkish *faqih* saying 'that the gate of *ijtihad* was not closed . . . by an external cause . . . but through the mere absence of *mujtahids*' (1969, p. 124). Ilallaq (1984) is among the few modern scholars who believe the gate of *ijtihad* has never been closed in theory or practice.

REFERENCES

Aghnides, Nicolas P., *Mohammedan Theories of Finance with an Introduction to Mohammedan Law and a Bibliography* (New York: AMS Press, (1916) 1969).

Hallaq, Wael B., "Was the Gate of Ijtihad Closed?" *International Journal of Middle East Studies*, 16 (1), March 1984, 3–41.

Macdonald, Duncan B., *Development of Muslim Theology, Jurisprudence and Constitutional Theory* (London: Darf Publishers, (1902) 1985).

Momen, Moojan, *An Introduction to Shi'i Islam* (New Haven: Yale University Press, 1985).

Mutahhari, Morteza, *Jurisprudence and its Principles (Fiqh and usul ul-fiqh)*, translated by Muhammad Salman Tawheedi (Albany, California: Moslem Student Association, n. d., circa 1983).

Schacht, Joseph, *An Introduction to Islamic Law* (Oxford: Clarendon Press, (1964) 1982).

Schacht, Joseph, *The Origins of Muhammadan Jurisprudence* (Oxford: Clarendon Press, (1950) 1985).

Tabataba'i, Hossein Madarressi, *An Introduction to Shi'i Law: A Bibliographical Study* (London: Ithaca Press, 1984).

Index